GEROPSYCHOLOGICAL ASSESSMENT AND TREATMENT

Linda Teri, Ph.D., is an Assistant Professor in the Department of Psychiatry and Behavioral Sciences, and Chief Psychologist of the Geriatric and Family Services Clinic, at the University of Washington Medical School in Seattle. Since receiving her doctorate in Psychology from the University of Vermont in 1980, she has been active in teaching, research, clinical work, and supervision in the areas of depression and geropsychology. She is the author of numerous papers and, with Peter Lewinsohn, co-authored *The Coping with Depression Course* and *Clinical Geropsychology.*

Peter M. Lewinsohn, Ph.D., is a Professor of Psychology and Director of the Geropsychological Services Program at the University of Oregon in Eugene. A diplomate in Clinical Psychology of the American Board of Professional Psychology, he is well known for his work on the behavioral assessment and treatment of clinical depression. He has published more than 100 articles and book chapters, and is the senior author of *Control Your Depression, The Coping with Depression Course,* and *Clinical Geropsychology.*

GEROPSYCHOLOGICAL ASSESSMENT AND TREATMENT
SELECTED TOPICS

Linda Teri, Ph.D.
Peter M. Lewinsohn, Ph.D.
Editors

Springer Publishing Company
New York

Springer Publishing Company, Inc.
536 Broadway
New York, New York 10012

86 87 88 89 90 / 10 9 8 7 6 5 4 3 2 1

Library of Congress Cataloging-in-Publication Data

Main entry under title:

Geropsychological assessment and treatment.
  Includes bibliographies and index.
  1. Geriatric psychiatry. 2. Behavioral assessment. 3. Behavior therapy. I. Teri, Linda.
II. Lewinsohn, Peter M. [DNLM: 1. Mental Disorders—in old age. 2. Psychology,
Clinical—in old age. WT 150 G3768]
RC451.4.A5G49   1986   618.97'689   85-17226
ISBN 0-8261-4790-9

Printed in the United States of America

Contents

38276

Contributors

Richard Hussian, Ph.D., is a Clinical Psychologist at the Terrell State Mental Hospital in Terrell, Texas. Previously at the Guilford County Mental Health Center in North Carolina and Director of Psychological Services at a long-term care facility in Greensboro, North Carolina, Dr. Hussian is experienced in providing direct and indirect services to the frail and institutionalized elderly. Known for his work with this population, Dr. Hussian is the author of *Geriatric Psychology: A Behavioral Perspective,* and *Behavioral Geriatrics: A Clinician's Guide.*

M. Powell Lawton, Ph.D., is currently Director of Research at the Philadelphia Geriatric Center, and Editor of the new APA journal, *Psychology and Aging.* He was awarded the Distinguished Research Contribution Award of Division 20 (Aging) of the APA, and the Kleemeier Award of the Gerontological Society. Dr. Lawton is best known for his work on environmental and functional assessment of older adults. He serves on numerous editorial boards and has authored more than 170 articles and 12 books, including *Environment and Aging,* and *The Psychology of Adult Development and Aging.*

Muriel D. Lezak, Ph.D., is currently Clinical Neuropsychologist at the VA Hospital, and Associate Professor of Neurology and Psychiatry, at Oregon Health Sciences University in Portland, Oregon. She is a Diplomate in Clinical Psychology and Clinical Neuropsychology, and a member of the Board of Directors of the International Neuropsychological Society. Dr. Lezak is the author of numerous publications and is known for her text *Neuropsychological Assessment.*

Alan H. Roberts, Ph.D., is currently the Director of the Behavioral Medicine Program at the Scripps Clinic and Research Foundation in La Jolla, California. His direct clinical and consulting experience includes working with clients and staff on issues in chronic pain management. Previously, he was a Professor in the Departments of Physical Medicine and Rehabilitation, and Psychology, at the University of Minnesota where he was also the Director of the Pain Clinic and the Pain Treatment Program. He has authored over 50 articles and chapters, and is a contributor to *Comprehensive Handbook of Behavioral Medicine* and *The Pain Clinic and Pain Treatment Program Procedure Manual*.

Leslie Schover, Ph.D. is currently an Assistant Professor of Psychology in Urology, at the M.D. Anderson Hospital and Tumor Institute of the Texas Medical Center, Houston, Texas. Prior to this, Dr. Schover was an Instructor in the Department of Psychiatry at Baylor College of Medicine, as well as the coordinator of an NIA Grant on sexual function and aging. She was a postdoctoral fellow for two years in the Sex Therapy Center at SUNY Stony Brook, NY, and is known for her clinical work and expertise in the design of sexual rehabilitation programs. Dr. Schover has written many articles and chapters dealing with the assessment and treatment of sexual dysfunction; her most recent book is *Prime Time: Sexual Health for Men Over 50*.

Preface

In recent years, the literature on the clinical assessment and treatment of older adults has been growing exponentially. Clinical gerontology is a rapidly growing field which can already boast of a growing cadre of highly skilled and competent researchers and clinicians. We are excited to share in this explosion of knowledge, especially as it pertains to the mental health needs of older adults.

We greatly appreciate the contributions of Drs. Hussian, Lawton, Lezak, Roberts, and Schover to this volume. Not only did they create the excellent chapters you are about to read but they also shared their knowledge and clinical experience in a series of workshops which were offered to practitioners and professionals-in-training in Eugene, Oregon, in 1983 ("The 2nd Annual Conference on Recent Advances in Clinical Psychology of Aging"). In writing the chapters and in leading the workshops, they modeled a high degree of dedication, scholarship, and clinical expertise.

We would also like to take this opportunity to extend our appreciation to those who helped coordinate the conference; especially to Mary Hecht, who repeatedly demonstrated a wonderful capacity for hard work and organization, and to Susan Taylor and Alyn Stanton, who were available when we needed them.

For their help in the production of this book, our thanks go to Teal Korn and Valerie Peterson for their consistent and excellent typing and to the publishers at Springer Publishing Company for their support and encouragement throughout the process.

Introduction

Linda Teri and Peter M. Lewinsohn

With the growing numbers of older adults in our population and the increasing recognition of their unmet mental health needs, there is an obvious need for effective assessment and treatment procedures for use with the elderly and for specially trained mental health practitioners. Persons over 65 currently constitute approximately 10 percent of our population; by 2025 it is estimated that proportion will increase to 15 percent (U.S. Bureau of Census, as cited in Botwinick, 1978). Among these older adults, psychological problems are common and frequently hinder physical diagnosis and treatment, community adaptation, and quality of life. Despite this, in 1975 only one APA approved doctoral program in clinical psychology offered a specialization in aging, and in 1980 there were still only four (Storandt, 1982). In addition, "fewer than 100 clinical psychologists in the entire country had been trained in one way or another to work with older persons" (Storandt, 1982, p. 11). Among other mental health professionals, the picture is equally dismal.

A recognized lack of sound clinical and empirically based assessment and treatment procedures for use with older adults also exists. Assessment and treatment procedures have typically been developed and evaluated for use with college and middle-aged populations so that their utility and effectiveness with older adults is unknown.

This picture is changing somewhat. In answer to the need for trained specialists, NIMH began providing funds for specialized training, and professional programs began offering programs for mental health specialists in geriatrics at a variety of professional levels (e.g., predoctoral, doctoral, and postdoctoral levels). A clinical and empirical base for assessment and treatment, while certainly not yet in abundance, is emerging—and emerging steadily. (cf. Hussian, 1981; Lewinsohn & Teri, 1983; Storandt, Siegler & Eliase, 1978; Zarit, 1980). Researchers and clinicians are recognizing that some current strategies need to be modified and some new strategies need to be developed.

Unfortunately, despite this recognized need for changes, much information is not yet published nor readily available for the practitioner or practitioner-in-training. It is our hope that this book facilitates the availability of such knowledge by providing the practitioner and practitioner-in-training with a practical yet scholarly guide to the assessment and treatment of some of the psychological problems facing older adults.

In planning this book, we had to decide what topics to include and what topics to omit. We were guided by several considerations. First, we were interested in maintaining a balance between assessment and treatment. Second, we were interested in focusing on problems of particular relevance to older adults. And third, we were interested in clinically relevant and empirically based techniques. Thus, the first two chapters deal with neuropsychological and functional assessment while the remaining three chapters focus on the treatment of sexual dysfunction, severe behavioral problems, and chronic pain.

We were also interested in limiting the size of this book so that it could be published in a timely fashion and be quickly available to professionals and professionals-in-training. Thus, this book was not intended to be a comprehensive textbook on how to assess and treat all problems faced by older adults. Rather we have chosen a selected number of clinical problems of special relevance to older adults for which empirically based techniques have been developed and evaluated for older adults.

Because of the above-mentioned considerations, we did not include chapters on other highly relevant topics such as bereavement and loss, retirement, substance and alcohol abuse, anxiety, and paranoia. While there is a growing body of literature on these topics, in our opinion they have not yet attained the kind of empirical data base to warrant their inclusion. It is our expectation and hope that by the time this book is published, there will already have been new empirical and clinical literature in these areas and that they could be included in a future book. We also chose to omit topics which had been included in our earlier publication: to wit, depression, dementia, social and daily living skills, insomnia, and stress (Lewinsohn & Teri, 1983).

The chapters in this and in our earlier book represent attempts to provide an integration of knowledge about specific assessment and treatment strategies for use with older adults. It is our hope that they can make significant contributions to the training of mental health practitioners and to the quality of clinical services to older adults.

In this topical organization, we are clearly revealing our applied behavioral orientation. Our first concern is to develop a clear definition of the problematic behavior (whether this be by means of neuropsychological assessment, functional assessment, or some combination of the two strategies). Our second concern is to develop a concrete and directly relevant approach to the personal, psychosocial, environmental, and physical events that surround the defined problem area. The clear specification of assessment and treatment goals facilitates objective evaluation. Without minimizing more traditional approaches, we are clearly advocating the utility of a time-limited, behavioral approach with older adults. The high structure, clear delineation of goals, increased therapist activity, and relevance of expected tasks serve to make a behavioral orientation particularly suitable to older adults (Hussian, 1981; Lewinsohn & Teri, 1983; MacDonald & Kerr, 1982; Richards & Thorpe, 1978).

One potential danger of this behavioral, structured, clearly delineated, topic-oriented focus is that the practitioner or practitioner-in-training may lose sight of the need to place this approach in its rightful larger context. There are certain general considerations that are important to the assessment and treatment of older adults that, if not taken into account, may adversely affect outcome. Prior to proceeding to the chapters, we briefly review these considerations here. For more detailed discussion of these issues, readers are referred to Gallagher, Thompson, and Levy (1980), Lawton et al. (1980), Lewinsohn, Teri, and Hautzinger (1984), and Pfeiffer (1980).

1. *The need to view older adults as unique individuals.* Older adults are not all the same. Although this sounds facile, it must be said particularly in a book of this type that attempts to make generalizations about "older adults" or "older adults with problem *x*." It is important to relate to people as whole, complex beings and not as oversimplified caricatures of a particular age or problem. Although such simplified generalizations help provide structure, this structure must remain flexible so that it takes into account the particular individual and his/her individual situation. Consistent with maintaining such flexibility, mental health professionals working with (or planning to work with) older adults would do well to investigate what age biases they possess and how these biases influence their work. (For an excellent discussion of these biases, readers are referred to Butler, 1969.)

2. *The need for comprehensive assessment.* It is crucial to address and evaluate the multiplicity of problems experienced by the older adult. While there are clients who seek help for particular problems, there are also clients for whom the presenting problem is more amorphous or for whom the presenting problem provides a distorted or partial picture of the situation. Thus, assessment should go beyond a unidimensional approach and incorporate traditional areas of assessment (such as intellectual and cognitive functioning, personality, affective and symptomatic complaints) and nontraditional areas (such as general competencies; social, familial, and occupational functioning; financial status, medical and physical considerations; nutritional needs; and any other factors relevant to the presenting problem). Assessment should be based upon information as varied as possible: from multiple sources (the older adult, his/her family and concerned others), in multiple ways (interviews, standard testing, behavioral observation), about multiple areas (functional and social competencies, physical and emotional health, financial status, social and environmental factors).

3. *The need for an interdisciplinary approach.* Although this book is developed by psychologists interested in problems with which psychologists commonly work, this focus is not meant to underemphasize the importance of contributions from other disciplines or to underemphasize the importance of an interdisciplinary approach.

The availability and utilization (when needed) of an interdisciplinary approach can ensure that assessment and treatment adequately address the plethora of needs the older adult may have. Although not every case will require different professionals or require the same combination of professionals, it is important for mental health practitioners working with the aged to be aware of the kinds of specialized services available and to have access to those services when needed.

4. *The need to be aware of factors that influence assessment and treatment.* On the client's part, sensory deficits (such as hearing loss or visual impairment), physical problems, and general unfamiliarity with psychological tests may make assessment difficult. The current generation of older people has not undergone the socialization to testing that the younger generation has (Lawton, Whelihan, & Belsky, 1980). Thus, the older client may not understand the purpose of the psychological evaluation. He/she may be fearful about the outcome of the assessment and the function it will serve and may deny or suppress certain problems of importance. On the evaluator's part, myths and stereotypes about older adults may interfere with conducting objective and adequate assessment and interpretation. They may be awkward at establishing and maintaining rapport that is critical to adequate evalua-

tion. Finally, the assessment procedures themselves may be inappropriate or biased against an accurate assessment of the older adult: (a) because of factors inherent in the test themselves, such as being speed-timed or motor-performance based (Botwinick, 1978), (b) because the tests may not facilitate clarifying overlapping symptomatology of older clients, (c) because the tests may not include items relevant to this age-group, and (d) because age-appropriate norms may not exist to enable differentiating responses of normal aging from those involving pathological processes.

The mental health professional seeking to work with older adults must keep these broad factors in mind while also understanding and implementing the approaches discussed in the chapters that follow.

This combination of specialized knowledge with clinical and empirical expertise embedded in a wide-ranging understanding and awareness of more general issues is the point of departure for ensuring that sound mental health services are provided to older adults.

References

Botwinick, J. (1978). *Aging and behavior* (2nd ed.). New York: Springer Publishing Company.

Butler, R. N. (1969). Age-ism: Another form of bigotry. *Gerontologist, 9,* 243–246.

Gallagher, D., Thompson, L. W., & Levy, S. (1980). Clinical psychological assessment of older adults. In L. Poon (Ed.), *Aging in the 1980's.* Washington, D.C.: American Psychological Association.

Hussian, R. A. (1981). *Geriatric psychology: A behavioral perspective.* New York: Van Nostrand Reinhold.

Lawton, M. P., Whelihan, W. M., & Belsky, J. K. (1980). *Handbook for mental health and aging.* Englewood Cliffs, N.J.: Prentice-Hall.

Lewinsohn, P. M. & Teri, L. (1983). *Clinical geropsychology.* New York: Pergamon Press.

Lewinsohn, P., Teri, L., & Hautzinger, M. (1984). Training clinical psychologists for work with older adults: A working model. *Professional Psychology, 15,* 187–202.

MacDonald, M. L., & Kerr, B. B. (1982). *Mental health interventions for the aging: Behavior therapy with the aging.* New York: Praeger.

Richards, W. S., & Thorpe, G. L. (1978). *The clinical psychology of aging: Behavioral approaches to the problems of later life.* New York: Plenum.

Pfeiffer, E. (1980) The psychosocial evaluation of the elderly patient. In E. W. Busse & D. G. Blazer (Eds.), *Handbook of Geriatric Psychiatry.* New York: Van Nostrand Reinhold, 275–285.

Storandt, M. (1982). Where have we been? Where are we going? In J. F. Santos & R. VandenBos (Eds.), *Psychology and the older adult.* Washington, D. C.: American Psychological Association, pp. 11–18.

Storandt, M., Siegler, I. C., & Eliase, M. F. (Eds.). (1978). *The clinical psychology of aging.* New York: Plenum.

Zarit, S. H. (1980). *Aging and mental disorders: Psychological approaches to assessment and treatment.* New York: Free Press.

GEROPSYCHOLOGICAL ASSESSMENT AND TREATMENT

I

Assessment

1

Neuropsychological Assessment

Muriel D. Lezak

Need for Assessment

In clinical practice, neuropsychological assessment is usually undertaken to aid in diagnosis, to provide information that can be of help in
planning for the patient, or to improve patient care or treatment.
Frequently, the neuropsychological assessment will serve both diagnostic and patient care purposes and the examination data may be used
for research as well. Much of the knowledge about brain function and
the mental changes that occur with aging has come from neuropsychological assessments performed for research purposes. The broad scope
of neuropsychological assessment of the elderly and its varied applications will be briefly addressed.

Neuropsychological Assessment
in Differential Diagnosis

For most neurodiagnostic purposes, the CT scan and other neuroradiologic techniques provide the pertinent information about the patient's neuroanatomic status. However, the degenerative diseases of
old age cannot yet be reliably identified by neuroradiologic techniques (de Leon, et al., 1980; Miller, 1983; Weisberg, 1979), so that
the most definitive diagnoses are often those arrived at through neuropsychological assessment. Thus, probably the most common diagnostic request for neuropsychological assessment of elderly persons
involves patients who appear to be demented. In the elderly particu-

larly, the symptoms of depression often mimic the early appearance
of irreversible dementing processes (McAllister, 1983; Salzman &
Shader, 1979; Small & Jarvik, 1982). Many depressed elderly patients
become socially withdrawn and unresponsive. They complain of memory problems and seem to have difficulty keeping track of what is
going on around them. Their thinking may become simplistic, and
their ability to care for themselves appears to have deteriorated. Elderly depressed patients who appear demented but whose depression
goes unrecognized may be deprived of the treatment and care that
would enable them to return to a happier state and a more constructive level of functioning. Neuropsychological assessment can help differentiate between dementia and depression by eliciting the characteristic patterns of deficit associated with dementia or by uncovering
areas of competency and intact intellect that have been masked by
the depression.

   Neuropsychological assessment can also be useful in identifying
the nature of an organic disease process (Fuld, 1978; Gainotti, Caltagirone, Masullo, & Miceli, 1980). For example, the patient whose functioning is obviously deteriorating may be suffering from Alzheimer's
disease which is, as yet, untreatable; or the mental changes may be the
result of a condition called normal pressure hydrocephalus (NPH) in
which there is a slow erosion of deeply buried brain structures as a
result of blockages in the normal flow of cerebral spinal fluid through
the brain's ventricles (Adams, 1980; Torack, 1978). Since NPH can
often be alleviated by surgery, it becomes very important to differentiate those persons with early organic dementia who are suffering from
NPH from other victims of dementia whose condition is not treatable.

Neuropsychological Assessment
to Document the Course
of a Condition

Few disorders are static. Rather, the patient may enjoy improvement
following some single event such as a stroke, or will display deterioration when stricken with a degenerative condition such as Huntington's
disease, multiple sclerosis, or Alzheimer's disease (Lezak, 1983, pp.
209–216). Whether deterioration or improvement is expected, repeated neuropsychological testing will provide a great deal of information about the rate at which change is taking place, its regularity, and
whether the changes that are occurring fit the expected pattern. Repeated neuropsychological assessment allows the patient's family to
plan for the future in the most realistic manner. Repeated testing is

also useful to evaluate treatment; for example, to indicate whether surgery has been effective in halting the growth of a tumor or whether drugs are making a patient with Parkinson's disease more or less alert and responsive.

Neuropsychological Assessment in Evaluating the Patient's Mental Status

Probably the most common use of neuropsychological assessment today is to provide information about the patient's mental condition and how it relates to his/her capacity for self-care, psychosocial adjustment, or rehabilitation, and to other issues concerning the patient's psychological competency. The mental condition of a person suspected of suffering from a dementing disorder or known to have had some brain disease such as a stroke must be taken into account when questions arise regarding the patient's capacity to handle finances or exercise judgment. Information obtained from a neuropsychological examination can be of help to persons responsible for the patient's welfare who have to make decisions about his/her living situation—for example, whether the patient can continue to live alone, what level of care and protection is needed, and so on. Thus, neuropsychological data are valuable in counseling not only the patient but the patient's family and others who need to know how much assistance the patient requires, the extent to which the patient may participate in making decisions, and even such specific behavioral details as whether the patient is capable of handling his/her own medication. Information about the patient's neuropsychological status is often useful to other professionals who share in the responsibility for the patient's welfare. For example, it is important for physical therapists or occupational therapists working with the patient to know that the patient has a limited ability to learn, is unable to generalize or conceptualize effectively, or tends to be inattentive to the left side of space.

Information about the patient's mental incapacities can be particularly illuminating to relatives when the mentally impaired patient shows little if any physical evidence of the psychological changes that have taken place. Family members looking at the patient are likely to see him/her as the same person they have always known and thus continue to hold the same expectations of the patient and of their relationships that they have had for perhaps the last 30 or 40 years. These expectations can create a great deal of unhappiness, stress, and guilt for family members who may interpret the patient's withdrawal, confusion, or irritability to be reactions to something wrong that they—the family members—have done or not done. Family members who appreciate that the patient's personality has changed as a result of the brain disorder can better understand their limitations as well as the patient's in being able to restore the familiar person that they once knew. Families that understand the patient's disability experience less stress and can care for the patient more effectively.

Neuropsychological Assessment in Geriatric Research

Neuropsychological assessment has provided much of the data base for the study of how aging affects mental abilities (Benton & Sivan, 1984; Botwinick, 1981; Craik, 1977). In documenting the normal age changes that occur in mental functioning, neuropsychological studies have shown the importance of using age-graded norms in mental examinations of elderly people (Lewinsohn, 1973; Prigatano & Parsons, 1976; Simpson & Vega, 1971). Only by comparing an aging person's performance on mental tests with those of other people in the same age range can a valid estimate be made of the examinee's mental capacity. For example, research has shown that mental and motor slowing occurs at known rates with advancing years. To compare the performance of a person of 70 on a speeded test with standards set by a much younger population usually results in the older person receiving a score at a *borderline* or *defective* level (Lezak, 1983, p. 245). Moreover, inappropriate age standards would not aid in identifying abnormal slowing in elderly persons.

Neuropsychological research has also shown that different brain disorders result in different patterns of cognitive dysfunction. Documentation of a specific pattern of mental dysfunction in which there is marked impairment of the ability to perform complex and organized visuomotor acts while many verbal skills remain intact illustrates how the data of neuropsychological assessment can provide information about some early changes in Alzheimer's disease (Fuld, 1982; Horenstein, 1977). Neuropsychological assessment has also been helpful in evaluating treatment for brain diseases. Cerebrovascular surgery, for example, has been used to relieve the effects of strokes or ward off impending ones. Monitoring the effects of such surgery with repeated testing has shown that, by and large, little consistent improvement in mental status can be expected from these operations (Matarazzo, Matarazzo, Gallo, & Wiens, 1979; Parker et al., 1984).

Neuropsychological Assessment Procedures

Approaches to
Neuropsychological Assessment

Two distinct methods of doing neuropsychological assessment and handling the examination data have evolved. The *clinical approach* is
based on history and observations. It is characterized by (1) an individualized examination in which the patient's needs and the circumstances of the examination are taken into account; (2) sensitivity to
such qualitative features of the examination as *how* the subject solves
the test problems, whether he or she is aware of errors and tries to
correct them, and so on; and (3) its multidimensional focus on the
patient's emotional behavior and capacities for self-control and self-
regulation as well as the purely cognitive data elicited by formal tests.
The *psychometric approach,* in contrast, is based primarily on test
scores. Its prominent features are (1) the use of a standardized examination which requires that the same tests be given in the same way to
all patients; (2) reliance on quantitative data, that is, test scores; and
(3) a primary focus on cognitive functions. In some neuropsychological
assessment batteries, the Minnesota Multiphasic Personality Inventory
(MMPI) (Dahlstrom, Welsh, & Dahlstrom, 1975; Hathaway & McKinley, 1951), which is also a psychometric examination technique, is
included to assess personality and emotional status. Each approach has
distinctive advantages and disadvantages.

Clinical Approaches to Neuropsychological Assessment. In the
clinical approach, the examination is adapted to the patient's particular
problems and takes into account the patient's specific limitations.
Thus, if the patient's memory functioning appears to be the major
problem, the examination will focus primarily on the patient's memory
performance and not dwell heavily on those functions which a cursory
review may have shown to be basically intact. The individualized clinical approach typically has a flexible focus that allows for in-depth
exploration of problem areas without taxing the patient by overtesting
when it is not needed. Moreover, in looking at how the patient goes
about answering questions or solving problems, the examiner can identify the patient's strategies and the idiosyncratic characteristics of his/
her speech or thinking or memory processes. One major problem of
the clinical approach, however, is that clinical judgments are subjective. In the absence of objective norms, it becomes difficult to make

reliable comparisons between subjects or of one subject over a period of time. Moreover, communications about the subjective data can easily be misinterpreted and are always vulnerable to suspicions of bias.

  Psychometric Approaches to Neuropsychological Assessment. The advantages of psychometric approaches to neuropsychological assessment are in many ways counterparts of the disadvantages of clinical approaches. Chief among the advantages of the psychometric approach is objectivity: presumably the same test can be given to a patient at different times or by different examiners and virtually identical findings will be forthcoming. Moreover, many psychometric assessment systems provide for a systematic review of functions. Quantified data permit the development of standardized test norms against which any individual subject's performance can be meaningfully compared. The disadvantages of the psychometric approach stem from the restrictions that standardization imposes on the administration and interpretation of the data (e.g. the requirement that every patient be given the same tests in the same way). Thus, the observations made in a psychometric assessment will be limited to those allowed by the instruments used in the examination. Moreover, a strictly psychometric approach loses the qualitative features of a patient's performance, which can result in very distorted data. For example, should an elderly patient take longer than 10 seconds to generate the correct response to a memory question on the Luria-Nebraska Neuropsychological Battery (LNNB) (Golden, Hammeke, & Purisch, 1980), that patient receives a failing score for the response even though it might be correct. The fact that the failure was due to slowness and not to a memory deficit is lost amid the test scores.

  Combining Clinical and Psychometric Approaches. The literature in clinical neuropsychology today reflects an ongoing debate between the adherents of a rigid battery approach and those examiners who favor a clinical assessment. However, most experienced neuropsychologists rely on both clinical and psychometric methods in their procedures. A standardized administration of standardized tests provides the needed objectivity, allows the examiner to compare a patient's responses with normal subjects of the same age or with prior test scores obtained by the patient, and generates psychometric data that can be readily documented and communicated as well as used for research.
  In addition to giving a standardized examination, the examiner

who employs a combined approach will individualize the examination by testing functions in which the patient may have demonstrated some difficulties and bypassing those tests which do not appear to be relevant for understanding the patient's problems. The examiner will also amplify those procedures which seem especially important for explicating the nature of the patient's deficits. For example, when giving the mental arithmetic section of the Wechsler Intelligence Scales (Wechsler, 1944, 1955, 1981), the examiner may request a patient who gives the wrong answer to repeat the question to see whether the patient heard it correctly or remembered the problem long enough to be able to solve it. Should the patient demonstrate a short memory span, the examiner may request the patient to do the problem on paper. In this way, although the patient may have displayed the inability to do *mental* arithmetic, the examiner will discover whether the patient can solve the problem at all. Observations made in this extended part of the examination will not be reflected in test scores, but may be of much greater importance than unqualified arithmetic test scores in counseling patients and their families about the patient's competency for financial management, for example. In this way, the eclectic examiner aims to achieve an individualized examination which is appropriate for each patient while at the same time retaining the many advantages of a standardized test.

Importance of a Combined Approach in Geriatric Neuropsychology. Perhaps more than in any other area of neuropsychological assessment, a combined approach is needed when examining the elderly patient. On the one hand, standardized data are absolutely essential for the appropriate evaluation of mental changes in elderly persons. On the other hand, the motor and sensory handicaps so common to elderly persons frequently require the sensitive examiner to go beyond the standardized test format if the patient's residual ability is to be assessed thoroughly. Thus, the examiner may allow the patient additional time to complete a response or use techniques that will allow the patient to compensate for attentional or memory deficits as well as other handicaps. Only by means of an individualized examination can a patient's strengths, limitations, and particular needs be appropriately assessed. The integrated interpretation that is generated by this approach takes into account the patient's history and unique circumstances as well as feelings and attitudes expressed in the course of the examination in order to provide a functionally meaningful evaluation of the patient's mental status. By including the qualitative aspects of the examination in the final interpretation, the examiner can develop recommendations that will be appropriate for the patient's rehabilitation needs and problems of everyday living.

The Neuropsychological Examination

What the Examiner Needs to Know. In order to plan a suitable examination and to be able to integrate the examination findings in a meaningful manner, the examiner needs to have a good deal of background information about the patient. The patient's history will provide such important demographic information as educational level and work history. In addition, the history will often inform the examiner about previous medical conditions, about relevant habits such as drinking or smoking, and about the patient's personal attitudes such as those about work and other activities, expectations, and self-regard. These and other aspects of the patient's life may affect performance on a neuropsychological test (Lezak, 1983). Thus the historical data complement observations made in the preparatory interview prior to the examination and during the course of the examination itself. By integrating information from the patient's history with the behavioral observations made in the course of the examination, the astute and sensitive examiner can gain a rich and useful picture of the patient. Such a perspective provides a meaningful context in which the test performance may be interpreted and recommendations formulated.

In addition, a well-trained neuropsychologist brings to the examination a comprehensive understanding of neuropathologic processes and how they relate to psychological brain functions. The examiner needs to know the nature of onset, the course, the most typical presentations, and the likelihood of occurrence of common neuropathologic conditions. Only with a background in the neurosciences can the examiner know what the neuropsychological dimensions of a particular symptom or disorder might be. Without this information, the examiner cannot generate diagnostic hypotheses. In cases in which the diagnosis has already been established, a naive examiner may not know what functions should be studied, or when a given performance differs from an expected pattern. When doing geriatric neuropsychological assessment, the examiner should have a very thorough understanding of the conditions most likely to afflict the elderly patient and of the functional disorders that may mimic the symptoms of brain disease.

The examiner also needs to have a conceptual framework for the functional organization of behavior from a neuropsychological standpoint. The neuropsychological schema employed by this author provides a tripartite conceptualization of behavior in which the *cognitive* functions have to do with the processing of information, the *executive* functions are responsible for the efficiency of information processing, and *emotional* capacity concerns feelings and motivation. Neuropsychological research supports the analysis of behavior into these three main divisions. Each of these divisions, in turn, can be broken down into discrete functional groupings that have neuroanatomic correlates, thus permitting the examiner to evaluate the neurological substrate by analyzing and measuring its functional product.

Neuropsychological Assessment of Cognitive Functions.

NEUROPSYCHOLOGICAL ASSESSMENT OF PERCEPTUAL FUNCTIONS. Perceptual functions can be analyzed in terms of whether they primarily involve *verbal* or *nonverbal* material and according to the receptive modality. Since most cognitive information has a *visual, auditory,* or *tactile* basis, there are six major categories of perceptual functions for which neuropsychological tests have been developed. For example, along the verbal dimension, *visual perception* can be tested by examining reading accuracy (e.g., Diagnostic Screening Procedure, Boder, 1973; Gates-MacGinitie Reading Tests, Gates & MacGinitie, 1965, 1969), *auditory perception* can be examined by evaluating speech comprehension (e.g., selected aphasia battery subtests, F. L. Darley, 1979; Token Test, Boller & Vignolo, 1966), and *tactile perception* can be examined by palm or fingertip writing in which the examiner traces numbers or letters on a sensitive area of the patient's skin, asking the patient to identify the figure traced (e.g., skin writing, Rey, 1964; Fingertip Writing, Russell, Neuringer, & Goldstein, 1970). Tests of *nonverbal visuoperceptual functions* include those requiring the subject to match designs (e.g., Coloured Progressive Matrices, Raven, 1965) or to identify unfamiliar faces (e.g., Test of Facial Recognition, Benton, Hamsher, Varney, & Spreen, 1983). *Auditory perceptual functions* can be examined by tone discriminations (e.g., tonal subtest, amnesia battery, Wertheim & Botez, 1961) or rhythm identification tests (e.g., Seashore Rhythm Test, Halstead, 1947; Boll, 1981). *Tactile perception* can be examined by tests using textured material such as different grades of sandpaper (e.g., Quality Extinction Test, Schwartz, Marchok, & Flynn, 1977).

Closely associated with perceptual functions is the capacity for *orientation*. Among the several aspects of temporal orientation for which tests or scoring schemes have been devised are knowledge of present time (hour? day of week? date?) (e.g., Temporal Orientation Test, Benton, Van Allen, & Fogel, 1964), appreciation of the passage of time (how long in hospital? how long since test began?) (e.g., Galveston Orientation and Amnesia Test, Levin, O'Donnell and Grossman, 1979; time estimation, Talland, 1965), and the integrity of chronology (i.e., the ability for accurate recall and ordering of significant life events) (e.g., confabulation questionnaire, Mercer, Wapner, Gardner, & Benson, 1977). Spatial orientation, too, can be examined in a number of ways: Tests asking the patient to identify body parts examine the intactness of the body schema (e.g., Personal Orientation Test, Teuber, 1964; Weinstein, 1965). Right/left orientation may be tested by a series of direct commands (e.g., "right-Left disorientation" in Strub & Black, 1977) or on a grid in which a patient indicates the direction of turns (e.g., *Standardized Road Map Test of Direction Sense,* Money, 1976). The accuracy of angular orientation may be assessed by asking the patient to match pairs of truncated radii with completed angles (e.g., Judgment of Line Orientation, Benton, et al., 1983).

NEUROPSYCHOLOGICAL ASSESSMENT OF MEMORY AND LEARNING.   Like tests of perception, tests of memory and learning examine these functions in both auditory and visual modalities and with respect to verbal and nonverbal content. There are tests for each modality and each kind of content for each of the four major divisions of memory and learning that commonly require evaluation: *immediate span, short-term storage, long-term storage,* and *retrieval.* For example, *immediate auditory memory span* is usually tested by finding out what is the longest string of digits the subject can repeat (e.g., Wechsler's Digit Span Subtest, Wechsler, 1944, 1945, 1955, 1981); a visual verbal counterpart can be made up of simple, easily verbalizable pictures. The *immediate span of auditory nonverbal* material is testable by tasks requiring the patient to reproduce a rhythmic series of taps; an example of a visual nonverbal test of immediate memory span consists of a sequence of nonsense designs that are difficult to verbalize (e.g., Recurring Figures Test, Kimura, 1963). Other major divisions of memory and learning—*short-term storage* (the working memory), *long-term storage* (learned material), and *retrieval* (the ability to recall or recognize once-learned material)—have each acquired a voluminous collection of tests specific for verbal and nonverbal content in both the auditory and visual modalities (Lezak, 1983, pp. 418–474). Additional parameters on which memory tests may differ are meaningfulness, familiarity, quantity of material presented, and the degree to which the material is organized. These are just some of the memory variables that have demonstrated relevance to particular brain disorders and are also sensitive to changes that occur with aging (Craik, 1977).

The typical neuropsychological examiner may use only a half-dozen or so memory tests frequently and perhaps a few more on rare occasions. Yet, since the first publication of Ebbinghaus's initial studies of human memory in 1885, hundreds of memory tests have been devised for particular patient populations or research questions. A resourceful examiner who wishes to pursue a memory complaint or problem to its fullest may want to take advantage of procedures that have been described in the human cognition as well as the neuropsychological literature.

NEUROPSYCHOLOGICAL ASSESSMENT OF CONCEPTUAL PROCESSES. Although the verbal/nonverbal dichotomy plays less of a role in conceptual processes, thinking should be examined from both of these aspects. A convenient way of considering tests of conceptual processes divides them into three separate groups: (1) *Verbal concept formation* can be tested by asking the subject to interpret proverbs (e.g., Proverbs Test, Gorham, 1956) or to identify similarities between objects or concepts (e.g., Stanford-Binet Intelligence Scale, Terman & Merrill, 1973, *passim;* Similarities Subtest of the Wechsler Intelligence Scales, Wechsler, 1944, 1955, 1981). (2) *Nonverbal concept formation* is usually tested by requiring the subject to classify multidimensional objects such as colored blocks by color, shape, or size (e.g., Kasanin-Hanfmann Concept Formation Test, Hanfmann, 1953). (3) *Sort-and-shift* tests examine both *concept formation* and *mental flexibility* in the verbal modality by means of tests asking for both similarities and differences between objects (e.g., Object Sorting Test, Goldstein & Scheerer, 1953), and in a somewhat nonverbalizable format, by requiring the patient to pick the conceptual category for multidimensional stimuli (e.g., different numbers of designs in different colors) and then shifting the category to be identified (e.g., Wisconsin Card Sorting Test, Berg, 1948; Parsons, 1975; Taylor, 1979). There are many different kinds of tests for assessing *verbal reasoning* including arithmetic reasoning (e.g., Luria, 1973; Stanford-Binet Intelligence Scales, Terman & Merrill, 1973, *passim*). *Nonverbal reasoning* tests may require mathematical constructions or visuospatial operations (e.g., Raven Progressive Matrices, Denes, Semenza & Stoppa, 1978; Raven, 1960).

NEUROPSYCHOLOGICAL ASSESSMENT OF CONSTRUCTIONAL AND VERBAL RESPONSE FUNCTIONS. The two kinds of tasks used to assess constructional response functions are *assembling* and *drawing*. Each of these may be administered in a copy or in a free-response format. For example, a test requiring the patient to build a replica of a three-dimensional block construction is a copy test, while another test, in which the patient is asked to build Tinker Toy designs using his/her imagination, is a free-assembly task (Tinker Toy Test, Lezak, 1982, 1983). A restricted construction, in which the patient neither copies nor is free to build what he/she pleases, is represented by puzzle tasks in which the patient must join pieces together to make the correct solution (e.g., Object Assembly subtest of the Wechsler Intelligence Scales, Wechsler, 1944, 1955, 1981). Drawing tests that are counterparts of these constructional tasks require the subject to copy designs, to draw from memory or imagination persons or specified objects such as bicycles or houses, or to draw a very restricted object, such as a clock face, which allows for little innovation or imagination (e.g., Lezak, 1983, pp. 403–406). The major division in neuropsychological assessment of verbal response functions is between *spoken* and *written responses*. They can be examined in terms of the kind of stimulation that elicits the response. For example, spoken responses elicited by spoken words may involve tests calling on the patient to repeat what is heard or to answer a set of formal questions such as those asked on the Wechsler Intelligence Scales. Oral reading is a common means of testing spoken responses to written words. The examiner will also note spontaneous speech that may not have been prompted by anything the examiner did. Written responses include writing to dictation, writing to copy, or free writing in which the subject is asked to make a sentence out of a set of words or write a story. All of these dimensions are examined in detail in aphasia tests designed to assess communication in speech and language disorders. (see F. L. Darley, 1979; Lezak, 1983, pp. 313–320). Since disorders of speaking and writing may occur with many different kinds of brain damage, a routine assessment of these functions should be included in neuropsychological examinations of elderly persons (Golper & Binder, 1981).

The Neuropsychological Assessment of Attentional Functions. While not cognitive functions in themselves, the attentional functions play an integral role in cognitive behavior (Craik & Byrd, 1981). Attentional functions may be disrupted at different levels of complexity so that their assessment requires a range of tests of increasing complexity. Immediate recall of a string of numbers or letters (i.e., the digit or letter span test) represents an attentional task at the simplest level (Spitz, 1972). Backwards operations—in which a subject must recite a string of digits in reverse, spell words backwards, recite familiar sequences, such as days of the week or months of the year in reversed order—gets at mental tracking operations as well (Bender, 1979). Other tests involving mental tracking may require the patient to add a number that must be remembered through a prior addition (e.g., Paced Auditory Serial Addition Test, Gronwall, 1977), or to alternate number and letter sequences on paper, keeping in mind the sequence and position at each point (e.g., Trail Making Test, Armitage, 1946; Davies, 1968).

The Neuropsychological Assessment of Executive Functions. The executive functions are necessary for appropriate, socially responsible, and effectively self-serving behavior (Lezak, 1983). They include the abilities (1) *to formulate a goal,* (2) *to plan,* (3) *to carry out goal-directed plans,* and (4) *to maintain an effective performance.* Because executive behavior is normally not elicited in the typical structured clinical examination, executive defects have not come to the attention of many examiners and few tests of these functions have been devised. Thus, much of the information about how the patient goes about handling his/her affairs—or not handling them—must be garnered from observation.

For example, difficulties with goal formulation typically will show up when there are problems of initiation. The examiner not only needs to observe what the patient does when the examiner makes no demands but should inquire from family or other close observers what the patient does when left to his/her own devices. The ability to plan can be assessed by asking the patient to provide specific plans (i.e., What are you going to do when you leave the hospital? How do you take care of your laundry?). Defects in planning may also become apparent when a patient is asked to make up a story to a picture and approaches the task in a disjointed, unsystematic manner.

The Tinker Toy Test (Lezak, 1982, 1983) was devised to examine how well people can carry out a task on their own. In this test, 50 Tinker Toy pieces are given to the patient, who is asked to make whatever he/she wants and to take as long a time as needed. Constructions can be scored for the number of pieces used, for their complexity, and for the appropriateness of whatever name the subject gives them. On the basis of both their complexity and the number of pieces used, Tinker Toy Test performances of brain-damaged dependent patients (i.e., requiring full-time care) can be distinguished from those of brain-damaged patients who are not dependent; and the constructions of both groups of brain-damaged patients can be distinguished from those of normal control subjects. Evaluation of a patient's capacity for effective performance—that is, ability to monitor, to self-correct, and to shift appropriately according to situational changes—comes best from observations of the patient's test performance and the character of the patient's interaction with the examiner.

Emotional capacity is also affected by disorders of executive functions. Defects in executive functions will be reflected in abnormal intensity of emotional response, in inappropriate emotional behavior, and in impaired ability to control affect-laden responses. Observations of the patient's emotional behavior will contribute to an understanding of the patient's general neuropsychological status.

Neuropsychological Test Batteries in Current Use

Along with the many tests of relatively discrete functions, there are comprehensive batteries that include tests of many different kinds of functions. These batteries are often used in conjunction with individual tests or with one another. Some investigators may use only one battery or none. The advantages of batteries are that they provide a review of many different functions, a standardized administration, and standardized norms. However, when the examiner rigidly and unquestioningly applies the battery in the same way to every patient, the examination will no longer be appropriate for any patient. Not only is there likely to be considerable undertesting when using a formal test battery, but there may be overtesting as well. Moreover, a naive examiner may take false confidence from using a well-publicized battery without evaluating either the limitations of the battery or how well the battery meets the assessment needs of each patient.

The Wechsler Intelligence Scales. This set of tests was originally developed as an intelligence test (Wechsler, 1944, 1955, 1981). The Wechsler Scales have a number of advantages over previous intelligence tests. They are relatively easy to administer. They are composed of 11 separate subtests, which are actually individual tests having their own norms (including age-graded norms). The subtests can thus be used individually or as part of a battery, as the patient's situation requires. Moreover, the Wechsler Scales present a balanced examination of a variety of functions including constructional ability and visual reasoning.

For neuropsychological purposes, however, the Wechsler Scales have some decided limitations. Their format is misleading to the naive examiner as individual subtests were assigned to either "Verbal" or "Performance" scales by David Wechsler when he designed this battery of tests in the 1940s, long before the data from factorial studies had explicated what the subtests test (Matarazzo, 1972). For a number of the subtests, these assignments to "Verbal" and "Performance" subdivisions bear little relationship to subtest content. For example, performance on the Arithmetic and Digit Span subtests is not functionally related to performance on the other subtests in the Verbal Scale. Another example of misleading scale assignment is the Picture Completion subtest of the Performance Scale as factor analysis has shown that it is as strongly associated with Verbal Scale Subtests as it is with the Performance Scale. Moreover, Picture Completion contains no "performance" elements since it asks for a verbal response! Yet neither Wechsler nor his heirs have changed subtest assignments to accord with the data.

Another pitfall for the naive examiner lies in the use of summed scores to obtain a "Verbal Scale," a "Performance Scale," or a "Full Scale IQ" score. Any time scores from disparate measures are summed, the information conveyed by the individual scores is obscured. This can readily be illustrated with students' grade-point averages. Using the standard formula, a student who has achieved two grades of A and two grades of F (or failure) on his report card will have a grade-point average of 2.0, which translates into a grade of C, a grade that represents neither the student's best performance nor his worst and is therefore uninformative if not frankly misleading. The same problem arises from averaging subtest scores from the Wechsler Scales or any other set of tests. When the Wechsler Scale subtest data are treated as discrete scores that can be compared with one another and used to elicit patterns of cognitive functioning, the Wechsler Scales contribute rich and valuable neuropsychological information. When the scores are summed, the component scores are obscured, and the summed score is meaningless.

The Halstead-Reitan Battery (HRB). This test battery is very popular with many clinicians who use it in combination with the Wechsler Intelligence Scales, and sometimes in combination with memory and other tests (e.g., Boll, 1981; Reitan & Davison, 1974). Its basic core consists of five tests which were originally developed by Halstead (1947), who was looking for tests that would be sensitive to frontal-lobe damage. It has proven useful in identifying the presence of brain damage since the variety of tests included in it tend to be sensitive to many kinds of cerebral function. Thus, a brain-damaged patient who does well on one of the subtests may perform poorly on another subtest that is more appropriate for his/her particular kind of disorder. Unfortunately, the HRB norms were developed on a very small population (29 subjects) with an average age of 28.9 (the youngest subject was 14 and the oldest was 51) (Halstead, 1947).

Besides giving scores on each of the five subtests (three scores are generated on a formboard test done by blindfolded subjects), the scoring system provides for an Impairment Index, which is simply the proportion of tests "failed," that is, performed below a cut-off score based on norms developed on the original normative population. Like an "IQ" score, the Impairment Index also obscures the data in that it is impossible to tell from the number alone the nature of the disorder the patient may be suffering. Moreover, a patient with a very discrete deficit may achieve a low (good) Impairment Index score and not be recognized as suffering from a brain disorder. In addition, the norms are so unsuitable for elderly persons that many neuropsychologically intact individuals over 70 will achieve scores in the impaired range (Bak & Greene, 1980; Prigatano & Parsons, 1976).

The adventures of the HRB are those of the psychometric approach generally. The fact that the administration and scoring systems are standardized allows for repeat testing, for comparisons between patients, and for the recognition of known patterns of performance for particular patient groups. The HRB came into general use at a time when many clinical psychologists had limited test repertoires. With its relatively broad range of tests, this battery demonstrated the importance of examining many different functions for neuropsychological purposes. In addition, many examiners have become very familiar with this test and with the extensive literature concerning it. This familiarity enhances the ability of the individual examiner to use the test and to interpret the findings. Many practitioners who employ the HRB— particularly those who combine it with other tests—have developed sensitive interpretive skills.

The limitations of the HRB are, like its advantages, those of psychometric tests. Thus, there is both overtesting and undertesting. Some of the material is redundant, such as that used to identify the side of a lateralized lesion. This redundancy results in unnecessary testing, particularly when a patient has already received a diagnosis or presents with obviously lateralized symptoms. The most prominent weakness of the HRB lies in the absence of a systematic review of memory functions. Many other functions are not examined by this battery either, such as the abilities to read, write, or spell effectively, to perform arithmetic calculations, to draw or copy nonverbalizable material, and so on. Moreover, as presently constituted, this battery is very time consuming in that it takes six to eight hours for the complete administration, which usually includes one of the Wechsler Scales and an objective personality test, such as the Minnesota Multiphasic Personality Inventory (MMPI) (Dahlstrom et al., 1975; Hathaway & McKinley, 1951). The Halstead-Reitan Battery also contains equipment that is bulky and difficult to transport. Among other problems inherent in the Halstead-Reitan Battery is that significant education effects have been found (Finlayson, Johnson, & Reitan, 1977). Perhaps even more important to the examination of elderly persons is the fact that at present there are no fully standardized age norms, although the sensitivity of this test to the effects of aging has been well demonstrated.

Luria's Neuropsychological Investigation. Scattered throughout the writings of the late Russian neuropsychologist A. R. Luria are descriptions of fragments of many of the different kinds of tests he used in the course of his very individualized neuropsychological examinations of patients (Luria, 1966, 1973). Many items from formal tests plus examination techniques that he developed or adapted from the neurologic examination were selected and organized by Anna-Lisa Christensen (1979) so that other investigators could apply Luria's very flexible and experimental examination approach. This loosely organized collection of techniques was turned into a psychometric instrument by C. J. Golden, who structured Christensen's functional grouping of examination procedures and isolated test items into "scales" and arbitrarily assigned numerical values on a three-point scale to these items and procedures. This instrument, the Luria-Nebraska Neuropsychological Test Battery, currently enjoys widespread popularity (Golden, 1981; Golden et al., 1980).

The advantages of Golden's battery stem mainly from the ease of administration and the seeming simplicity of interpretation. The scoring system developed by Golden is relatively easy to learn and interpretation is based on high (abnormal) scores, both in terms of overall score level and of elevations on particular scales. Moreover, the test is portable and takes no more than an hour or two to administer. Dr. Golden and his colleagues have published many articles showing that this battery distinguishes between selected groups of brain-damaged persons, psychiatric patients, and normal subjects (Golden, 1981; Golden et al., 1980). However, they have neglected to point out that the neurologists' mental-status examination as well as any number of other tests also allow such discriminations to be made.

Unfortunately, this instrument, which promised to do so much with relatively little effort, is riddled with defects. In the first place, the so-called scales are not composed of homogeneous items and thus are not scales at all. Rather, they consist of collections of heterogeneous items that examine different facets of similar functions. Moreover, the scales are not only poorly described but tend to be confounded in that many of them test both more and less of what they purport to examine

(Delis & Kaplan, 1982; Spiers, 1981). For example, correct but slow responses can result in failure on some items on the Memory Scale. Thus the patient's score may suggest memory impairment when the problem is quite different. This defect has particular relevance for elderly persons who may make slow responses for any number of reasons and still be very competent to perform the required task. Many of the items on the Expressive Speech scale depend on a patient having intact receptive speech functions. Thus, an abnormally high score on this scale is just as likely to reflect a receptive problem as an expressive one, but the score could lead to an erroneous interpretation (Crosson & Warren, 1982; Delis & Kaplan, 1982, 1983). Another problem with this battery results from Luria's special interest in left-hemisphere damage, making this collection of test items heavily biased toward the examination of functions with verbal components to the relative neglect of visuospatial and gestalt functions. Moreover, the effects of aging are purportedly controlled for by applying the same correction factor to all subjects 45 years of age and older without regard to the fact that different functions tend to decline at different rates, and that overall the rate of decline increases with advancing age. The many questionable aspects of Golden's reformulation of Christensen's attempts to organize Luria's testing techniques in a systematic fashion cast serious doubts on the validity of test interpretations based on Golden's system.

Special Considerations When Examining Elderly Persons

Physical and attitudinal problems can complicate the examination of elderly persons. Thus the examiner must be sensitive both to the patient's physical status and capacities and to the kinds of fears and misunderstandings that may interfere with the elderly patient's ability to cooperate satisfactorily.

Sensory Disabilities.   When examining any person over the age of 45, the examiner must check for both visual and auditory competency. Patients who wear reading glasses should use them for the examination whenever possible. Sometimes patients who have been hospitalized hurriedly may not have brought their reading glasses with them. Examiners in hospital settings should be prepared for this problem by having reading glasses available as part of the standard testing equipment.

While most older people will willingly admit to visual changes, many hard-of-hearing persons find it difficult to reveal an auditory handicap—preferring to guess words they can make out with difficulty, if at all, to asking the examiner to speak more loudly or more clearly. Since auditory deficits are very common in an older population, the examiner must be alert to signs of impaired hearing, such as a patient cocking his head or making a consistent pattern of errors in response to conversation or spoken questions. It is a kindness, when a hearing deficit is suspected, to inquire about it and, if the patient admits to the problem, to advise the patient to obtain an audiological consultation with the possible goal of getting a hearing aid. Unfortunately, it is not possible to provide the patient with a hearing aid for the neuropsychological examination. When a patient is hard of hearing, the examiner must speak loudly or even shout if necessary. If the patient's auditory handicap is too severe, then the examination must be limited to visually presented material until the patient has acquired an effective hearing aid.

Motor Handicaps. A number of elderly persons have motor problems that may slow their responses, impair finely controlled movements, or—in the case of a full-blown paralysis—prevent the patient from making any motor response at all. Besides motor deficits that result from neurologic disease, many elderly persons suffer from bursitis, arthritis, or other bone or joint diseases that limit their capacity to give complete and swift motor responses. In these cases, the examiner must be discriminating, in both selecting tests and interpreting test performances. For example, a right-handed patient with a right-handed paralysis may have difficulties on a drawing or writing task. If the patient is at all capable of using a hand, the examiner may want to include tests that normally have a time limitation. When the patient cannot complete the test in the alloted time, rather than discontinuing the test, the examiner will gain a great deal of information simply by allowing the patient to finish the task or at least to continue letting the patient work until fatigue, boredom, or frustration becomes excessive. In short, the examiner should feel free to modify standard tests in order to test the limits of the elderly patient's motor capacity. When interpreting performance on a speed-dependent task, motor problems must be taken into account.

Problems That May Compromise Cooperation. Many elderly people become set in their ways and increasingly fearful of change, of anything that might disrupt their schedule, and of anything that is new or surprising. These fears are particularly likely to occur in patients whose physical or mental disabilities prevent them from functioning with full independence or maintaining their normal social activities and family responsibilities. Thus, while some elderly patients welcome the neuropsychological examination as an interesting and stimulating diversion, others may regard it as an intrusion on their privacy or fear that they will look foolish or that their poor performance may be held against them. In some cases, these concerns have a basis in reality. Thus, it is very important that the examiner give explanations at a level that the patient can understand. When a patient's worst fears are founded—as when the examination is being undertaken to evaluate competency—careful explanation must be made not only of the examination, but of its purpose and the alternatives the patient may have available.

Fatigue is a significant problem for anyone who is ill. Older patients suffering a brain disorder may be abnormally susceptible to fatigue (Lezak, 1978). Moreover, at the upper age levels, fatigue becomes an increasingly great problem. Within the first month or two following a stroke, for example, many patients will have no more than 15 minutes to a half-hour of peak efficiency a day. An examination undertaken later in the day, after the patient has engaged in an activity, or even immediately after having had to do the work of eating a meal, will only tell the examiner how poorly the patient does when fatigued. Thus, the examination of many older persons, particularly those who have had a stroke or are suffering from some other central nervous system disorder, may have to be conducted in many brief visits extended over a period of days if the patient is to perform at his or her best.

Distractibility is another problem that besets persons who have sustained significant brain damage (Lezak, 1978). The examiner needs to guard against this problem by testing in a quiet, preferably familiar place, and guarding against auditory and visual distractions as much as possible. Of course, the examiner may deliberately introduce distractions to test the patient's capacity to withstand them; but then the examiner should keep distractions at a minimum.

Relationship to Intervention

Utilization of Evaluation

Clinical Assessment Must Always Have a Stated Purpose. Essentially all referrals are for one of three purposes: for patient care, for the welfare of the patient's family, or for an institutional or community benefit. In many cases, more than one purpose will be served by the assessment. Referrals for neuropsychological assessment should contain a formulation of the problem that will allow the examiner to make an appropriate response (e.g., would retraining help this patient master enough Activities of Daily Living to return to the family's care?).

Clinical Assessment Must Always Be Responsive to the Referral Purpose. In general, the end product of neuropsychological assessment will be recommendations concerning care or treatment for the patient, management, or other recommendations for the family and for other persons involved with the patient. (For example, a nursing home may wish to know whether a patient can benefit enough from retraining to be able eventually to return to his family's care at home.) Even when the referral request is simply for diagnosis, it is incumbent upon the examiner to make recommendations when he/she has obtained information in the course of the examination that can be used on behalf of the patient or those associated with the patient. Sometimes the referral may be addressed to an issue that, upon examination, turns out to be only one of several that are of concern. For example, a referral may ask for a review of memory functions when executive function disabilities are contributing far more than poor memory to the patient's social debilitation. In this case, the examiner needs to study and report on the executive functions as well as identify all of the other relevant issues that can be addressed by responsible neuropsychological assessment.

All Findings and Recommendations Must Be Conveyed in an Intelligible Report. Any person making an appropriate referral of a patient for neuropsychological assessment has the right to expect a report in which all of the relevant findings are communicated in language that any intelligent lay person can understand. There is no behavioral observation or set of scores that cannot be translated into good everyday English. Since many reports will be used, reports must be written in a way that makes them comprehensible to all of these people. Otherwise, the report will not serve its purpose. Reports should not contain jargon, whether it be technical terminology or scores that cannot be deciphered by persons with little or no background in statistics or psychometrics.

Integration of Assessment Findings into Intervention

The findings of neuropsychological assessments may be used directly in the treatment of elderly persons or indirectly, to facilitate the treatment given by other therapists, such as speech pathologists or other members of a rehabilitation team. Memory problems are among the most common disorders that trouble brain-damaged persons or interfere with their ability to benefit from rehabilitation. For some patients, there are treatments that can be of direct help; when this is not possible, the findings of the neuropsychological assessment can contribute to rational and humane management. Examples of interventions for memory and other prominent problems are given below.

Treatment of Memory Problems. Among the many kinds of memory problems that beset brain-damaged persons are those that are as much or more the product of attentional disorders than anything else (Craik & Byrd, 1981). When an attentional problem has been identified, the attendant "memory disorder" can often be ameliorated through counseling, training geared to teaching subjects to focus and direct their attention, or a combination of these techniques. Highly distractible patients who are capable of self-direction, insight, and self-awareness can be taught how to reduce distractors in their environment, how to set up a situation that will be conducive to learning, and how to use repetition and rehearsal to overcome the effects of distraction. When rehabilitation efforts are compromised by a patient's distractibility, the therapist may be able to use these same techniques to enhance the patient's learning.

In each case, the nature of the memory disorder must be identified for appropriate treatment to be instituted. If the patient's memory problem lies in his/her inability to consolidate new information, no amount of attention training or removal of distractions will improve the memory performance significantly. The aware patient who can function independently can be counseled on the use of memory aids, such as notebooks, bulletin boards, and wristwatch alarms. However, if the patient does not appreciate that there is a problem or is incapable or being motivated to do anything about it, then the patient will probably not benefit from treatment, whether it be direct or indirect. When the memory-impaired patient has demonstrated that he or she is unable to benefit from *any* memory-enhancement techniques, the neuropsychological report should make management, not treatment, recommendations that will give practical guidance to the patient's family or caretaker and spare them false hopes.

Hemi-inattention Problems. Some patients, particularly those with right-sided brain lesions involving the sensory cortex, suffer from decreased or absent awareness of the side of their body or of events presenting to the side of their body opposite the brain lesion. This condition is called hemi-inattention or unilateral neglect. Subtle inattention problems may interfere with the patient's ability to read or to navigate safely on a sidewalk or crossing the street (Diller & Weinberg, 1970). Although gross inattention is usually obvious to even the casual observer, subtle defects may become apparent only through careful neuropsychological study (e.g., Denes et al., 1978). When they are identified, they are often amenable to a treatment program which calls the patient's attention to the disorder and teaches the patient to use verbal cues to heighten awareness of the neglected side (Diller & Weinberg, 1977).

Anosognosia. This cryptic-looking term means impaired awareness of one's own illness or defects. Like hemi-inattention, when it is grossly present it is obvious. However, it can be a subtle symptom of an early dementing process, of right-hemisphere or of frontal-lobe disease. Patients who do not fully appreciate the nature or extent of their disabilities are unable to cooperate intelligently in their rehabilitation. When working with these patients, rehabilitation therapists may puzzle over the patient's lack of cooperation without understanding that the patient's reluctance to cooperate results from defects in cerebral processing. Identification of the nature of the patient's lack of motivation can pave the way for rational counseling and training that enables patients to appreciate their deficits and actively participate in their treatment program.

Special Issues Re: Elderly

In the interpretation of the data of neuropsychological examinations and their application to the care and treatment of old people, there are three major sources of misinterpretation. Neglect of any one of them can result in serious error. (1) Test scores must be evaluated in relation to age norms. This is particularly important when examining functions which tend to change significantly with age, such as those involving motor speed, solving novel problems, and memory. (2) The examiner must be alert to evidence of depression. Significant depression can masquerade as dementia, or the overriding impoverishment of responses due to depression can mask a pattern of neuropsychological deficits that would indicate the presence of a medically treatable condition. (3) The examiner must be alert to the possibility that an elderly person may be suffering from a chronic disease that can have neuropsychological ramifications—such as diabetes mellitus (Holmes, Hayford, Gonzales, & Weydert, 1983; Pulsinelli et al.,

1983) or high blood pressure (Wilkie & Eisdorfer, 1971). The examiner needs to be knowledgeable about the elderly patient's medical status and to be alert to the neuropsychological ramifications of various diseases.

Case Illustration

First Neurologic Examination and Report

This 66-year-old CPA was examined for approximately two hours to evaluate his neuropsychological status relative to recent complaints of memory problems. Mr. X was examined by means of interview and the following tests: Wechsler Adult Intelligence Scale—Revised (Information, Arithmetic, Similarities, Digit Span, Picture Completion, and Block Design subtests), subtracting serial sevens, Rey's Auditory-Verbal Learning Test, the Complex Figure Test (Osterreith figure), Babcock and PVAH paragraph recall test, Controlled Oral Verbal Fluency Test, and Sentence Building (Stanford-Binet). In addition, he was given an abbreviated sensory examination (visual fields and finger recognition).

Background Information.   This senior partner in a prominent accounting firm reported that he has had bouts of depression for at least a decade and that he had had a serious drinking problem which he overcame some years ago. He reported suffering a mild stroke several years ago and, as a result, has lost vision in the lower left quadrant of his visual fields. He denies any other sequelae of this event. In the spring of this year, against his judgment, his firm undertook a major expansion which is creating financial problems. He has been troubled by depression since this summer and dates his memory problems to this summer as well.

Observation.   This well-groomed, congenial and very cooperative gentleman was alert, oriented, and appropriate in his demeanor. Speech production was a little slower than ordinary but within normal limits. Response latencies tended to be long except when doing arithmetic problems, when they were very short. Vocabulary, grammar, and syntax were in line with his education and occupation, although at times he tended to be repetitive in the format of his responses, as though less appreciative of verbal style than is customary for experienced financial counselors. Thinking tended to have a practical bent and was focused. Affect was somewhat muted. He described himself as depressed, but his mood seemed to be characterized more by seriousness and preoccupation than by evident sadness.

Test Performance. On gross visual field examination, Mr. X was not aware of stimuli presented to the lower left quadrant. Twice out of several trials he confused the third and fourth fingers of his left hand. He also indicated his left thumb when asked to show the right one, but this was the only instance of L–R confusion.

His performance on verbal tests was somewhat variable. Verbal fluency was excellent, and he displayed good category-based strategies for recalling words. In contrast was a just *average* score on a test of simple verbal abstracting (categorizing) ability in which he gave a surprising number of concrete answers and also confused relationships between specific concepts (e.g., "egg and seed alike?" "produced by something"). Although his recall of common information was a little better (*high average*), he gave wrong answers or no answers to questions on topics familiar to most persons of his age and background.

Arithmetic performance, however, was fast and excellent. His score on story problems was in the *superior* ability range. Mental tracking, as examined by serial sevens, was generally adequate—certainly well within normal limits for both speed and accuracy.

On tests of visual reasoning and visuospatial construction he obtained scores just in the *high average* ability range, but again he displayed some surprising difficulties. In reasoning about incomplete pictures, he tended to be slow in responding but failed on this count only once. However, he did miss some fairly obvious answers as well as several of the more difficult ones. Response times on the block design copying task were so slow that, although he successfully copied all of the designs, two of them were completed outside of the time limits. This slowing resulted from difficulties suggestive of a very mild constructional disability and some perseveration in reproducing incorrect solutions, although he readily perceived his errors. The constructional disability became obvious when he copied the Complex Figure, as his approach was fragmented, his proportions were somewhat distorted, he drew in one line too many, and he was unable to copy a diamond correctly, reproducing it as a crude triangle.

With the exception of a digit span forward and backward of 6 and 5, which was *within normal limits* for a man of his age, Mr. X's performance on all memory tests—verbal and visual, immediate and delayed, for meaningless and for meaningful material—was *below normal limits* and seemed to support his claims of memory impairment. However, he recalled perfectly an arithmetic question containing approximately 30 syllables (well above the normal adult range) after some interference, showing that when he was not attending to memory but to doing something he did well, his memory performance improved. This suggests that his memory may be somewhat better than he demonstrated here. In addition, the pattern of overall failure on memory items, regardless of their nature, also supports the possibility that at least some of his memory disturbance results from anxiety and interfering preoccupations.

Summary.   This man of originally at least *superior* intellectual endowment is no longer functioning at that level in a number of areas. The most salient deficits appear as a mild constructional disability and as a generalized "memory" problem. In addition, some subtle difficulties show up in verbal retrieval, verbal expression, and verbal abstraction. The constructional deficits and the mild problems of verbal abstraction and conceptual organization may be accounted for by the reported stroke. It is not possible at this time to estimate the extent to which his memory complaints stem from an organic problem or reflect his current anxiety and state of mental distractions due to depression and his financial concerns. It is certainly possible that his awareness and focus on memory complaints represent his awareness of failing mental faculties and results, at least in part, from his efforts to make sense for himself of his loss of mental efficiency. One may suspect that the office turmoil of this year, with its changes in routine activities and customary places, has brought Mr. X's stroke-related disabilities to light, at least for him. Thus in part, his current distress may reflect his growing awareness of these disabilities. This apparently lateralized pattern of deficts does not appear to be due to a progressive condition.

Recommendations.

1. Although relatively mild, Mr. X's difficulties in handling complex configurational relationships may compromise efforts to do complex planning or organization (such as laying out the strategy for a complicated financial program or dealing with the many details of his firm's growth), create a great deal of stress for Mr. X, and probably overtax his mildly limited abilities in this area. With his experience and

wisdom, he can probably serve best as an advisor and supervisor of younger accountants.

2. Should Mr. X continue to have the same degree of concern about his memory when he is no longer as depressed and distracted as he is now, a reevaluation would be in order.

Second Neurologic Examination and Report

This 68-year-old CPA requested a second neuropsychological evaluation on the recommendation of his physician, after suffering a second CVA two months ago. He was examined by means of interview and the following tests: Wechsler Adult Intelligence Scale—Revised (selected subtests), mental tracking (serial sevens, alphabet and months reversed), clock face, line bisection task, Hooper Visual Organization Test, sentence building, Sentence Repetition subtest of the Multilingual Aphasia Examination, Logical Memory subtest of the Wechsler Memory Scale (Babcock format), Complex Figure Test (Taylor figure), Category Test (Halstead-Reitan, card format).

Subjective. Mr. X complained about memory problems and difficulty in concentrating, but denied significant changes in thinking. He acknowledged that because he fatigues easily he now works a shorter day and is too tired to pick up work in the evening as he has done in the past.

Objective. Mr. X was alert, oriented, and socially appropriate. Speech was unremarkable. Thinking tended to be focused on practical, concrete issues and a little repetitive, but was unexceptional in conversation.

Although his demeanor and bearing gave Mr. X the superficial appearance of stolid geniality, he was unable to maintain this facade when reporting the events six months ago when he lost one sibling, was under a great deal of work pressure, and then unexpectedly lost a second sibling. In relating this, Mr. X broke into tears several times and appeared to suffer acute distress at this emotional display. He reported that only thoughts of his siblings' deaths elicit these crying spells, but he cannot think of these recent losses without tears. His report was supported in that he did not cry or seem emotionally labile at any other time, although a number of topics were discussed and discouragingly poor performance on some tasks was very evident. In general, he seemed to be mildly but not inappropriately depressed. He gave the impression of emotional fragility, that is, if pushed too hard, he would not be able to maintain his emotional composure. At the end of the examination Mr. X asked for help with his smoking habit and a number of recommendations and much encouragement were given.

When he dried his tears, Mr. X seemed to be unaware that some drops remained on his left cheek, suggesting diminished tactile appreciation. However, no testing for tactile perception was conducted.

TEST PERFORMANCE.   Well-learned verbal skills and visual reasoning abilities remained at *high average* to *superior* levels, essentially unchanged from the previous examination. Visuospatial organization, as elicited by freehand design copying, showed significant improvement since the first examination. Moreover, visual memory appears intact. Mental tracking, which was examined more closely this time, is intact for all practical purposes as Mr. X made relatively few errors. However, he performed mental tracking tasks at what appeared to be a great cost in effort and energy: his face reddened when doing serial subtractions and reversed operations, and he worked slowly and with considerable hesitation.

In contrast to these areas in which he continues to perform without significant impairment, Mr. X displayed a number of deficits which had not been previously observed.

1. Verbal memory, which was moderately impaired before, was seriously defective in two aspects: immediate recall for digits forward is only 4 (compared to 6 in 1981), at the *defective* level; digits backward is also 4 (compared to 5), in the *borderline defective* range. His ability to recall details of a little story was virtually nil, either on immediate recall or recall following a delay during which he performed other tasks that served as distractors. Thus, both immediate recall when given more material than can be held in immediate attention span and verbal learning were significantly impaired in this examination. However, his span of recall for meaningful verbal material (i.e., sentences) is virtually intact although susceptible to occasional errors (e.g., "Wednesday" for "Tuesday" in the 24-syllable sentence; most adults can recall sentences of this length with perfect accuracy).

2. Despite a score in the *superior* ability range (the top 5%) on a test of commonsense reasoning and practical judgment, Mr. X displayed a serious lapse of judgment in stating he would, "Get up and yell fire," if he were the first person to see smoke and fire at the movies. A pattern in which this particular defective response occurs along with many good ones suggests a breakdown of judgment and active reasoning in a bright,

socially experienced person who can still call upon well-indoctrinated social learning in most situations calling for social judgment, but whose judgment deteriorates when confronted with new or emotionally charged issues. Mr. X also demonstrated some inability to apply new information to conceptual problem solving which, in the light of a few instances of mild verbal perseveration, suggests a more general problem with conceptual shifting and mental flexibility.

3. Ability to do mental arithmetic has dropped from *superior* to low in the *high average* range. Mr. X either made calculation errors or did not perform the required calculations on several items answered correctly one and a half years ago.

Assessment.

1. This man of once *superior* ability continues to perform at or close to his original capacity on many learned skills and on tasks involving visuospatial concepts and visual reasoning. The major deficits appearing on this examination are in verbal attention span and verbal learning, practical judgment and conceptual thinking, and mental arithmetic. These deficits appear to be sufficient to compromise Mr. X's ability to practice his profession independently, without outside review of his work.

2. The emotional lability displayed by Mr. X suggests that he is functioning under more stress (depression, fatigue) than he cares to admit.

Recommendations.

1. Mr. X should be counseled regarding the need for external review of his work at this time. It should be stressed that this examination was conducted so soon after his most recent stroke that some of his current problems may still reflect the effects of acute processes and thus may diminish significantly within the next several months. However, at least for two or three months, Mr. X's work needs to be reviewed.

2. The possibility of his playing a much less active role in his firm should probably be considered if he does not show significant improvement in the next few months. However, this recommendation could have far-reaching emotional ramifications and should probably be raised only after consultation with his psychiatrist.

3. More rest and reduced work hours should ameliorate Mr. X's

emotional labililty if it is primarily due to fatigue. If he continues to experience uncontrollable crying, it is more likely symptomatic of depression, and psychiatric help should be considered.

4. Since this examination was conducted so soon after his last stroke, Mr. X may show significant improvement in the next month or two. If he does not have any more strokes, his energy returns, and he feels that he is performing more effectively, another examination in four to six months would show whether the problems observed in this examination are permanent or transient and whether he can resume full professional responsibility.

References

Adams, R.D. (1980). Altered cerebrospinal fluid dynamics in relation to dementia and aging. In L. Amaducci, A.N. Davison, & P. Antuono (Eds.), *Aging of the brain and dementia.* New York: Raven Press.

Armitage, S.G. (1946). An analysis of certain psychological tests used for the evaluation of brain injury. *Psychological Monographs, 60,* (Whole No. 277).

Bak, J.S., & Greene, R.L. (1980). Changes in neuropsychological functioning in an aging population. *Journal of Consulting and Clinical Neuropsychology, 48,* 395–399.

Bender, M.B. (1979). Defects in reversal of serial order of symbols. *Neuropsychologia, 17,* 125–138.

Benton, A.L., Hamsher, K. deS., Varney, N.R., & Spreen, O. (1983). *Contributions to neuropsychological assessment.* New York: Oxford University Press.

Benton, A.L., Van Allen, M.W., & Fogel, M.L. (1964). Temporal orientation in cerebral disease. *Journal of Nervous and Mental Disease, 139,* 109–119.

Benton, A.L., & Sivan, A.B. (1984). Problems and conceptual issues in neuropsychological research in aging and dementia. *Journal of Clinical Neuropsychology, 6,* 57–63.

Berg, E.A. (1948). A simple objective test for measuring flexibility in thinking. *Journal of General Psychology, 39,* 15–22.

Boder, E. (1973). Developmental dyslexia: A diagnostic approach based on three atypical reading-spelling patterns. *Developmental Medicine and Child Neurology, 15,* 663–687.

Boll, T.J. (1981). The Halstead-Reitan Neuropsychology Battery. In S. B. Filskov & T. J. Boll (Eds.), *Handbook of clinical neuropsychology.* New York: Wiley–Intersciences.

Boller, F., & Vignolo, L.A. (1966). Latent sensory aphasia in hemisphere-damaged patients: An experimental study with the Token Test. *Brain, 89,* 815–831.

Botwinick, J. (1981). Neuropsychology of aging. In S. B. Filskov & T. J. Boll (Eds.), *Handbook of clinical neuropsychology.* New York: Wiley–Intersciences.

Christensen, A.L. (1979). *Luria's neuropsychological investigation. Text* (2nd ed.). Copenhagen: Munksgaard.

Craik, F.I.M. (1977). Age differences in human memory. In J.E. Birren & K.W. Schaie (Eds.), *Handbook of the psychology of aging.* New York: Van Nostrand.

Craik, F.I.M. & Byrd, M. (1981). Aging and cognitive deficits: The role of attentional resources. In F.I.M. Craik & S.E. Trehub (Eds.), *Aging and cognitive processes.* New York: Plenum Press.

Crosson, B., & Warren, R. L. (1982). Use of the Luria-Nebraska Neuropsychological Battery in aphasia: A conceptual critique. *Journal of Consulting and Clinical Psychology, 50,* 22–31.

Dahlstrom, W.G., Welsh, G.S., & Dahlstrom, L. E. (1975). *An MMPI handbook. Vol. 1. Clinical interpretation* (Rev ed.). Minneapolis: University of Minnesota Press.

Darley, F.L. (1979). *Evaluation of appraisal techniques in speech and language pathology.* Reading, Ma: Addison-Wesley.

Davies, A. (1968). The influence of age on Trail Making test performance. *Journal of Clinical Psychology, 24,* 96–98.

de Leon, M.J., Ferris, S.H., George, A.E., et al. (1980). Computed tomography evaluations of brain-behavior relationships in senile dementia of the Alzheimer's type. *Neurobiology of Aging, 1,* 69–79.

Delis, D., & Kaplan, E.F. (1982). The assessment of aphasia with the Luria-Nebraska Neuropsychological Battery: A case critique. *Journal of Consulting and Clinical Psychology. 50,* 32–39.

Delis, D., & Kaplan, E.F. (1983). Hazards of a standardized neuropsychological test with low content validity: Comment on the Luria-Nebraska Battery. *Journal of Consulting and Clinical Psychology, 51,* 396–398.

Denes, F., Semenza, C., & Stoppa, E. (1978). Selective improvement by unilateral brain-damaged patients on Raven Coloured Progressive Matrices. *Neuropsychologia, 16,* 749–752.

Diller, L., & Weinberg, J. (1970). Evidence for accident-prone behavior in hemiplegic patients. *Archives of Physical Medicine and Rehabilitation, 51,* 358–363.

Diller, L, & Weinberg, J. (1977). Hemi-inattention in rehabilitation: The evolution of a rational remediation program. In E.A. Weinstein & R.P. Freidland (Eds.), *Advances in neurology* (Vol. 18). New York: Raven Press.

Finlayson, M.A.J., Johnson, K.A., & Reitan, R.M. (1977). Relationship of level of education to neuropsychological measures in brain-damaged and non-brain-damaged adults. *Journal of Consulting and Clinical Psychology, 45,* 536–542.

Fuld, P.A. (1978). Psychological testing in the differential diagnosis of the dementias. In R. Katzman, R.D. Terry, & K.L. Bick (Eds.), *Alzheimer's disease: Senile dementia and related disorders. Vol. 7. Aging.* New York: Raven Press.

Fuld, P.A. (1982). Cognitive changes associated with Alzheimer's dementia. In R.N. Malathesa (Ed.), *Neuropsychology and cognition.* Netherlands: Martinus Nijhott.

Gainotti, G., Caltagirone, C., Masullo, C., & Miceli, G. (1980). Patterns of neuropsychologic impairment in various diagnostic groups of dementia. In L. Amaducci, A. N. Davison & P. Antuono (Eds.), *Aging of the brain and dementia.* New York: Raven Press.

Gates, A.I. & MacGinitie, W.H. (1965, 1969). *Gates-MacGinitie Reading Tests.* New York: Teachers College Press, Teachers College, Columbia University.

Golden, C.J. (1981). A standardized version of Luria's neuropsychological tests. In. S. Filskov & T.J. Boll (Eds.), *Handbook of clinical neuropsychology.* New York: Wiley–Interscience.

Golden, C.J., Hammeke, T.A., & Purisch, A.D. (1980). *Manual for the Luria-Nebraska Neuropsychological Battery.* Los Angeles: Western Psychological Services.

Goldstein, K.H., & Scheerer, M. (1953). Tests of abstract and concrete behavior. In A. Weider (Ed.), *Contributions to medical psychology* (Vol. 2). New York: Ronald Press.

Golper, L.C., & Binder, L.M. (1981). Communicative behaviors in aging and dementia. In J. Darby (Ed.), *Speech evaluation in medicine and psychiatry* (Vol. 2). New York: Grune & Stratton.

Gorham, D.R. (1956). A Proverbs Test for clinical and experimental use. *Psychological Reports, 1,* 1–12.

Gronwall, D.M.A. (1977). Paced auditory serial-addition task: A measure of recovery from concussion. *Perceptual and Motor Skills, 44,* 367–373.

Halstead, W.C. (1947). *Brain and intelligence.* Chicago: University of Chicago Press.

Hanfmann, E. (1953). Concept Formation Test. In A. Weider (Ed.), *Contributions toward medical psychology.* New York: Ronald Press.

Hathaway, S.R., & McKinley, J.C. (1951). *The Minnesota Multiphasic Personality Inventory Manual* (rev. ed.). New York: Psychological Corporation.

Holmes, C.S., Hayford, J.T., Gonzalez, J.L., & Weydert, J.A. (1983). A survey of cognitive functioning at different glucose levels in diabetic persons. *Diabetes Care, 6,* 180–185.

Horenstein, S. (1977). The clinical use of psychological testing in dementia. In C.E. Wells (Ed.), *Dementia* (2nd ed.), Philadelphia: F.A. Davis.

Kimura, D. (1963). Right temporal lobe damage. *Archives of Neurology* (Chicago), *8,* 264–271.

Levin, H.S., O'Donnell, V.M., & Grossman, R.G. (1979). The Galveston Orientation and Amnesia Test. A practical scale to assess cognition after head injury. *Journal of Nervous and Mental Disease, 167,* 675–684.

Lewinsohn, P.M. (1973). *Psychological assessment of patients with brain injury.* Unpublished manuscript, Eugene, Oregon, University of Oregon.

Lezak, M.D. (1978). Living with the characterologically altered brain injured patient. *Journal of Clinical Psychiatry, 39,* 592–598.

Lezak, M.D. (1982). The problem of assessing executive functions. *International Journal of Psychology, 17,* 281–297.

Lezak, M.D. (1983). *Neuropsychological Assessment* (2nd ed.). New York: Oxford Press.

Luria, A.R. (1966). *Higher cortical functions in man.* (B. Haigh, trans.). New York: Basic Books.

Luria, A.R. (1973). *The working brain: An introduction to neuropsychology.* (B. Haigh, trans.). New York: Basic Books.

Matarazzo, J.D. (1972). *Wechsler's measurement and appraisal of adult intelligence* (5th ed.). New York: Oxford University Press.

Matarazzo, R.G., Matarazzo, J.D., Gallo, A.E., Jr., & Wiens, A.N. (1979). IQ and neuropsychological changes following carotid endarterectomy. *Journal of Clinical Neuropsychology, 1,* 97–116.

McAllister, T.W. (1983). Overview: Pseudodementia. *American Journal of Psychiatry, 140,* 528–533.

Mercer, B., Wapner, W., Gardner, H., & Benson, D.F. (1977). A study of confabulation. *Archives of Neurology, 34,* 429–433.

Miller, V.T. (1983). Lacunar stroke. *Archives of Neurology, 40,* 129–134.

Money, J. (1976). *A Standardized Road Map Test of Direction Sense.* Manual. San Rafael, Ca: Academic Therapy Publications; Chicago: Stoelting.

Parker, J.C., Smarr, K.L., Gamache, M., et al. (1984). *Neuropsychological outcomes following carotid endarterectomy: A two-year analysis.* Paper presented at the 12th Annual Meeting of the International Neuropsychological Society, Houston.

Parsons, O.A. (1975). Brain damage in alcoholics: Altered states of unconsciousness. In M.M. Gross (Ed.), *Alcohol intoxication and withdrawal, experimental studies,* No. 2. New York: Plenum Press.

Prigatano, G.P., & Parsons, O.A. (1976). Relationship of age and education to Halstead Test performance in different patient populations. *Journal of Consulting and Clinical Psychology, 44,* 527–533.

Pulsinelli, W.A., Levy, D.E., Sigsbee, B., et al. (1983). Increased damage after ischemic stoke in patients with hyperglycemia with or without established diabetes mellitus. *American Journal of Medicine, 74,* 540–544.

Raven, J.C. (1960). *Guide to the Standard Progressive Matrices.* London: H.K. Lewis; New York: Psychological Corporation.

Raven, J.C. (1965). *Guide to using the Coloured Progressive Matrices.* London: H.K. Lewis; New York: Psychological Corporation.

Reitan, R.M., & Davison, L.A. (1974). *Clinical neuropsychology: current status and applications.* New York: Hemisphere.

Rey, A. (1964). *L'examen clinique en psychologie.* Paris: Presses Universitaires de France.

Russell, E.W., Neuringer, C., & Goldstein, G. (1970). *Assessment of brain damage. A neuropsychological key approach.* New York: Wiley–Interscience.

Salzman, C., & Shader, R.I. (1979). Clinical evaluation of depression in the elderly. In A. Raskin & L. Jarvik (Eds.), *Psychiatric symptoms and cognitive loss in the elderly.* Washington, DC: Hemisphere Publishing Co.

Schwartz, A.S., Marchok, P.L., & Flynn, R.E. (1977). A sensitive test for tactile extinction: Results in patients with parietal and frontal lobe disease. *Journal of Neurology, Neurosurgery, and Psychiatry, 40,* 228–233.

Simpson, C.D., & Vega, A. (1971). Unilateral brain damage and patterns of age-corrected WAIS subtest scores. *Journal of Clinical Psychology, 27,* 204–208.

Small, G. W., & Jarvik, L.F. (1982). The dementia syndrome. *Lancet,* 1443–1446.

Spiers, P.A. (1981). Have they come to praise Luria or to bury him? The Luria-Nebraska Battery controversy. *Journal of Consulting and Clinical Psychology, 49,* 331–341.

Spitz, H.H. (1972). Note on immediate memory for digits: Invariance over the years. *Psychological Bulletin, 78,* 183–185

Strub, R.L., & Black, F.W. (1977). *The mental status examination in neurology.* Philadelphia: F.A. Davis.

Talland, G.A. (1965). Three estimates of the word span and their stability over the adult years. *Journal of Experimental Psychology, 17,* 301–307.

Taylor, L.B. (1979). Psychological assessment of neurosurgical patients. In T. Rasmussen & R. Marino (Eds.), *Functional neurosurgery.* New York: Raven Press.

Terman, L.M., & Merrill, M.A. (1973). *Stanford-Binet Intelligence Scale. Manual for the Third Revision, Form L-M.* Boston: Houghton Mifflin.

Teuber, H.-L. (1964). The riddle of frontal lobe function in man. In J.M. Warren & K. Akert (Eds.), *The frontal granular cortex and behavior.* New York: McGraw-Hill.

Torack, R.M. (1978). *The pathologic physiology of dementia.* New York: Springer-Verlag.

Wechsler, D. (1944). *The measurement of adult intelligence* (3rd ed.). Baltimore: Williams & Wilkins.

Wechsler, D. (1945). A standardized memory scale for clinical use. *Journal of Psychology, 19,* 87–95.

Wechsler, D. (1955). *Wechsler Adult Intelligence Scale. Manual.* New York: Psychological Corporation.

Wechsler, D. (1981). *WAIS-R manual.* New York: Psychological Corporation.

Weinstein, S. (1965). Deficits concomitant with aphasia or lesions of either cerebral hemisphere. *Cortex, 1,* 154–169.

Weisberg, L.A. (1979). Computed tomography in the diagnosis of intracranial disease. *Annals of Internal Medicine, 91,* 87–105.

Wertheim, N., & Botez, M.I. (1961). Receptive amusia: A clinical analysis. *Brain, 84,* 19–30.

Wilkie, F., & Eisdorfer, C. (1971). Intelligence and blood pressure in the aged. *Science, 172,* 959–962.

2

Functional Assessment

M. Powell Lawton

The Need for Assessment

Functional Assessment and
Other Clinical Assessments

The purpose of most clinical assessment is to gain maximum knowledge of a person's assets and liabilities in as objective a fashion as possible with the least expenditure of time and professional resources. The traditional psychological test battery fits this purpose, as does the medical and mental examination, the nursing-care assessment, the intake interview, and other approaches. Functional assessment is similar to these approaches and yet there are also important differences. Functional assessment is broader, more eclectic, and less profession-specific than other forms of assessment. It is "an attempt to evaluate the most important aspects of the behavior, the objective, and the subjective worlds of the person through standardized methods that can be applied by people with a wide variety of backgrounds and training" (Lawton & Storandt, 1984, 236–276).

Thus functional assessment is above all evaluative: There is an implied asset-versus-liability, positive-versus-negative judgment made about every attribute being assessed. This evaluative stance is not always present in clinical assessment. Describing the quality of personal relationships or the unique pattern of personal needs in a psychiatric examination does not necessarily require that one way of relating to others or of experiencing the self is judged as superior to another.

Second, most professions have their favorite domains on which assessment is concentrated: activities of daily living for the nurse, cognition for the psychometrist, and so on. Functional assessment, by contrast, has the grandiose aim of evaluating every important realm of life—not just behavior, not just the subjective world, but even more yet. Some domains of everyday functioning that have not usually been included in clinical assessment batteries, such as amount of social contact or environmental quality, are defined in the realm of functional assessment.

Third, functional assessment is necessarily cross-disciplinary and usually capable of being performed by people with specific assessment training but not necessarily full professional training. This fact has to some extent lessened the appeal of functional assessment technology for the highly professionalized: If it is not arcane and available only to the select few it must not be any good!

In retrospect one might wonder why functional assessment is considered part of the professional's armamentarium if, in fact, nonprofessionals can be trained to use the instruments. The fact is that the kinds of assessments to be discussed augment every traditional assessment procedure in a way that counteracts professional myopia. There is more to the total life of a person than any profession-specific approach commonly elicits. Thus the clinician's own treatment-relevant base of knowledge becomes enriched.

Further, the professional who becomes familiar with the technology of functional assessment will then have added two more skills to her/his capability. First the clinician, regardless of profession, then becomes the person who can organize, train, and supervise others whose task is to perform the assessments. Second, the clinician becomes the expert to whom others turn for the development of new assessment technologies for special purposes relevant to their unique client population, their agency, or a particular profession.

What Attributes of Older People Are Candidates for Assessment? One could assemble a list of assessment instruments that have been used by others and answer empirically the question, "what has gerontology considered worthy of assessment?" The state of the art does not, however, necessarily represent where the technology should go in the future. Much preferable is a conceptual framework based on general knowledge of older people that is capable not only of anchoring existing approaches to assessment but of indicating areas of neglect and ideas regarding where assessment efforts of the future should be directed. This author's conception of "the good life" (detailed in Lawton, 1983a) offers one such framework.

The good life is indicated by positively assessed qualities in four major sectors: behavioral competence, psychological well-being, perceived quality of life, and objective environment. Behavioral competence is the evaluated quality of behavior in domains that by normative social judgment have been considered necessary for adaptation to the external world. Psychological well-being represents the person's subjective judgment of the total, generalized quality of self in its own terms and in relation to the external world, including the mood and affective states associated with such cognitions. Perceived quality of life is the person's subjective judgment of the quality of her experience in any of several limited areas of interaction with the external world. Finally, the objective environment is the physically measured or consensually judged quality of all that lies outside the person. These capsulized definitions require some elaboration. This discussion will be followed by a brief consideration of how the sectors are related, and then an overview of how this structure suggests an approach to functional assessment.

Behavioral competence. It is convenient to arrange five major domains of behavior in a hierarchy of complexity, as shown in Figure 2.1. The ordering of the five levels represents a hierarchy of "complexity" in the sense that the minimum requirements for behavior at higher levels presume some involvement at lower levels. Behavior in domains at the rightmost side of Figure 2.1 involve substantial contributions of lower domains. The model is also hierarchical within domains; examples of increasingly differentiated and complex behaviors may be seen as one reads from bottom to top in each domain. A third dimension perpendicular to the plane of Figure 2.1 represents the evaluative dimension for any behavior, that is, behavioral competence by socially normative standards.

Physical health is indicated at the cellular, tissue, organ, or system level. Operationally the presence of a diagnosable illness or physical condition signals a deviation from full competence.

Functional health represents the acknowledgment that different illnesses and different people are associated with different degrees of disability and ability. Thus measures in this domain denote the competence of very basic behaviors that are necessary to sustain life or live in ordinary social contexts.

Cognition represents the competence of the person in a variety of areas such as orientation, memory, problem solving, perceptual functioning, psychomotor skills, and information processing.

Time use (or "effectance," which White, 1959, defined as ". . . what the organism wants to do when otherwise unoccupied or

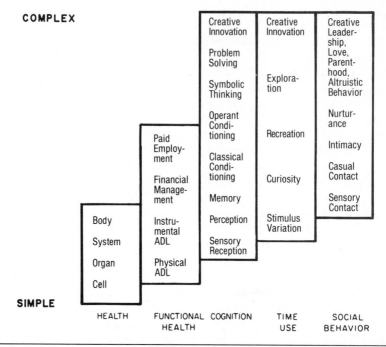

COMPLEX

HEALTH	FUNCTIONAL HEALTH	COGNITION	TIME USE	SOCIAL BEHAVIOR
				Creative Leader-ship, Love, Parent-hood, Altruistic Behavior
		Creative Innovation	Creative Innovation	
		Problem Solving		
		Symbolic Thinking	Explora-tion	
		Operant Condi-tioning		Nurtur-ance
	Paid Employ-ment		Recreation	Intimacy
		Classical Condi-tioning		Casual Contact
	Financial Manage-ment		Curiosity	
		Memory		Sensory Contact
Body	Instru-mental ADL	Perception	Stimulus Variation	
System		Sensory Reception		
Organ	Physical ADL			
Cell				

SIMPLE

Figure 2.1. Hierarchy of behavioral competence. (Copyright, Gerontological Society of America. Reproduced with permission from M. Powell Lawton, "Environment and Other Determinants of Well-being in Older People," *The Gerontologist*, Vol. 23, pp. 349–357, 1983.)

gently stimulated by the environment," p. 302) refers to complex instrumental behaviors and noninstrumental behaviors of the "discretionary" type. Thus this category includes both paid work and leisure-time activity.

Social interaction includes interactions with significant others, small groups and large aggregates.

One should note that the concept of normative competence is easy to apply in domains of lower complexity, but more difficult to apply in domains of higher complexity (such as time use and social interaction), where matters of personal preference become increasingly important.

Psychological Well-being. Various constructs that have been notoriously difficult to operationalize make good sense as a sort of core of psychological well-being, such as ego strength, self-esteem, or positive mental health. However, no hierarchical framework has been proposed for the psychological well-being sector, and measurement has used indicators that are considerably more distant from this hypothetical core. The necessity to define psychological well-being by multiangulation and successive approximation is responsible for the fact that such indicators go by so many names. This chapter cannot afford the space for a discussion of the research evidence that has attempted to define and distinguish one variety of psychological well-being from another, but reviews of this research may be found in George (1981) and Lawton (1982). Further specification of the domains of psychological well-being will be made when instruments are described below.

Perceived Quality of Life. As is the case with psychological well-being, no theoretically based organizing structure defines the sector of perceived quality of life. There are a limited number of domains of everyday life for which evaluations can be made, however. Consensus is virtually complete that marriage, family life, friends, work, housing, neighborhood, free-time activity, and income or standard of living belong on every list of the most salient perceived quality of life domains. Therefore there is a relatively high degree of consensus regarding the major domains, although some interesting variations occur in the hands of the several major investigators in this area (Andrews & Withey, 1976; Campbell, Converse, & Rodgers, 1976; Flanagan, 1979). The basis for evaluation of perceived quality of life is usually "satisfaction," although "importance" is sometimes used separately or in conjunction with satisfaction. Flanagan (1979) for example, asked systematically about the importance of 15 domains of life quality for each person. He then obtained a rating of "how well met" the person's needs were in each domain. Satisfaction with one's health and the self are very central concerns as well, but because they have no obvious external referent they are excluded as members of this sector.

Objective Environment. The environmental sector is notable for being outside the person, as contrasted with the previous three sectors. Objective environment is defined by anything outside the person that can be counted, measured in physical units, or evaluated with a very high degree of consensus among many judges. The rationale for separating objective and subjective environment so sharply rests partly on the idea that the meaning of one person's perception of an environmental attribute cannot be understood fully until we know the extent to which it corresponds to or deviates from some externally defined standard.

The past decade has seen some empirical efforts to dimensional-ize the objective environment. Usually these taxonomies result in some blending of objective and subjective environment (Kahana, 1982; Wind-ley, 1981). Where the components have been limited to aspects of the objective environment, their coherence is not always self-evident (Lawton & Cohen, 1974).

For the time being, then, a basic atheoretical set of categories at least illustrates the varieties of environment that must be considered (Lawton, 1970). The *physical environment* is composed of the natural or person-made environment exclusive of people. The *personal environment* includes the people with whom one has significant one-to-one contact. The *small-group* environment refers to the formal or informal groups with which one interacts where some interaction is face-to-face. The *suprapersonal environment* refers to the aggregate characteristics of the people in one's geographically proximate environment, such as age mix, racial character, or average health. The *social environment* includes institutionalized social influences that impinge on the person through government, economic forces, norms, values, and other macro-social factors. Each of the domains of the environment may be mea-sured in terms that are independent of a single person's perception. The subjective aspect of one person's view of the environment constitutes a domain of perceived quality of life, rather than objective environment.

Relationships Among the Sectors of the Good Life.   For any per-son, the good life may be enhanced through well-being in any of the sectors. Thus, for example, separate contributions to the good life may be made by performing a job well, by an optimistic attitude to life, by a positive evaluation of one's family, and by having a good home. It is likely, however, that if life is favorable in one sector, it is also favor-able in the other sectors. Thus our interventions often make such presumptions as: cognitive training will enhance psychological well-being; psychotherapy will enhance marital satisfaction; or a better neighborhood will lead to more social interaction. However, one must also recognize that it is possible for a person to strive for improvement in one sector and achieve such an improvement without corresponding improvement in other sectors (discussed at greater length in Lawton, 1983a). The related but partly autonomous sectors of the good life are pictured graphically in Figure 2.2, where the shaded areas represent overlap among the various sectors.

The point of this discussion is that people do seek improvement in their lives in many different domains. Our assessments should be complete enough to acknowledge that since people espouse these mul-

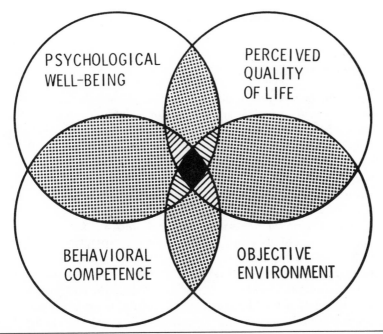

Figure 2.2. Four sectors of the good life. (Copyright, Gerontological Society of America. Reproduced with permission from M. Powell Lawton, "Environment and Other Determinants of Well-being in Older People," *The Gerontologist,* Vol. 23, pp. 349–357, 1983.)

tiple goals, it is worthwhile to seek improvement in one of the sectors without demanding that our intervention simultaneously remake the person's life in every area.

This conception of the good life helps us see in broader perspective, then, all that could and should be assessed. As will be seen later, some sectors and domains are liberally supplied with usable assessment instruments while others are very poorly covered. For example, in the behavioral competence sector, where the conceptual structure seems clearest, two useful deductions are possible. First, the division into domains allows us to see how much better-developed our measures of functional health and cognition are, as compared to time use and social behavior and to some extent physical health. Second, the implied evaluative third dimension for Figure 2.1 suggests that we should have instruments that make good discriminations at every level of functioning. Putting together the model of Figure 2.1 and our review of existing instruments thus will identify missing or poorly represented domains and ranges of competence within domains.

Assessment Procedures

Components of Adequate
Assessment and Rationale

This section will begin by discussing some of the characteristics of a good assessment tool. The greater portion will be devoted to a review of some of the frequently used measures with some indication of how well they perform in relationship to these quality criteria. The section will conclude with a brief sketch of several of the major assessment packages, that is, those designed to assess systematically a number of the sectors of the good life and the domains within them.

   Quality Criteria for Assessment Instruments. Classical texts in psychometric methods (e.g., Nunnally, 1978) provide comprehensive guidelines by which measurement accuracy may be enhanced. In much more brief form, some of these characteristics will be described here.
   INTRADOMAIN COMPREHENSIVENESS. A necessary beginning point is the definition of a domain and its anchoring within some larger theoretical framework. A measure must have "construct validity," that is, a clear specification of what is included and what is excluded from the domain. Once such a definition is in hand, an effort must then be made to represent systematically in individual measurement items each of the important subdomains. The entries within any column of Figure 2.1 are only illustrative, but one can readily see that a truly comprehensive measure of time use, for example, would require a number of dimensions. One dimension might deal with basic accounting for time, as in the time budget. Another might focus on all that a person does at work; another on organizational activities; still another on hobbies and leisure activities, and so on. Intradomain comprehensiveness also demands that the instrument discriminate "good" from "bad" (or "high" from "low") across the full range of variation. Some measures discriminate well at low levels but have such a constricted upper range that everyone "passes." Some domains, such as the time budget, have scales ranging from zero (never performed the activity) through a variety of levels (performed it for 24 hours) and are thus ideally discriminating. Most domains cannot be so readily differentiated. For example, a measure capable of ranking patients with Alzheimer's disease in terms of their cognitive ability would be useless in ranking nonimpaired people. Thus for many purposes a group of measures, each of which is most useful along a portion of the continuum of difficulty, will be preferable to a single measure for an entire domain.

NORM COMPREHENSIVENESS. Strictly speaking one can claim to have norms that allow a person's score to be compared with scores from other people only when the norms have been derived on a representative sample of all people. A national probability sample is the ideal sample on which to base norms. A nonrepresentative sample risks having the norms be unduly influenced by certain segments of the population.

Few assessment instruments used with older people have good norms. In fact, a problem with many otherwise good measures is that their standardization was done only on younger people or with insufficiently large or biased samples of older people. An example was the early Wechsler Adult Intelligence Scale (WAIS, Wechsler, 1958), whose older sample consisted of an elite, convenience sample of people in one city studied for another research project (the revised WAIS-R remedied this problem up to age 75, Wechsler, 1981). Thus a very specific criterion is whether the measure has norms for the older ages. Since so few instruments were derived from even locally representative samples, successively less acceptable compromises are purposively diverse samples, restricted but large samples with carefully detailed background characteristics, and finally least desirable, convenience samples whose characteristics are incompletely specified.

For many purposes subgroup norms are desirable, for example, by gender, age, race, or urban–rural residence, all of which are theoretically possible to derive from a large representative sample. More difficult but particularly useful are norms for specific service-recipient or applicant groups (for example, the elderly in state hospitals or applicants to a home-health agency).

SUBJECT AND SETTING VERSATILITY. The content and format of an instrument need to be examined to determine whether they offer any inherent limitations to the kind of subject who will be evaluated in a particular setting. For example, some devices may be purged of any visual stimuli so as to allow the blind to be evaluated. Language likely to be problematic to some subgroups can usually be modified (for example, regionalisms or technical terms). Sometimes one has specific interest in people living in a particular setting and therefore designs the content to apply only to people living in that setting. Conversely, an all-purpose instrument must be carefully purged of content that applies only to specific groups in specific settings such as adolescents, urban dwellers, Hispanics, or institutional residents.

STRUCTURAL VERSATILITY. This refers to options in the measurement form that afford freedom of use. For example, multiple forms of an instrument (shown empirically to be equivalent) permit repeated measurement with minimal practice effect. The choice of a short form or a long form to measure a single attribute offers the user greater flexibility. Normative data for each subscale free the user from the necessity of giving all subscales.

MISSING-DATA VERSATILITY. All functional assessment suffers frequently from items whose responses are missing for a variety of reasons. There is no real protection against such problems. One can prorate scores based on the total number answered, but especially where items are graded in terms of difficulty there is always the risk that the missing item is not at the mean difficulty level. It is possible to convert a set of item scores to a rating that does not demand that every item be answered. In effect this procedure allows the rater to prorate in a way that subjectively weights the importance of the items and of other non-item cues such as the person's expression, voice, or gestures. Considerably greater flexibility is possible when a domain may be measured by either (or both) a cumulative item score and a rating based on all available information, including item scores.

SOURCE-OF-DATA VERSATILITY. The realities of clinical or research assessment frequently include subjects whose own responses are unavailable, unreliable, or not complete. Depending on the situation, it may be more important to have information from the best available source, rather than necessarily from the subject. Ideally one ought to have normative data on how the responses or scores obtained alternatively from the subject, family member, or a professional deviate from one another. Such information is rarely available, however. In its absence, the instrument should specify which domains, scales, or items may use substitute sources of data. Usually these items will be those capable of being answered objectively. Items should not be answered by proxy if the respondent would have to judge how the subject would evaluate or respond affectively to the item.

EXAMINER VERSATILITY. As mentioned earlier, most functional assessment, unlike clinical psychological assessment, is meant to be performed by people with widely varying backgrounds. Often the interviewer will be a research assistant or service worker who is intelligent and has had experience working with people but has not had extensive training in assessment. Therefore the demands on the interviewer made by the instrument should be modest. An administration manual should spell out in detail exactly how each question should be asked and scored. The manual should also orient the user to more general principles of interviewing older people, such as how to deal with anxiety or sadness evoked by questions or how to recognize fatigue. Suggestions for training interviewers should also be included.

The amount of training required will vary considerably with the complexity of the procedure. The greatest amount of training is required when the interviewer is also expected to make subjective ratings, such as summary ratings representing an entire domain. In general, the less reliance is placed on such ratings, the greater the versatility of the instrument.

SENSITIVITY. The sensitivity of an instrument is its ability to measure change when change in that characteristic has actually occurred. This criterion is very important for attributes that are known to change, such as affect, perceived control over a particular situation, or amount of social interaction. There is no effective index of sensitivity. In judging whether an instrument meets this criterion, one depends largely on whether there is research evidence that change in the score has taken place in situations where change is likely to have occurred. A common error in choosing a measure is to use an instrument designed to measure a relatively stable trait when one wishes to evaluate change, for example, the effect of an intervention.

RELIABILITY. Reliability is the ability of a test to evoke the same response from the same person when the condition being measured has not changed. Many of the measures being used in gerontology did not have adequate determination of their reliability when they were first designed. In general, the user should seek measures that have good test–retest reliability, and good internal consistency. A corollary problem to the general lack of age norms (discussed earlier) is the frequent absence of information regarding reliability specifically for the 65+ age-group or for subgroups among the aged. Response error becomes more frequent when various factors such as hearing, fluency in English, physical health, mental status, or motivation are less than optimal. Thus it would be very helpful to the user to be able to compare various measures in regard to their relative reliability with intact and impaired people or with service-receiving groups. When observers' ratings are required, their reliability also should be reported and comparative data on the variations in reliability associated with levels of professional education and with amount of training made available.

VALIDITY. This represents the degree to which an instrument actually measures the construct it purports to measure. Many of the measures reported in the gerontological literature are based on face validity, that is, the researcher's a priori attempt to phrase items that sound like manifestations of the construct. The best measures are those whose items were originally constructed on the basis of an exhaustive sampling of those characteristics which, on the basis of the literature on a particular construct, should reflect the construct. While this is a necessary first step, succeeding steps should include empirical selection of the best items through a variety of methods: determining which items are most related to other criteria such as total score, independent measures of the criteria, outcomes that imply the presence of the criterion or correlations with other related instruments plus showing a lack of correlation with measures not presumed to represent the criterion (discriminant validity). (An example of the steps in this successive pattern of test development may be found in the Philadelphia Geriatric Center Morale Scale (Lawton, 1975).

DISCRIMINATING POWER. Reliability and validity are necessary prerequisites for a measure to classify accurately those who have a characteristic and those who do not. However, the efficiency with which the classification can be performed is an additional and necessary characteristic to know. Two questions must be addressed. First, what percentage of those classified by the measure as having the trait do not have it (false positives)? Second, what percentage of these classified as not having the trait do have it (false negatives)? There are a great many errors of interpretation, exceptions, and non-criterion-related reasons possible for a person to respond to an item in a given way. Response styles such as agreement, denial or social desirability require some consideration when judging the discrimination power of an instrument. The overall percentage of correct classifications in a standardization sample is an excellent guide to the usefulness of a measure.

ACCEPTABILITY TO THE OLDER SUBJECT. The usefulness of a measure may be reduced considerably by failure to consider structural and content features that may be inappropriate to the age, cohort, or health status of the potential subject. Items to which the subject responds directly are usually better when the language and sentence structure are relatively simple. Rankings of several attributes (for example, "Arrange these six activities in an order representing how much you like them") are often difficult, and rating scales composed of even as many as four points may screen out some less-competent subjects from responding. Paired comparisons are usually possible, but as the total number of items goes beyond four or five, problems of attention and motivation may be introduced by the repetition of the same item in successive pairs. Of course, for highly competent, well-educated, and normally motivated people these factors are relatively unproblematic. However, in service-providing situations these types of limitations may be serious and the instruments should be constructed for the lowest common denominator.

Currently Used Measures

Having established this set of criteria for judging their quality, a number of measures of domains in each of the four sectors of the good life will be discussed. By no means do all meet all of the quality criteria just discussed. Their strengths and weaknesses in this respect will be discussed. Most of the measures chosen were designed for the older client as respondent and all will have a considerable range of examiner versatility.

Measures of Behavioral Competence

Physical Health. One may categorically suggest that no clinical or research assessment should be done without some attempt to evaluate the person's level of biological health. In many situations exhaustive physical examination, history, and laboratory data are available, but these are notoriously resistant to scaling and comparison. Three classes of measures may be considered here: self-ratings, health behavior, and health conditions. *Self-rated health* in its simplest form is represented by the ubiquitous question, "How would you rate your health; would you say it is excellent, good, fair, or poor?" The validity of this item has been shown to be surprisingly good (Maddox & Douglas, 1973; Tissue, 1972), to the point where one can recommend its use if one has time to accommodate only one item. However, self-rated health has been shown repeatedly to overlap so substantially with psychological well-being that other approaches are strongly recommended (Okum & Stock, 1984).

Health behavior, such as frequency of physician visits, hospital days, or days sick in bed are relatively objective. Yet health behavior is affected substantially by such factors as income, family situation, accessibility of services, and preference. Empirically such measures have been less than ideally predictive of other health criteria (Lawton, Moss, Fulcomer, & Kleban, 1982).

Health conditions, as reported by the subject on a checklist, may be suggested as the most desirable measure, since people generally know their conditions. The Cornell Medical Index (Brodman, Erdmann, Lorge, & Wolff, 1949) is by far the most comprehensive. It is, however, too long (195 items), it mixes psychophysiologic symptoms with physical conditions, and it has had relatively little use in psychometric treatment. A more usable index is the checklist of 40 conditions designed by Rosencranz and Pihlblad (1970), which contains weighting for seriousness as well as an inquiry about the amount of disability consequent to each condition. The Linn, Linn, and Gurel (1968) Cumulative Illness Scale requires a physician to rate the severity of 13 organ systems. The Wyler, Masuda, and Holmes (1968) Seriousness of Illness Scale is scaled by consensual severity ratings of about 100 diagnostic symptoms and complaints.

Functional Health. Functional health might be referred to as "biological health expressed in action through everyday activities." Although this attribute is difficult to distinguish statistically from physical health, the ability to perform self-maintaining activities represents the single most important item of information to measure, because deficits in these areas are so closely linked to service needs. A good measure of basic activities of daily living (ADL) should include toileting, eating, dressing, ambulation, transfer in and out of bed, bathing, and grooming. Most ADL measures (Katz, Downs, Cash, & Gratz, 1970; Lawton & Brody, 1969; Mahoney & Barthel, 1965) include these features, but they are all constructed so as to require observers' ratings. Alternative forms for self-response may be found in the OARS (Duke University, 1978) and the Multilevel Assessment Instrument (MAI, Lawton et al., 1982), about both of which more will be said later.

A more complex set of self-maintenance skills, "instrumental activities of daily living" include telephone use, money management, laundry, shopping, housekeeping, cooking, transportation use, and self-medication (Lawton & Brody, 1969). Self-rating versions of these skills were created for the OARS (Duke University, 1978).

In clinical practice it is often necessary to determine why some tasks are not performed independently, what kinds of difficulties interfere with their performance, who gives help, and what kind of help is needed. To some extent some of the assessment packages to be discussed later standardize these inquiries.

Of course there are many other important functions that could be measured in greater detail and for which one can sometimes find ready-made measures. Range of motion, the ability to move different body parts in different places, is an example of a set of functions that is critical to measure in a rehabilitation setting and for which adequate clinical guides exist (Granger, 1974). Thus, the set of basic functions listed here represents an open-ended list that requires augmenting, depending on the subject and the setting.

Cognition. The measurement of intellectual functioning is a highly developed specialty that requires full professional training. Nonetheless, in the typical functional-assessment setting, an early determination may be necessary to decide whether a referral for full evaluation is necessary. The measures of cognitive functioning to be discussed here are easily performed by nonpsychologists, but should never be thought of as anything more than preliminary screening devices.

By far the most frequently used measure is the Kahn-Goldfarb (Kahn, Goldfarb, Pollack, & Peck, 1960) Mental Status Questionnaire (MSQ), a 10-item test measuring basic information and orientation (date, birthdate, name of place, name of president, for example). A variation that attempts to control for education and presumably past attainment is the Short Portable MSQ (Pfeiffer, 1975). Such measures are invaluable in identifying gross instances of mental impairment (Gurland et al., 1977–78). They lack any attempt to assess memory, a feature that is added to the MSQ-type items in the Mini-Mental Status Examination (Folstein, Folstein, & McHugh, 1975). A six-item short MSQ that includes memory and cognitive processing has also been reported (Katzman et al., 1983).

Memory is exceedingly complex and is not a candidate for assessment in any way other than for gross screening. Similarly, elaboration in depth of the many components of cognitive functioning such as sensory-motor functioning, problem solving, or abstract thinking may be done only by specialists in these areas.

Time use. The previous three domains of behavioral competence have the advantage of long traditions of measurement. By contrast, the next two, time use and social behavior, have been less-frequently recognized as candidates for functional assessment. There is no approach to measuring time use that has been used by more than a few investigators (see Bull, 1982, for a longer review of the measures that have been reported). It is worth separating uses of time that involve friends and family from other uses of time, the latter being focused on activities themselves. The time budget, an attempt to log minute by minute the activities of specific days, is the most complete method for measuring time use (Chapin, 1974; Moss & Lawton, 1982). However, it is far too complicated for use in clinical functional assessment situations (Carp, 1978). One thus recommends that a checklist requesting an estimate of the frequency with which a finite number of activities are performed be used. Such lists may be found in many studies, but none has attained the status of a "scale" or been used by any substantial number of researchers other than its originators (Gordon & Gaitz, 1976; National Council on the Aging, 1975; Sherman, 1973).

It may be desirable to separate organizational participation from social behavior and from the other kinds of informal or solitary activities that appear on the above checklists (see for example Cutler's list of organizational types, 1976).

All of these measures of time use are expressed as frequencies of participation. Estimates of the quality of the activity belong in the perceived quality of life sector.

Social Behavior. Like time use, social behavior has been addressed for measurement purposes less seriously than have health and cognition. One reason for the neglect is that many approaches have unthinkingly mixed three separate aspects of social relationships. First, the *existence* of social objects and their physical *proximity* are properly attributes of the personal environmental domain of the objective environment sector. Second, the *quality* of the social relationship is a domain in the perceived quality of life sector. Finally, only the *frequency* of social contacts belongs in the behavioral competence sector. The three aspects are in real life impossible to separate, but since the three have appreciable freedom to vary independently of the others, it is recommended that each be measured separately.

Instruments to assess social behavior have been difficult to establish. While almost everyone obtains counts and frequencies of contacts with relatives and friends (see, for example, Tamir and Antonucci, 1981), these measures have typically not been scaled in the psychometric sense. Thus it is difficult to answer the questions, "How much contact is a lot? How much contact is a little?"

The most complete inquiry into the amounts, objects, and conditions of social contact has been provided by Sokolovsky and Cohen (1981), in their Network Analysis Profile. The Profile inquires exhaustively into the structure of a person's social network and has been scored to represent a variety of types and varieties of social contact. The inquiry, however, is too long for use in the functional assessment setting. Included in the MAI (Lawton et al., 1982) are questions that yield a standardized index of frequency of contacts whose information requires 8 to 10 minutes to obtain. A variety of other approaches, usually not scaled, are discussed by Kane and Kane (1981) and Mindel (1982).

Psychological Well-being

The domains of psychological well-being are not easily distinguished from one another either conceptually or empirically. The summary of measures that follows is thus for convenience based on the nomenclature used in the literature.

Life satisfaction. Neugarten, Havighurst, and Tobin (1961) provided a conceptual definition of life satisfaction that is still the model for a clinically derived, research-operationalized attempt to express the essence of what is referred to as "successful aging." The measure that resulted, the Life Satisfaction Indices A and B (and a frequently used shortened version, the LSI-Z, Wood, Wylie, and Sheafor, 1969), did not, however, systematically include items representing each of the five components of their definition: zest, resolution and fortitude, congruence between desired and attained goals, positive self-concept, and mood tone. While the LSI has performed admirably as a general criterion of psychological well-being, its factor structure has been difficult to define (Adams, 1969; Bigot, 1974; Hoyt & Creech, 1983). Empirical research has not succeeded in characterizing exactly what the LSI measures, but it seems to represent a highly generalized cognitive estimate of the extent to which the person's actual life has measured up to expectation (George & Bearon, 1980). The LSI is easy to administer in oral interview format (about 8 to 12 minutes) and its language is moderately comprehensible to relatively unsophisticated people.

Morale. The measurement of morale has a long history in gerontology. A very comprehensive review and set of critical essays on morale appears in Nydegger (1977). In practice, morale, like life satisfaction, does not represent a single construct. Empirically, however, the correlation between the LSI and one of the most-frequently used morale measures, the Philadelphia Geriatric Center Morale Scale (Lawton, 1975), is almost as high as the retest reliabilities of the measures. Thus one is not confident that the two scales measure different aspects of psychological well-being. However, the PGC Morale Scale has demonstrated a highly stable factor structure across different investigators (Lawton, 1975; Liang & Bollen, 1983; Morris & Sherwood, 1975).

The revised PGC Morale Scale consists of 17 items written in highly simplified language, with a dichotomous response format that facilitates its use with relatively low-competent people. It takes 10 to 15 minutes for most people and yields factors named age-related morale, agitation, and lonely dissatisfaction.

Negative affect. One facet of psychological well-being is clearly the absence of negative subjective states such as worry, anxiety, depression, and other signs of distress (named "demoralization" by Dohrenwend, 1980). People in poor mental health show greater demoralization. In addition, many people without clinically manifest disorders also report such symptoms. A major national study of happiness identified a cluster of five such subjective experiences that were labeled "negative affect" (Bradburn, 1969). The content of these items is very similar to many items contained in the agitation factor of the PGC, the nonsomatic items of the Langner (1962) Twenty-Two Item Screening Inventory, and the State-Trait Anxiety Inventory (Spielberger, Gorsuch, & Lushene, 1970). Unlike life satisfaction and morale, negative affect has repeatedly demonstrated its conceptual and empirical coherence (Andrews & Withey, 1976; Bradburn, 1969). The Bradburn scale (1969) is a highly efficient measure that takes only a minute or so to administer. For longer and more reliable scales, the Langner has worked well with the aged (Gaitz & Scott, 1972), while Lawton, Kleban, and diCarlo (1984) reported a 10-item negative affect factor with many desirable psychometric qualities. The State-Trait Inventory has been used on older people with promising results, although age-specific norms are not available (Himmelfarb & Murrell, 1983).

Depression. The definition of negative affect given above deliberately included depressive symptoms because most such items cluster with and are indistinguishable in a psychometric sense from anxiety and other negative affects. It is important to know that depressive affect is a frequent symptom among older people, but the incidence of major clinical depression appears to diminish with age (Gurland, 1976). Because depression is so important clinically, it is important to measure depression separately from other forms of mental health. There are several useful measures available, each of which takes approximately 15 to 25 minutes for most older subjects. Three of them were designed for younger people but have been used successfully with older clients. The Zung (1965) Self-Rating Depression Scale consists of 20 items, a number of which are physiologic symptoms of the type that are frequent in younger depressives but which could indicate physical disorders that become more prevalent with age; indeed, this latter fact may be a disadvantage in using the Zung with the elderly. The Beck Depression Scale (Beck et al., 1951) consists of 21 items; the subject must check multipoint ratings whose structure differs for each item, making it difficult for some older subjects. The Center for Epidemiologic Studies Depression Scale (CES-D, Radloff, 1977) is especially useful because it consists of only 20 items and contains almost no physiologic or vegetative symptoms. The only relatively brief scale reported to date that was designed with older people in mind is the Geriatric Depression Scale (GDS, Brink et al., 1982). While little research using this scale has been reported as yet, it shows considerable promise.

Any of these depression scales is useful in functional assessment situations when there is some reason to suspect depression. How high a score must be on any of these scales to strongly hint of clinical depression is as yet unknown, however. The score itself and the clinical meaning of the responses to the separate items, unlike many of the other assessment measures discussed in this chapter, must be interpreted by a clinical psychologist and are appropriate in a screening battery only when this professional resource is present.

Positive Affect. One of the great contributions of Bradburn's (1969) research was his discovery that while both positive affective states and negative states are related to happiness, they are unrelated to one another. His positive affect scale (1969) consisted of five items denoting pleasant, ego-affirming, or novel experiences. Research has shown that positive affect is associated with activity, social behavior (Bradburn, 1969; Lawton, 1983b), and extraversion (Costa & McCrae, 1980) as well as general happiness.

Clinicians sensitized to identifying psychopathology have often neglected to concern themselves with the assessment of active pleasures (but see MacPhillamy and Lewinsohn, 1982, for in-depth explorations of pleasant experiences), in parallel fashion with neglect of the time use and social behavior domains of behavioral competence. The Positive Affect Scale, especially when used with the Negative Affect Scale (together they form the 10-item Affect Balance Scale (Bradburn, 1969), provides a complementary look at psychological well-being and is highly recommended as a component of functional assessment.

Happiness. Perhaps the most-used indicator for the psychological well-being sector is the single item, "Taking all things together how would you say things are today—would you say you're very happy, pretty happy, or not too happy these days?" (Gurin, Veroff, & Feld, 1960). While a single item is not a dependable measure of anything, it is important to recognize that happiness has frequently been thought of as *the* ultimate criterion of psychological well-being. Some evidence is at hand suggesting that happiness has a stronger component of affect, while satisfaction is more cognitive (Andrews & McKennell, 1980). Psychometrically acceptable measures of the affective and cognitive aspects of psychological well-being could be extremely useful. It is thus surprising that no multi-item happiness scale has been developed. A scale bearing the "happiness" label is actually considerably broader in what it measures. The Memorial University of Newfoundland Happiness Scale (MUNSH, Kozma & Stones, 1980), in fact, is a mixture of items from the PGC and LSI, and an expanded set of positive affect and negative affect items, all 24 of its items having been validated against the "happiness item" above. Thus to call it a scale of happiness seems like something of a misnomer. What the MUNSH does allow is a superior overall measure of psychological well-being that combines the affective and the cognitive indicators. It also balances temporally enduring ("trait") with transitory ("state") affects and positive with negative statements, features not present in other measures.

Self-Esteem. Although the Self-Esteem Scale (Rosenberg, 1965) was derived and standardized on adolescents, its usefulness has been shown with older people (George & Bearon, 1980; Dobson, Powers, Keith, & Goudy, 1979). The content of most of its 10 items reflects the person's evaluation of him-/herself. Yet, in at least one investigation the Rosenberg scale failed to demonstrate its factorial separateness from other well-being measures or discriminant validity among its correlates (Lawton et al., 1984). A measure of the quality of the self would be invaluable. For the present, however, what the Rosenberg and other similar instruments measure is difficult to distinguish from many of the well-being instruments discussed above.

In conclusion, it is clear that the dimensions of psychological well-being are not as well-articulated as those of behavioral competence. Most of the measures discussed here are useful but also require further study by specialists in geropsychology for more precise understanding. How a person stands in relation to other older people in general can best be determined through the LSI, provided the items and the response format are identical to those used in the national Harris survey (National Council on the Aging, 1975, 1981), which provides national norms. The LSI is lacking in the affective side of psychological well-being, however. The PGC offers one subscale in the negative-affect domain, in addition to the cognitive-evaluational element shared with the LSI. The separate scales of the Affect Balance Scale offer something unique in tapping the positive as well as the negative affect domain. While research on the MUNSH has thus far been reported primarily by its originators, it has the advantage of systematically representing the cognitive and affective aspects of well-being. Once its predictive performance is better known, it will be a candidate for the best of the all-purpose measures of psychological well-being.

Perceived Quality of Life

A smaller body of research exists on perceived quality of life among the aged, and there is a relative dearth of well-standarized age-specific measures of domains in this sector. It thus is desirable to indicate at the outset how several investigators have approached measurement across all the domains. The two major research investigations of perceived quality of life (Andrews & Withey, 1976; Campbell et al., 1976) used fairly similar single-item ratings (framed in terms of "satisfaction" or related constructs) for each of a set of domains such as friendships, marriage, amount of education. Within the limits of the single item, such questions (displayed for easy use in Herzog, Rodgers, & Woodworth, 1982, pp. 95–106) at least afford the first cut of information relevant to this sector. The only other systematic effort to define and measure the domains of psychological well-being resulted from the coding of open-ended responses to several general questions about what in the person's life had caused satisfaction, worry, or change (Flanagan, 1979). Categories such as those among the 15 domains of Flanagan then were used to determine the importance and degree of satisfaction associated with aspects of everyday life.

According to the Harris Survey (National Council on the Aging, 1981), the domains for which people are most likely to report dissatisfaction are personal security (crime), health, and income. Health satisfaction is properly an indicator (though not a particularly good one) of self-rated health. A three-item measure of perceived security forms part of the Multilevel Assessment Instrument (Lawton et al., 1982). Less frequent as a source of dissatisfaction according to the Harris Survey is perceived residential quality. Multi-item scales of perceived environmental quality (with little replication by different investigators) have been derived by Campbell et al. (1976), Carp and Carp (1982), and Lawton et al. (1982).

Not represented in the Harris Survey list are three domains that are of critical importance to overall well-being, often problematic to the older client, and yet rather poorly represented in current assessment instruments: time use, friends, and family. Time use was shown to be one of those most central to overall quality of life (Campbell et al., 1976). The only multi-item index of satisfaction with time use known to this author is a four-item index obtained by Lawton, Kleban, and diCarlo (1984) as a factor from a large pool of psychological well-being and perceived quality of life items.

For some people the perceived quality of relationships with others is even more central than time use. The construct "loneliness" captures some of this quality; the UCLA Loneliness scale shows some promise with older people (Russell, 1982). However, loneliness is too specific a quality. Different measures are also required for friends and for relatives, since they serve quite different functions for people (Hess, 1979; Wood & Robertson, 1978). Bengtson and Schrader

(1982) reported a Positive Affect Index for older people's relationships with children (p. 154). No attempt to scale multi-item indices of quality of friends has been located.

Because people involved in the service system are likely to have multiple needs, inquiry into these perceived quality of life domains is always appropriate. A rule of thumb might be that for routine purposes a short set of the best single items might be sufficient for all domains except time use, friends, and family. Longer item sets might be used for these latter domains and any others that appear problematic.

Objective Environment

Physical Environment.   One of the few well-standardized measures in this domain is the Physical and Architectural Feature checklist (Moos & Lemke, 1980), which applies only to planned residential environments that offer some additional supportive services. Carp and Carp (1982), Lawton and Kleban (1971), and Windley and Scheidt (1982) have produced factor-analytically derived measures that represent adequately certain limited aspects of neighborhood environments (for example, concentration of stores or amount of traffic). A list of housing deficits (for example, presence of plumbing, cracks in floors, heating system breakdowns) from the Department of Housing and Urban Development's Annual Housing Survey (U.S. Bureau of the Census, 1975) discriminates acceptable housing from grossly inadequate housing. Regrettably there is as yet no simple standardized checklist that one can use in ordinary residential environments to reflect the dimensions important for livability. The deficits in the Annual Housing Survey list are found in only a small minority of homes and thus differentiate poorly through most of the range of housing.

If one considers the availability of supportive services an important aspect of the objective environment, the Older American Resources and Services Multidimensional Functional Assessment Questionnaire (OARS, Duke University, 1978), which will be described in greater detail below, provides a classification of services for the elderly and detailed specifications on measuring their quantities.

Personal Environment.   The personal environment does not constitute a measurement problem, since it consists of the number and the kinds of people with whom one has face-to-face or other personal contact. Typical measures are household composition, presence of a spouse, number and type of relatives, number of friends, or number of neighbors known.

Suprapersonal Environment. Theoretically any characteristic of a person can also be used to describe an aggregate of people. Age, sex, race, ethnicity, or health mix may be salient to the everyday life of the person being assessed. These characteristics may be measured in any context. For example, Lawton and Nahemow (1979) found that high age concentration of neighborhoods where housing for the elderly was placed was associated with greater well-being and social activity. More complex suprapersonal characteristics such as resident social resources or activity levels were used by Lemke and Moos (1981) in supportive housing settings; they could be easily adapted for other community settings.

Social Environment. The social environment has the most diverse components. The defining features of the social environment are a mix of physical, suprapersonal, attitudinal, and policy or program features. Some components are the aggregated behaviors of people in a circumscribed area, for example, the crime rate of a block, a neighborhood, or a community. Other components may represent an assessment of the policies, programs, and practices of an organization (Lemke & Moos, 1980). Several researchers have defined "psychosocial" attributes of a treatment context, which are measured by rating scales. For example, Kahana (1982) measured institutional environment on scales representing such qualities as the segregate or congregate characteristics or amount of control or structure in the psychosocial environment. Lieberman and Tobin (1983) used such environmental variables as warmth, cue richness, and tolerance for deviance. Moos, Gauvain, Lemke, Max, and Mehren (1979) constructed a Sheltered Care Environment Scale with dimensions such as cohesion, independence, and physical comfort.

Life Events. Life events such as retirement, residential relocation, or bereavement are phenomena that "happen" to people to some extent, yet different events in the lives of different people have varying degrees of volitional or endogenous components. It seems clear to this writer that "change in health" of the subject, which appears on most of the standard life-events lists (e.g., Holmes & Rahe, 1967) is not an environmental event, while the health of significant others is such an event. Life-event scales tailored to older people have been devised (Amster & Krauss, 1974), which seem preferable to those designed for the population at large. In any case, for conceptual clarity health items referring to the self should not be used if an indicator of external stress is desired.

Comprehensive Functional
Assessment Instruments

Some assessment packages were designed to measure a broad spectrum of characteristics of older people. The instruments to be discussed here each represent reasonably well the domains of behavioral competence, moderately well the sector of psychological well-being, and less well the sectors of perceived quality of life and objective environment. The first one to be designed and in by far the most common use is the Duke OARS (sometimes referred to as the OMFAQ, or OARS Multidimensional Functional Assessment Questionnaire, Duke University, 1978). The OARS is an interview instrument whose content deals with physical health, activities of daily living, mental health, social behavior, and economic resources. The final score for the OARS consists of a profile of five six-point rating scales completed by a trained person, each rating based on the rater's judgment of the items representing each domain. A total score can be obtained by summing the ratings. The OARS has the great advantage of having norms derived from several large representative samples of older people (Fillenbaum & Smyer, 1981). It also has considerable versatility because the five basic ratings may be done even if some information has to be obtained from an informant or is missing. This latter feature is also a disadvantage, in that raters must be given substantial training for their task. Another disadvantage is that using ratings only inadequately utilizes item data. The OARS' domain comprehensiveness is limited also because cognition and psychological well-being must be collapsed into a single rating (called "mental health"), as must time use and social behavior.

The Comprehensive Assessment and Referral Evaluation (CARE, Gurland et al., 1977–78) is indeed the most comprehensive assessment presently available, affording high domain and intradomain comprehensiveness. The CARE is notable for inquiring deeply enough into every function to minimize both false negatives and false positives. Data are available from large samples in both New York and London. The major disadvantage is its extreme length; the entire CARE requires anywhere from 75 to 120 minutes for many clients. However, shorter homogeneous scales have been designed and extensive standardization data presented (Golden, Teresi, & Gurland, 1984; Teresi, Golden, Gurland, Wilder, & Bennett, 1984). The CARE was designed explicitly to serve the need for a clinical instrument in community mental health. It is very strong in its measurement of clinical syndromes but is based on an empirical rather than theoretical conception of behavior.

The Philadelphia Geriatric Center Multilevel Assessment Instrument (MAI, Lawton et al., 1982) was designed to represent all of the domains of behavioral competence, psychological well-being, and the housing and neighborhood satisfaction domains of perceived quality of life. While it allows summary rating scales for seven domains (health, activities of daily living, cognition, time use, social behavior, psychological well-being, and environment) to be used, it offers item indices to be calculated for each of these domains and a number of subdomains. It also has the unique feature of presenting psychometric data on full, mid-length, and short forms (averaging 60, 40, and 20 minutes, respectively), allowing flexibility in terms of time requirements. This feature is enhanced by being able to use selected indices and omit others. The standardization sample did not constitute a representative sample, but descriptive data are available separately for community residents and several service-recipient groups.

Newest on the scene is the Self-Evaluation of Life Function (SELF) Scale (Linn & Linn, 1984), a 55-item self-report scale that measures physical disability, symptoms of aging, self-esteem, social satisfaction, depression, and personal control. While the SELF also has no integrating conceptual base, it has excellent psychometric characteristics that make it a good choice for a comprehensive assessment where time is very limited.

The four instruments described here will certainly not be the last packages to be developed. The practitioner will be well-advised to remain alert to improved assessment batteries as they appear in the literature.

Some Neglected Candidates for Assessment

The Minnesota Long-Term Care Plan (1981) adds three assessment tasks which do not involve direct client assessment but which are seen as important in "gatekeeping" for long-term care (that is, exercising control over the match between type of care prescribed and the needs of the person):

- Assessment of caregivers' needs for support.
- Assessment of the resources available for caregiving from both formal agencies and informal sources such as family, neighbors, or friends.
- Determination of the assistance to be given, taking account of the person's capacities, her preferences, and the supply of available supports.

These recommendations reflect the fact that formalized assessment has been aimed only at client assessment. The three elements noted above have been ignored by most of us because they are difficult to manage in a quantitative fashion. Our standard assessment instruments do, to be sure, determine the number and relationship of family members and those others who constitute the person's informal network. In a rather unsatisfactory way some instruments sometimes attempt to determine these people's potential availability for assistance. Some have included an audit of local formal support agencies as an adjunct to their individual assessment systems (i.e., the Aging Needs in Manitoba survey, Havens & Thompson, 1976). However, the notion of "caregiving capacity"—a construct with elusive attributes which include willingness to help, the competence of the caregiver, knowledge of resources, and so on—so far as I know has been approached only clinically. The same is true of the caregivers' needs for support. The final element, the recommendation of a specific service, includes an interesting factor that is not usually mentioned in the assessment context, that is, the preference of the client. While our assessment technology is not yet up to the task of determining service preference in any formal way, one can only applaud the idea that this is an all-important but too-frequently forgotten factor in service choice. As the situation stands, however, integrating the diverse factors of client capacity, caregiving resources, and client preferences to equal a service recommendation is a clinical, rather than a quantitative, task. The gap between descriptive knowledge of client, caregiver, and context and the specification of the optimum service is still very wide and thus represents a prime target for continuing research attention.

Approaching the Older Person for Assessment

A perennial problem for all explicit mental health services offered to older people is the fact that the idea of seeking mental health services is foreign to today's cohort of elderly people. They are not used to thinking in mental health terms, and many are apt to be put off by the idea that someone wants to assess them psychologically. These problems can often be obviated by defining the process as a conversation designed to learn more about the client's needs. People readily accept the necessity of talking about such matters as health, social life, or activities. There is rarely any resistance to answering most questions in the domains of morale, life satisfaction, or positive affect. Depression,

sadness, bereavement, and major psychotic symptoms are more difficult to talk about. Some modes of handling these problems will be
discussed below.

The Threat of a "Test." Anything that appears to be a "test" of
cognitive processes, memory, psychomotor function, and the like may
cause considerable anxiety. Where only the grossest kind of screening
is required (as in the MAI or the OARS), most of the mental status
questions can be embedded into the interview so that they appear to
be routine. For example, rather than asking the 10 MSQ items serially,
the interview can begin with the request, "What is today's date, any-
way?" as if the examiner needs help. Birthday and address also fit
easily into a "face sheet" context. Naming the presidents, of course, is
clearly a test item, but they can be saved for later in the interview.
Where many demanding cognitive tests are to be given, they usually
will be best saved for the end or for a second session, since once in a
while a subject will be disturbed enough to refuse to continue; the
chance to obtain other less-threatening information is thus jeopar-
dized. In any case, when the "test" nature of the material is apparent,
one might as well acknowledge that fact, while assuring the client that
the object is to understand strengths and weaknesses. The professional's major task, however, is less to reduce the client's anxiety (that
task frequently cannot be achieved) than to appreciate fully the strain
she/he is enduring, and to respond in a way that shows this sensitivity.

Denial. There is some risk that denial or a set toward social
desirability will obscure the discriminating capacity of measures of psychological well-being. The best antidote for this tendency is to build up
trust and a feeling of familiarity in the client through preliminary conversation and careful staging of the assessment process so as to precede
the psychological well-being items with less-threatening areas of assessment. Thus, other things being equal, these questions may be best
placed in the second half of the assessment contact.

Emotionally Threatening Questions. Questions with obvious affective content should not come at the end of the session, however,
because such inquiries sometimes "open up" the client emotionally in
a way that demands some subsequent opportunity to neutralize the
engendered affect. Interview content relating to daily activities or to
the characteristics of housing or neighborhood is good for this sealing-
over process.

Occasionally—in our experience maybe once in 10 or 15 research interview occasions—questions with strongly affective connotations will visibly upset the client, sometimes to the point of tears. Such behavior may be more frequent with people in clinical situations. There is no need to explain to the experienced clinician how such an event should be handled. However, as will be discussed later, there is a high probability that the functional assessment interview will be performed by people with less than complete professional training. The supervising clinician must understand that such displays of sadness are very upsetting to the interviewer, who may, in turn, require some support.

It is necessary for the interviewer to understand that it is not necessarily undesirable for a client to be reminded of loneliness or loss. The annals of interviewing are full of instances where the display of affect or the recounting of sad occasions in the client's life has resulted in a positive cathartic or even therapeutic experience. However, this does not mean that such an event should turn the tone of the assessment in a therapeutic direction. Most older interviewees seem to view a crying episode as an intrusion and are glad to be helped to end it. An acknowledgment by the interviewer that many people feel sad when a question reminds them of something unpleasant helps reassure the person that he/she is not alone in responding this way. Often simply a short pause, followed by a suggestion to proceed with more questions, is enough to bring an end to the upset. Novice interviewers need to be told firmly that it is not their task to explore the affectively toned situation in depth. If the older person needs to continue talking about an emotionally loaded preoccupation, this need will be apparent to the interviewer. Training should include learning the criteria to be used to decide when a referral for evaluation or counseling is appropriate. The general rule is to run a middle course that acknowledges and legitimates the negative affect while encouraging the concentration on the task of the moment, that is, the interview.

Attending to the Interview. An interviewing problem more frequent than overt sadness is maintaining attentiveness throughout the hour or so that may be required to complete the interview. The more experience the client has had with academic pursuits or with mental health professions earlier in life, the more comprehensible will be the interview context and the format of the questions, and therefore, the less problematic will be paying attention. Most older clients are not so sophisticated, however; accordingly the interviewer needs to accommodate to that lack of experience in a variety of ways.

The major accommodation is recognition of the fact that the task demands may not be immediately evident nor the communications regarding the demands clear. The interviewer's speech patterns require deliberate and self-conscious modification. Most important is to slow down the pace of speech, since an increase in "processing time" is one of the few age-related changes that have been validated (Botwinick, 1984). The complexity of such processing demands is reduced by keeping the questions and the explanations short and simple. The interviewer will have to curb his/her natural tendency to elaborate instructions or to offer many alternative ways of asking a question. Long sentences and redundancy beyond some low level make the message incomprehensible. For the hard of hearing, slow and distinct speech are superior to mere loudness. But a versatile interviewer will be able to sustain a louder voice over an extended period of time for the select few who seem to need it.

The body language of the interviewer is as important as what he/she says. Eye contact is by far the most effective way of keeping the interviewee engaged. Unless there are signals from the older person to the contrary, a deliberate closing of the physical distance between interviewer and interviewee also helps. Where special attention is required (for example, to listen to a series of response alternatives or to ask for a complex judgment), the deliberate inclination of the interviewer's face, body, or arms toward the person can underline the importance of the client's mustering the necessary concentration.

When in doubt, simultaneous auditory and visual aids are desirable, as in any interview situation. Where there is a repetitious format, such as a Likert scale, or a series of questions framed in the same way, having a copy in front of the person while the responses are read can sometimes help. The interviewer needs to be able to read the signals from the client, however. Some clients simply cannot use the displayed cards and the effort is therefore wasted. For a few, the visual display may even actively interfere with the client's ability to think about the question. In both cases the interviewer should not hesitate to discontinue the visual display.

Loquaciousness. The final problem to be discussed is the fairly frequent tendency of some interviewees to wish to talk far beyond giving an adequate response to a question. If the interviewer will have later extended contact with the client, then the additional information and opportunity for mutual interchange will be useful and there is little problem in allowing digressions. However, most interview situations have built-in time limitations and very often that occasion may be the only one where interviewer and client interact. Thus the most usual task will be to allow the right amount of informal talk but still push through to an efficient completion of the interview. The best rule of thumb is to plan for an informal, conversational preamble of no more than five minutes, and then to proceed through the interview whenever possible from question to question without extraneous conversation. This procedure paces the task so as to limit its length and helps maintain the interviewee's set toward attentiveness and productiveness. Most clients accept the "rules" of the interview context by acceding to requests such as "Let's go on to the next one" or "Could we talk about that after we've finished these questions?" Sometimes interruption or refusal to discuss an extraneous topic is necessary; even such active measures do not alienate most interviewees. In contrast to such task orientation, the interviewer should plan to spend some unstructured time with the client once the interview is over. Virtually without exception the interviewee will let the interviewer know if he is tired and would rather the session terminate.

Proxy Interviews and Their Problems

Formalized assessment cannot proceed without taking account of the realities of most assessment situations. One of these realities is that the person most in need of assessment frequently is the one least likely to be able to respond in a valid manner. Of course, staff and observer ratings and sometimes relatives' ratings (Ellsworth, Foster, Childers, Gilbert, Kroeker, 1968) are familiar sources of data for pathological populations. Relatively infrequently attempts have been made to use the same instruments for both self-report and observer report. In functional assessment the principle of using the best available source of data to complete an index demands that the measures presented to either party be identical.

Most available instruments have used this principle by assertion, that is, with no empirical knowledge of the degree of distortion or error introduced by the source of the information. To some extent this is defensible; for some purposes, error-prone knowledge is better than no knowledge at all. Nonetheless, we badly need extended investigations of the types of informants, information, and conditions of inquiry for which proxy responses may be most valid. Only a few hints are given by existing empirical knowledge. Edwards and Danziger (1982) found that collaterals' ratings of depression, activities of daily living, memory, judgment, and problem solving correlated only .30 (median) with *S*s' responses. However, agreement was increased considerably when the informant was asked whether the older person knew when he was born, what day it was, or who the president was, rather than having to give an overall rating of "mental status." One may conclude that the more concrete the judgment, the greater the likelihood of a valid estimate.

In using an informant for instruments like the OARS or the MAI, this concreteness is maximized. Both of these instruments, however, adopted the convention that questions requiring subjective judgments would not be asked of informants (for example, psychological well-being or perceived quality of life). It remains to be tested, however, whether this exclusion is necessary.

If distortion occurs, its direction is a further issue. Edwards and Danziger (1982) found no consistency for relatives to overstate or understate a patient's condition. Rubenstein, Schairer, Wieland, and Kane (1982), on the other hand, found that the most impaired persons' self-ratings regularly underestimated impairment when compared to those done by a collateral. Where a major decision is known to hinge on the response (for example, in legally mandated screening programs whose purpose is to determine eligibility for long-term care), substantial disparities among self-estimates, professional estimates, and family estimates are almost certain to abound.

The Relation of Assessment to Intervention

The ultimate purpose of assessment in service-giving contexts is to assist professionals in their efforts to work with older people. There are a number of direct and indirect ways that this can occur. These multiple pathways to intervention all have the goal of identifying a problem and helping match the intervention to the needs and capabilities of the older client. This self-evident larger goal may be served by achieving a number of more specific goals.

Objective and Orderly Planning

The major problem with clinical practice performed in the absence of formalized assessment is that the worker necessarily looks at a client from a perspective determined by that professional's own background, interests, theoretical position, and preferences. These determinants of professional practice are not only inevitable; they are, within limits, desirable sources of variation in approach, simply because clients also

vary in their needs. Thus professional variation increases the chance
that an appropriate professional match will be attained.

However, some regulating features are necessary to keep the
assessment focused on the client, rather than the assessor's own
predilections. Formalized assessment is one such mechanism. Instruments are best when the function they purport to assess is clearly
defined and the indicators of the function are objective. With such
definitions in front of them, assessors are encouraged to filter out
personal bias, social stereotypes, and preconceived ideologies of how
people "ought" to be. The assessor thus becomes able to adjust internal anchoring points for judging what is a lot or a little desirable or
undesirable, healthy or pathological, to what is actually observed in
practice.

A related favorable result of formalized assessment is that attention is directed toward a holistic view of the person rather than a
limited view. The built-in myopias associated with different professions
were alluded to at the beginning of this chapter. Having to proceed
systematically to assess many domains in all four sectors of well-being
absolutely ensures that one will not see only the psychopathological
symptoms, the loneliness, or the physical disability. The assessment
battery will train each user to appreciate how closely related many
domains of functioning can be, yet at the same time underline the
instances that demonstrate how an impairment in one domain can be
counteracted by a strength in another.

Helping the Family

The families of older clients should benefit from an objective view and
report of the older person's status. They too are subject to personal
and social sources of distortion. Guilt feelings about their inability to
do more for their older relative than they have been able to accomplish
are a potent source of tension in relatives. Interpreting to them the
facts about their relative, how their functioning compares to that of
other people, and what they can expect in the future not only helps rid
them of irrational expectations and guilt but even more importantly
can help them focus on concrete tasks in behalf of their relative.

Assessing Change in the Client

Research in psychotherapy has underlined powerfully how difficult it is
for the therapist to assess change in the client. Functional assessment
helps overcome this problem because it defines specific functions

clearly and offers a systematic framework for identifying those functions in which change can be expected to occur. Global estimates of change (e.g., overall improvement) are notoriously subject to distortion. A change in the level of performance on an important task or in the number of depression symptoms, for example, have far greater sensitivity than a qualitative impression or a gross rating.

Human service workers often formulate intervention goals that are far too ambitious. In other instances they may deny any possibility of improvement, given the enormity of a particular impairment. The concept of a profile of abilities that can change in small ways is essential to grasp if one is to work with people with chronic disabilities. The differentiation of functioning into many separate domains and levels of performance within each domain allows the worker to gain some respect for small improvements, an essential element of maintaining one's professional motivation.

Interprofessional Communication

In many settings where older people are clients, human service is necessarily multidisciplinary and very unlikely to be dominated by any one profession. From every point of view such multiple perspectives are desirable. One of the costs of multidisciplinarity is the effort required by members of different professions to communicate with each other. The functional assessment technology helps to catalyze this process. In order to be able to function as a team all members of a team must make certain each understands critical terms such as "activities of daily living" or "life satisfaction" in the same way. Such definitions ought to be part of the documentation of professional practice. Once they are learned, there is far greater ease in sharing observations about clients with one another.

Social Planning and the Allocation of Resources

The formalized and standardized individual assessment procedure has the great advantage of being able to represent in aggregate form how any given group stands in relation to others. Social agencies are often surprised to learn these overall characteristics of their own clients. As normative data on large and probability-sampled aggregates become available, the ability to compare one's own clientele with the "average" or with clients from other agencies or service types becomes a potent help in planning. For example, subtle changes in the health of new admissions to a residence may signal the growth of a new client segment and the need to reconsider whether the existing program is still suitable. Data on community samples may help determine unmet needs for service planning. Because agency personnel will have become familiar with the meaning of a single client's scores, they will have a much clearer idea of the meaning of aggregate scores.

Fulfilling Formal Assessment Requirements

A major service-delivery goal is to "channel" prospective clients to services that will meet the client's needs at the least public cost and with the least restriction of personal freedom. Screening and referral agencies, often serving whole counties or regions, have sprung up in response to the need to defer institutionalization by steering people to appropriate community-based services. Motivation is strong to develop assessment techniques that can differentiate those for whom institutional placement is appropriate from those who can remain in the community (McAuley & Prohaska, 1981). This goal has not always resulted in a requirement for quantitative assessment of the type discussed in this chapter. However, the importance of quantitative assessment is strongly suggested (for example, in Minnesota—see Minnesota Long-Term Care Plan, 1981) and may well become mandatory.

At this point, some cautions are in order regarding this use of assessment. Even the best assessment cannot, by itself, determine who should enter an institution. Therefore it is heartening to find in a review of 19 state screening programs that 14 of them specify that screening must be done by a team consisting of two or more people, thus ensuring that clinical expertise is dominant (Knowlton, Clauser, and Fatula, 1982). The training for and monitoring of these programs must consistently emphasize, first, being sure that the formal assessment instrument is necessary, but, second, keeping in mind that the measures should be considered a tool rather than a decision. While the cost of making a team decision exceeds the cost of a nonteam assessment, putting the decision in the hands of a team provides the very precious protection for the individual that a cutting score cannot provide.

The problem of source of data in a formal gatekeeping situation cannot be overlooked, since it is possible that responses given by the client, family, informant, personal health professional, or others might show a bias related to a desired decision. This situation is one of those that justifies the use of the clinical judgment as the final factor in the decision. It is recommended that even when a major bias is suspected, the client's and/or informants' responses should be obtained for the assessment instrument. Only in this way can one know exactly the gap between the client's and the professional's judgment.

The important point to keep in mind is that older clients are far more likely than younger clients to have problems that span the many domains of the good life from biological health to environmental resources. Approaching their problems requires exceedingly concrete attention to the kinds of attributes that appear in the functional assessment, such as whether the client can perform housework or the amount of pleasure received from interactions with friends. Neuropsychological assessment and a thorough understanding of the person's psychodynamics may be necessary, but chances are that clinical practice will find the functional assessment even more frequently necessary.

Detailed Case Illustrations

A Mental Health Center Client

Mr. J. was the 78-year-old, widowed father of a physician. Both father and son recognized some critical signs of depression in Mr. J., including a constant feeling of impending doom, a loss of interest in everything, and disturbances of sleep and appetite. What bothered them most, however, was that Mr. J. was leaving bills unpaid, forgetting to lock the front door of his central-city residence, and required reminders of appointments. It was no problem getting him to a mental health clinic, where the team study procedure, including a neurologic examination, a brain scan, and neuropsychological testing, showed definitively that his problem was *not* an organically based dementia but a depressive reaction so profound that it simulated a memory deficit. Transmission of this conclusion to the family, while reassuring to Mr. J.'s son, had no apparent therapeutic effect on Mr. J.'s own depression.

The final diagnostic team conference was rich in diagnostic material on physical health, cognitive functioning, and psychopathology. While antidepressive medication was prescribed, their consensus was that a behaviorally oriented intervention would be required to cut into his now firmly established pattern of passivity, helplessness, and hopelessness. The team realized, however, that it knew very little about Mr. J.'s daily life. The MAI portions dealing with instrumental activities, time use, and social behavior were given by the social worker. Some excerpts from these responses follow:

Instumental activities	*Answers*

Q.15 Goes out of house. . . .
Comment: But they forced
me to go to the
July 4 picnic.

Once a month.

Q.17 Own and drive a car now?
Comment: But I haven't
driven for 6
months.

Yes.
(*Note:* Correct response
would thus be "No" for
Q.17).

Q.32 a. Goes shopping for
groceries?

Don't shop at all.

    b. Why?

My daughter-in-law brings
them.

    c. *Can* go shopping for
groceries?

No. I wouldn't know how
anymore.

Q.34 a. Does own housework?

Do with help.

    b. Why have help?

My son says the place is a
mess if my daughter-in-law
doesn't help.

    c. *Can* do housework?

I could do it, but I never
want to.

Q.38 a. Does manage own
money?

Do with help.

    b. Why have help?

My son asks me if I want
this or that, but he pays all
the bills. I'd just let them
go.

    c. Can manage money?

Sure I could, it just . . . I
don't know . . . I'm a mess.

Activity

Q.47 Frequency of participation
in 16 activities, past year
Item o (visit from friend or
relative who lives at
distance)

4 to 10 times.

Item b [attended church
(synagogue)]

3 or less.

The remaining 14 items

Never.

Q.46 What do you like to do
most?

All I do is eat and watch
TV.

Social interaction

Q.55 (Summary of 6 questions
enquiring about "relatives
to whom you feel close")

		Frequency			
		Phone	*S visits other*	*Other visits S*	*Where live*
John	Son	2–4/week	3/year or less	2–4/week	Local
Lisa	Daughter-in-law	2–4/week	3/year or less	2–4/week	Local
Tim	Grandson	Never	3/year or less	1/week	Local
Mary	Daughter	2–4/week	Never	4–10/year	Another city
Edie	Sister	1/week	Never	2–3/month	Local
Ellen	Sister	2–4/week	Never	1/week	Local

Q.57 In past year, how often
have you
   a. (Visited friends)   Never.
   b. (Had friends visit S)   Once a week.
   c. (Received phone calls   2–4 times a week.
       or letters from friends)
   d. (Met a friend some   Never.
       other place)

Impressions gained from the previous clinical contacts had been dominated by Mr. J.'s depression, self-doubt, and apparent confusion, and had also yielded the impression of vegetative, isolated behavior. These excerpts from the MAI resulted in a somewhat altered picture:

1. When forced to make the distinction between "does perform" and "can perform," Mr. J. begins by denigrating his ability ("a mess," "I never want to") but does, perhaps grudgingly, admit or imply that he probably could perform the tasks if he had to. This approach to the ADL questions suggests that he retains enough self-regard to avoid total dependence. A completely resigned person would without hesitation say he could not perform the tasks.

2. Mr. J. is close to being a true shut-in. He responds to very strong pressure to visit his son and does go out for medical care, but otherwise almost never leaves the home.

3. His social life, on the other hand, is richer than that of most people. One would never have known this fact without requesting the specific details regarding the number of contacts with

people. He speaks of himself as "lonely," "I'm no good to any-
body," "I just sit alone all day." Yet both family members and
freinds are very attentive.

4. The social contact is, just as clearly, all passive: Relatives and
friends do *all* the visiting and telephoning. The MAI does not inquire
how Mr. J. experiences this concern and outgoingness of his significant
people, but the great contrast between how much visiting they do and
how little he does offered the chance to inquire about his perception of
the disparity. He indicated that the more they visited and called, the
more he was convinced that they were wasting their time on him. "I'm
glad they don't just let me die, but I don't enjoy the visits. What do I
do for any of them?" He is thus concerned about reciprocity of social
exchange, though he does nothing about it now.

5. The passivity is also reflected in the great void in time use.
The Physical Self-Maintenance ADL activities (not reproduced above)
were all performed independently, and Mr. J. presumably turned on
the television and answered the phones and doorbells by himself, but
in every other way he was the recipient of stimulation from the environment. His life is truly improverished in the sense of novelty, intrin-
sically motivated activity, or personal control.

This knowledge, gained in about 10 minutes with the abbreviated
MAI, in turn, led the team to feel that some greater detail would be
desirable in order to be able to work with Mr. J. to change the pattern
of dependence, depression, and isolation. Thus some self-generated
time budgets were requested by the worker as a baseline against which
to measure and feed back knowledge of change in how his days were
spent. Inventories of pleasant and unpleasant events were given both
to identify reinforcers for therapeutic intervention and as further bases
for highlighting change. This detailed knowledge about Mr. J.'s daily
life proved to be essential for the ensuing cognitive therapy, which
followed the principle of helping Mr. J. set tasks for himself that
produced increments of self-controlled behavior.

A Community Resident Applying for an Institution

Mrs. S. was an 86-year-old person whose husband had died four years
previously. She had found her single-family detached home and its
yard too much to care for and had moved to an apartment a short
distance away. Two daughters and their families lived nearby and
were attentive to Mrs. S.'s needs. Mrs. S. had always been a flam-
boyant and sociable person, with a buoyant egotism that made people

enjoy being entertained by her without being too oppressed by her preoccupation with her own thoughts and needs. In the new apartment she readily made several friends but seemed not to be interested in keeping up with friends who lived elsewhere. To her relatives, she became increasingly demanding of their full attention and critical of her daughters during their visits. She visited a retirement residence suggested by her son-in-law and decided that this would satisfy her social needs. It had a long waiting list, however. During the third year of her widowhood she withdrew from her apartment-building friends, became afraid to drive her car, and found excuses for not accepting or for canceling arrangements suggested by her daughters to visit their homes or go out for entertainment with them. She began to eat less, lost some weight, and in a period of just a few months it was clear that she was losing her once-admirable agility. At the same time her memory became problematic, especially about such matters as whether she had taken her medicine or eaten. In this rundown condition, she slipped and fell in the apartment and had to spend a few days at the hospital. Upon returning to her apartment, she appeared to have lost all motivation to help herself. Her children and their families attempted to care for her by being present six or more hours per day. They had to call upon a homemaker, however, for occasional assistance. The homemaker's impression was that Mrs. S. was very impaired and that there was a real risk of undernutrition and physical accidents in the apartment.

The agency had the homemaker administer the full MAI. Some excerpts (it took almost 80 minutes because of Mrs. S.'s slowness of response and tendency to forget what question was asked):

Q.1	Today's date?	Month correct; previous year, wrong date.
Q.2a	How long lived here?	Don't know.
Q.13	Address?	(Address of previous house given.)
Q.33ff	(Instrumental activities of daily living?)	(Responded that she performed all activities without help.)
Q.60	As much pep as last year?	Yes.
Q.67	Get upset easily?	No.
Q.96	Major problems with memory?	No.
Q.97	Know time, day, season?	No.

These few responses showed quite conclusively the combination of cognitive impairment and denial of problems that is characteristic of many very impaired people. She was not so impaired, however, as to fail to understand many of the questions. Consequently, it was very desirable to do the entire MAI. Even though her pathology seemed evident from the beginning, the strength of her denial showed especially in the psychological well-being and perceived cognitive functioning domains. Had the homemaker not had the benefit of actually observing Mrs. S.'s inability in self-care ADL, it would have been desirable to ask one of the daughters to be an informant for the MAI.

The overall score of 5 on the cognitive functioning scale was in the marginal range, low enough to warrant the agency's requesting a psychiatric consultation. The psychiatrist felt that Mrs. S. was in the early stages of Alzheimer's disease. (It might be mentioned that often really early stages of the illness occasion a great deal of anxiety and some recognition of the confusion in oneself. The high level of denial is at least suggestive of an illness that has already progressed into a middle stage.)

Although the MAI and the consultation indicated that Mrs. S. clearly met all the criteria for admission to a nursing home, her daughters wished to continue to help her. They and the psychiatrist agreed that with help she could probably spend several more months in her own apartment followed by several more months in the home of one of them. The assessment results were accepted by the family, however, so that they felt free to make the application for institutional care as Mrs. S. continued to decline.

References

Adams, D. L. (1969). Analysis of a life satisfaction index. *Journal of Gerontology, 24,* 470–474.

Amster, L. E., & Krauss, H. H. (1974). The relationship between life crisis and mental deterioration in old age. *International Journal of Aging and Human Development, 5,* 51–55.

Andrews, F. M., & McKennell, A. C. (1980). Measures of self-reported well-being: Their affective, cognitive, and other components. *Social Indicators, 4,* 127–155.

Andrews, F. M., & Withey, S. B. (1976). *Social indicators of well-being.* New York: Plenum Press.

Beck, A. T., Ward, C. H., Mendelson, M., Mock, J., & Erbaugh, J. (1951). An inventory for measuring depression. *Archives of General Psychiatry, 4,* 561–571.

Bengtson, V. L., & Schrader, S. S. (1982). Parent–child relations. In D. J. Mangen & W. A. Peterson (Eds.), *Social roles and social participation (pp. 115–185)*. *Minneapolis: University of Minnesota Press.*

Bigot, A. (1974). The relevance of American life satisfaction indices for research on British subjects before and after retirement. *Age and Ageing, 3,* 113–121.

Botwinick, J. (1984). *Aging and behavior* (3rd ed.). New York: Springer Publishing Company.

Bradburn, N. M. (1969). *The structure of psychological well-being.* Chicago: Aldine.

Brink, T. L., Yesavage, J. A., Lum, O., Heersema, P. H., Adey, M., Rose, T. L. (1982) Screening tests for geriatric depression. *Clinical Gerontologist, 1,* 37–44.

Brodman, K., Erdmann, A. J., Lorge, I. & Wolff, H. G. (1949). The Cornell medical index: An adjunct to a medical interview. *Journal of the American Medical Association, 140,* 530–534.

Bull, N. C. (1982). Leisure activities. In D. J. Mangen & W. A. Peterson (Eds.), *Social roles and participation* (Vol. 2, pp. 447–538). Minneapolis: University of Minnesota Press.

Campbell, A., Converse, P. G., & Rodgers, W. (1976) *The quality of American life.* New York: Russell Sage Foundation.

Carp, F. M. (1978). Effects of the living environment on activity and the use of time. *International Journal of Aging and Human Development, 9,* 75–91.

Carp, F., & Carp, A. (1982). Perceived environmental quality of neighborhoods. *Journal of Environmental Psychology, 2,* 4–22.

Chapin, F. S., Jr. (1974). *Human activity patterns in the city.* New York: Wiley.

Costa, P. T., & McCrae, R. R. (1980). Influence of extraversion and neuroticism on subjective well-being: Happy and unhappy people. *Journal of Personality and Social Psychology, 38,* 668–678.

Cutler, S. J. (1976). Membership in different types of voluntary associations and psychological well-being. *Gerontologist, 16,* 335–339.

Dobson, C., Powers, E. A., Keith, P., & Goudy, W. J. (1979). Anomia, self-esteem, and life satisfaction: Interrelationships among three scales of well-being. *Journal of Gerontology, 34,* 569–572.

Dohrenwend, B. P. (1980). *Mental illness in the United States.* New York: Praeger.

Duke University Center for the Study of Aging. (1978). *Multidimensional functional assessment: The OARS methodology* (2nd ed.). Durham, NC: Duke University.

Edwards, D. F., & Danziger, W. L. (1982). *Congruence between patients and collateral source in interviews for dementia.* P. W. J. Rehabilitation Institute. St. Louis: Washington University School of Medicine.

Ellsworth, R. B., Foster, L., Childers, B., Gilbert, A., & Kroeker, D. (1968). Hospital and community adjustment as perceived by psychiatric patients, their families, and staff. *Journal of Consulting and Clinical Psychology Monographs, 32,* 1–41 (5, Pt. 2).

Fillenbaum, G. G., & Smyer, M. A. (1981). Reliability of the OARS multidimensional functional assessment questionnaire. *Journal of Gerontology, 36,* 428–434.

Flanagan, J. C., (1979). *Identifying opportunities for improving the quality of life of older age groups.* Palo Alto, CA: American Institute for Research.

Folstein, M.F., Folstein, S. E., & McHugh, P. R. (1975). "Mini-Mental State": A practical method for grading the cognitive state of patients for the clinician. *Journal of Psychiatric Research, 12,* 189–198.

Gaitz, C. M., & Scott, J. (1972). Age and the measurement of mental health. *Journal of Health and Social Behavior, 13,* 55–67.

George, L. K. (1981). Subjective well-being: Conceptual and methodological issues. In C. Eisdorfer (Ed.), *Annual review of gerontology* (Vol.II, pp. 345–382). New York: Springer Publishing Company.

George, L. K., & Bearon, L. B. (1980). *Quality of life in older persons: Meaning and measurement.* New York: Human Sciences Press.

Golden, R. R., Teresi, J. A., & Gurland, B. J. (1984). Development of indicator scales for the Comprehensive Assessment and Referral Evaluation (CARE) interview schedule. *Journal of Gerontology, 39,* 138–146.

Gordon, C., & Gaitz, C. M. (1976) Leisure and lives: Personal expressivity across the life span. In R. H. Binstock & E. Shanas (Eds.), *Handbook of aging and the social sciences.* New York: Van Nostrand Reinhold.

Gurin, G., Veroff, J. & Feld, S. (1960). *Americans view their mental health.* New York: Basic Books.

Gurland, B. J. (1976). The comparative frequency of depression in various age groups. *Journal of Gerontology, 31,* 283–292.

Gurland, B. J., Kuriansky, J., Sharpe, L., Simon, R., Stiller, P., Birkett, P. (1977–78). The comprehensive assessment and referral evaluation (CARE)—rationale, development, and reliability. *International Journal of Aging and Human Development, 8,* 9–41.

Havens, B., & Thompson, E. (1976). Aging needs. Assessment schedule. Department of Health and Community Services, Province of Manitoba, Winnipeg.

Herzog, A. R., Rodgers, W.L., & Woodworth, J. (1982). *Subjective well-being among different age groups.* Ann Arbor, MI: Institute for Social Research.

Hess, B. B. (1979). Sex roles, friendship, and the life course. *Research on Aging, 1,* 494–515.

Himmelfarb, S., & Murrell, S. A. (1983). Reliability and validity of five mental health scales in older persons. *Journal of Gerontology, 38,* 333–339.

Holmes, T. H., & Rahe, R. H. (1967). The social readjustment rating scale. *Journal of Psychosomatic Research, 11,* 213–218.

Hoyt, D. R., & Creech, J. C. (1983). The life-satisfaction index: A methodological and theoretical critique. *Journal of Gerontology, 38,* 111–116.

Kahana, E. (1982). A congruence model of person–environment interaction. In M. P. Lawton, P.G. Windley, & T. O. Byerts (Eds.), *Aging and the environment: Theoretical approaches* (pp. 97–121). New York: Springer Publishing Company.

Kahn, R. L., Goldfarb, A. I., Pollack, M., & Peck, A. (1960). Brief objective measures for the determination of mental status in the aged. *American Journal of Psychiatry, 117,* 326–328.

Kane, R. A., & Kane, R. L. (1981). *Assessing the elderly.* Lexington, MA: Lexington Books.

Katz, S., Downs, T. D., Cash, H. R., & Gratz, R. C. (1970). Progress in development of the index of ADL. *Gerontologist, 10,* 20–30.

Katzman, R., Brown, T., Fuld, P., Peck, A., Schechter, R., Schimmel, H. (1983) Validation of a short orientation-memory-concentration test of cognitive impairment. *American Journal of Psychiatry, 140,* 734–739.

Kozma, A., & Stones, M. J. (1980). The measurement of happiness. *Journal of Gerontology, 35,* 906–912.

Langner, T. S. (1962). A 22-item screening score of psychiatric symptoms indicating impairment. *Journal of Health and Human Behavior, 3,* 269–276.

Lawton, M. P. (1970). Ecology and aging. In L. A. Pastalan & D. H. Carson (Eds.), *Spatial behavior of older people* (pp. 40–67). Ann Arbor: Institute of Gerontology, University of Michigan.

Lawton, M.P. (1975). The Philadelphia Geriatric Center Morale Scale: A revision. *Journal of Gerontology, 30,* 85–89.

Lawton, M.P. (1982). The well-being and mental health of the aged. In T. Field, A. Stein, H. Quay, L. Troll, & G. E. Finley (Eds.), *Review of Human Development* (pp. 614–628). New York: Wiley–Interscience.

Lawton, M. P. (1983a). Environment and other determinants of well-being in older people. *The Gerontologist, 23,* 349–357.

Lawton, M. P. (1983b). The dimensions of well-being. *Experimental Aging Research, 9,* 65–72.

Lawton, M. P., & Brody, E. M. (1969). Assessment of older people: Self-maintaining and instrumental activities of daily living. *Gerontologist, 9,* 179–186.

Lawton, M. P., & Cohen, J. (1974). Environment and the well-being of elderly inner city residents. *Environment and Behavior, 6,* 194–211.

Lawton, M. P., and Kleban, M. H. (1971). The aged resident of the inner city. *Gerontologist, 11,* 277–283.

Lawton, M. P., Kleban, M. H., & diCarlo, E. (1984). Psychological well-being in the aged: Factorial and conceptual dimensions. *Research on Aging, 6,* 67–97.

Lawton, M.P., Moss,, M., Fulcomer, M., & Kleban, M.H. (1982). A research and service-oriented Multilevel Assessment Instrument. *Journal of Gerontology, 37,* 91–99.

Lawton, M.P., & Nahemow, L. (1979). Social areas and the well-being of tenants in planned housing for the elderly. *Multivariate Behavioral Research, 14,* 463–484.

Lawton, M. P., & Storandt, M. (1984). Assessment of older people. In P.

McReynolds & G. J. Chelune (Eds.). *Advances in psychological assessment.* (Vol.6). San Francisco, CA: Jossey-Bass.

Lemke, S., & Moos, R. H. (1980). Assessing the institutional policies of sheltered care settings. *Journal of Gerontology, 35,* 96–107.

Lemke, S. & Moos, R. H. (1981). The suprapersonal environments of sheltered care settings. *Journal of Gerontology, 36,* 233–243.

Liang, J., & Bollen, K. A. (1983). The structure of the Philadelphia Geriatric Center Morale Scale: A reinterpretation. *Journal of Gerontology, 38,* 181–189.

Lieberman, M. A., & Tobin, S. S. (1983). *The experience of old age.* New York: Basic Books.

Linn, M. W., & Linn, B. S. (1984). Self-Evaluation of Life (SELF) Scale: A short comprehensive self-report of health for the elderly. *Journal of Gerontology, 39,* 603–612.

Linn, B. S., Linn, M. W., & Gurel, L. (1968). Cumulative illness rating scale. *Journal of the American Geriatrics Society, 16,* 622–626.

MacPhillamy, D. J., & Lewinsohn, P. M. (1982). The Pleasant Events Schedule: Studies on reliability, validity and scale intercorrelation. *Journal of Consulting and Clinical Psychology, 50,* 363–380.

Maddox, G. L., & Douglas, E. (1973). Self-assessment of health: A longitudinal study of elderly subjects. *Journal of Health and Social Behavior, 14,* 87–93.

Mahoney, F. I., & Barthel, D. W. (1965). Functional evaluation: The Barthel Index. *Rehabilitation, 14,* 61–65.

McAuley, W. J., & Prohaska, T. R. (1981). Professional recommendations for long-term care placement: A comparison of two groups of institutionally vulnerable elderly. *Home Health Care Services Quarterly, 2,* 41–57.

Mindel, C. H. (1982). Kinship relations. In D. J. Mangen & W. A. Peterson (Eds.), *Social roles and social participation* (Vol. 2) *Research Instruments in Social Gerontology* (pp. 187–229). Minneapolis: University of Minnesota Press.

Minnesota long-term care plan. (1981). Minnesota Department of Health, Minneapolis.

Moos, R. H., Gauvain, M., Lemke, S., Max, W., & Mehren, B. (1979). Assessing the social environments of sheltered care settings. *Gerontologist, 19,* 74–82.

Moos, R. H., & Lemke, S. (1980). Assessing the physical and architectural features of sheltered care settings. *Journal of Gerontology, 35,* 571–583.

Morris, J. N., & Sherwood, S. (1975). A retesting and modification of the Philadelphia Geriatric Center Morale Scale. *Journal of Gerontology, 30,* 77–84.

Moss, M., & Lawton, M. P. (1982). The time budgets of older people: A window on four lifestyles. *Journal of Gerontology, 37,* 115–123.

National Council on the Aging. (1975). *The myth and reality of aging in America.* Washington, DC: Author.

National Council on the Aging. (1981). *Aging in the eighties: America in transition.* Washington, DC: Author.

Neugarten, B. L., Havighurst, R. J., & Tobin, S. S. (1961). The measurement of life satisfaction. *Journal of Gerontology, 16,* 134–143.

Nunnally, J. C. (1978). *Psychometric theory* (2nd ed.). New York: McGraw-Hill.

Nydegger, C. (1977). *Measuring morale: A guide to effective assessment.* Washington DC: Gerontological Society.

Okun, M. A. & Stock, W. A. (1984). Research synthesis of the health–subjective well-being relationship. *International Journal of Aging and Human Development, 19,* 81–172.

Pfeiffer, E. (1975). A short portable mental status questionnaire for the assessment of organic brain deficit in elderly patients. *Journal of the American Geriatrics Society, 23,* 433–441.

Radloff, L. W. (1977). The CES-D Scale: A self-report depression scale for research in the general population. *Applied Psychological Measurement, 1,* 385–401.

Rosenberg, M. (1965). *Society and the adolescent self-image.* Princeton NJ: Princeton University Press.

Rosencranz, H. A., & Pihlblad, C. T. (1970). *Journal of Gerontology, 25,* 129–133.

Rubenstein, L.Z., Schairer, C., Wieland, G.D., & Kane, R. (1984). *Systematic biases in functional status assessment of the elderly: Effects of different data sources. Journal of Gerontology, 39,* 686–691.

Russell, D. W. (1982). The measurement of loneliness. In L. A. Peplau & D. Perlman (Eds.), *Loneliness.* New York: Wiley–Interscience.

Sherman, S. (1973). Leisure activities in retirement housing. *Journal of Gerontology, 28,* 351–358.

Sokolovsky, J., & Cohen, C. (1981). Measuring social interaction of the urban elderly: A methodological synthesis. *International Journal of Aging and Human Development, 12,* 233–244.

Spielberger, D., Gorsuch, R., & Lushene, R. (1970). *STAI Manual for the State-Trait Anxiety Inventory.* Palo Alto, CA: Consulting Psychologists Press.

Tamir, L. M., & Antonucci, T. C. (1981). Self-perception, motivation, and social support through the family life course. *Journal of Marriage and the Family, 43,* 151–160.

Teresi, J. A., Golden, R. R., Gurland, B. J., Wilder, D. E., & Bennett, R. G. (1984). Construct validity of indicator-scales developed from the Comprehensive Assessment and Referral Evaluation Interview Schedule. *Journal of Gerontology, 39,* 147–157.

Tissue, T. (1972). Another look at self-rated health. *Journal of Gerontology, 27,* 91–94.

U.S. Bureau of the Census. (1975). *Annual Housing Survey: Indicators of housing and neighborhood quality.* Washington, DC: U.S. Government Printing Office.

Wechsler, D. (1958). *The measurement and appraisal of adult intelligence.* Baltimore: Williams & Wilkins.

Wechsler, D. (1981). *WAIS-R Manual: Wechsler Adult Intelligence-Revised.* New York: Psychological Corporation.

White, R. W. (1959). Motivation reconsidered: The concept of competence. *Psychological Review, 66,* 297–333.

Windley, P. G. (1981). The effects of ecological/architectural dimensions of small rural towns on the well-being of older people. In P. Kim & C. Wilson (Eds.), *Toward mental health of the rural elderly.* Landover, MD: University Press of America.

Windley, P. G., & Scheidt, R. J. (1982). An ecological model of mental health among small-town elderly. *Journal of Gerontology, 37,* 235–242.

Wood, V., & Robertson, J. (1978). Friendship and kinship interaction: Differential effects on the morale of the elderly. *Journal of Marriage and the Family, 40,* 367–375.

Wood, V., Wylie, M. L., & Sheafor, B. (1969). An analysis of a short self-report measure of life satisfaction: Correlations with rater judgments. *Journal of Gerontology, 24,* 465–469.

Wyler, A. R., Masuda, M., & Holmes, T. H. (1968). Seriousness of illness rating scale. *Journal of Psychosomatic Research, 11,* 363–374.

Zung, W. W. K. (1965), A self-rating depression scale. *Archives of General Psychiatry, 12,* 63–70.

II

Treatment

3

Excess Disability in the Elderly: Exercise Management

Alan H. Roberts

The tragedy of life is what dies inside of a man while he lives.

—*Albert Schweitzer*

Two clear trends have emerged in the past two decades that have major implications for health care professionals and their patients (U.S. Department of Health and Human Services, 1979). The first and most striking of these trends is the aging of our nation's population and the growing concern for their health care. During the twentieth century, the elderly population has been growing at a much more rapid rate than the general population. More than 25 million persons in the United States—one out of every nine Americans—is at least age 65. If this trend continues, the proportion will reach one in five within the next 50 years. The significance of this demographic shift for health care providers may be appreciated if one considers that while persons over the age of 65 account for 11 percent of the population, they account for more than 30 percent of visits to specialists in internal medicine at this time.

The second important trend is the increasing prevalence of chronic disease. It has been estimated that over 30 million adults suffer from one or more chronic diseases that impair function (U.S. Department of Health and Human Services, 1979). Musculoskeletal disorders represent the most common cause of chronic impairment and disability in both men and women in all age-groups, but the highest prevalence of musculoskeletal disorders occurs in the elderly (U.S. Department of Health and Human Services, 1981). Other major groups of disorders accounting for disability include cardiovascular, respiratory, digestive, and emotional disorders (U.S. Department of Health and Human Services, 1981). These too are overrepresented in the elderly.

In years to come we can expect increasing numbers of patients with a variety of chronic musculoskeletal disorders and other chronic impairments. Many of these will be elderly persons for whom a lesser degree of physical impairment may result in greater disability, with loss of independence and an accelerated decline in the quality of life. It is obvious that special effort will be required to anticipate the needs of these patients and implement programs to reduce functional disability to the lowest possible levels.

Functional disability, the degree to which illness or impairment interferes with activities of daily living, is a preferred measure of health status among the elderly. Functional disability can be evaluated by targeting the number of days lost from work, including homemaking; time spent in bed; or inability to bathe, dress, or travel independently. Based upon these measures, disability increases among older age-groups, but there is no abrupt increase at age 65 or any other age; instead, the process is progressive, becoming apparent in middle age and building steadily thereafter. Those at risk are not confined to a particular age-group (Butler & Newacheck, 1982).

Excess Disability

The concept of *excess disability* is intended to address the problem that large numbers of people, with or without chronic illness or disease, are more functionally disabled than is necessary. There is no clear operational definition for *excess disability*. It requires a clinical judgment that has a value judgment as a component.

Contrast, for example, a quadriplegic who is unable to walk, with a paraplegic, not otherwise physically impaired, who is unable to leave his or her bed and use a wheelchair. In most instances, the paraplegic would be judged to be suffering from disability in excess of physical limitations imposed upon him/her by a spinal cord injury, while the quadriplegic would not.

At times, however, the degree to which disability is excessive is not so readily apparent. What judgment might we make about a 68-year-old woman who has had chronic low back pains for seven years after twisting her back getting out of an automobile? Since that incident she has continued to have severe and debilitating pain. She spends most of her day reclining and is unable to perform more than minimal self-care chores and tasks. She has had many medical evaluations and tests with no positive medical findings. It is apparent that she is severely physically disabled.

Does the fact that there are no medical findings prove that there is no organic basis for her pain and disability? If the judgment is made that she is not a malingerer, that she truly "experiences" the pain that she says she has, is she disabled by her pain or is she "excessively" disabled by her pain?

How would one judge a woman with polymyositis and pulmonary fibrosis, severe connective tissue disorders, that are still active after 13 years of treatment? She has an exogenous Cushing's syndrome with symptoms of diabetes. Because of steroid treatments she has osteoporosis and possibly compression fractures of her spine. Because of these she has severe pain. She is clinically and admittedly depressed. For the past three months she has been bedridden with muscle pain, back pain, and headaches. After dressing herself in the morning, she retires to the couch for the majority of the day and is unable even to sit for long periods of time. How much of her disability can be attributed to her medical problems? How much of it is excessive? With an appropriate program of rehabilitation, how much more is she capable of doing? Could her day-to-day functioning be improved enough to make a meaningful difference in the quality of her life?

Questions like these are not always easy to answer. They require clinical judgments based upon experience with patients with similar medical problems combined with careful and extensive behavioral analyses of situational factors that may be influencing the patient's disability. These analyses require a combination of both medical and psychological expertise. Both physicians and psychologists involved in making these kinds of assessments must have knowledge and experience of rehabilitation methods and their potential.

If the patients' problems are seen only in the light of the patients' presumed underlying problem (e.g., paraplegia, poor motivation, osteoporosis, pain of unknown origin) then the patients' potential for increased functioning may be overlooked or underestimated. In contrast, if the clinician attends to what the patient does or does not do, then it is often possible to use learning technology to increase, decrease, or maintain selected behaviors to bring about improvements in function. These improvements in function may occur in the absence of change in the underlying medical or psychological problems.

Physical Deconditioning and Excess Disability

One of the common sources of excess disability in the aged, and one which is often overlooked, is physical deconditioning. Current social attitudes militate against even moderate physical activities in the elderly (Bassey, 1978). There is a general attitude of disapproval of all but mild exertion for older people. It is frequently assumed that too much exercise for those in older age-groups will lead to injury, exhaustion, or illness. As people grow older, they expect their health to decline (Costa & McCrae, 1980).

Sidney and Shephard (1976, 1977) have found marked differences between the positive attitudes of elderly people toward exercise and what they actually do. In one study (1977) they found that their subjects reported above-average activity, while at the same time they had high heart rates and a corresponding lack of endurance fitness. When asked to join an exercise program, those subjects who refused said they were active enough already, that their weight was normal, and that their fitness was above average. All of these perceptions were inaccurate. Sidney and Shephard (1976) have attributed these discrepancies to a conditioned belief that, at retirement, a person should slow down and "enjoy a well-earned rest." This belief limits expectations about engaging in physical activity.

Sidney and Shephard speculated that their subjects may have worried about the possible dangers of exertion, while at the same time misunderstanding the amount of exercise necessary to maintain good physical condition. They also observed that in the unfit elderly, feelings of fatigue occurred very early so that even minimal work was perceived as significant effort. In another survey by Perry (1982) only one-fifth of a group of elderly residents of a high-rise apartment were exercising at levels necessary to maintain minimal fitness.

Lack of physical exercise and training decreases strength, flexibility, and endurance, and these, in turn, contribute to increasing disability, even in the absence of physical illness. Moderate amounts of exercise are needed for the maintenance of the integrity of the cardiovascular system, bones, muscles, and ligaments. Since it is reasonably speculated that physical activity may protect people against coronary artery disease, diabetes, and hypertension, it is possible that lack of physical activity may increase physical illness and disease, which in turn may become disabling (cf. Holloszy, 1983).

The most common presenting complaint of patients judged to be excessively disabled is that of pain. It is not surprising therefore that behavioral methods used to manage excess disability are for the most part extensions of methods developed to help manage disability due to chronic pain.

Chronic Pain and Excess Disability

Historically, chronic pain (which is usually defined as pain which persists for six months or more despite appropriate medical or surgical intervention) was treated with drugs, surgery, or psychiatric intervention. When patients continued to complain of chronic pain in the absence of definitive medical findings, the etiology of the pain was usually thought to be psychogenic. Some underlying psychiatric dysfunction requiring treatment with psychotherapy or psychoactive medication was assumed to exist. One survey of patients referred with a diagnosis of chronic pain of unknown etiology reported that this problem accounted for as much as one-third of referrals for psychiatric consultations (Pilling, Bronnick, & Swensen, 1967).

In 1968, Wilbert E. Fordyce published two reports describing the use of behavioral management techniques for treating problems associated with chronic pain (Fordyce, Fowler, & DeLateur, 1968; Fordyce, Fowler, Lehmann & DeLateur, 1968). Following the publication of these papers, the use of behavioral methods to treat chronic pain increased rapidly. Instead of presuming an underlying medical or psychological cause for disability, the behavioral methods focused directly upon the actions or behaviors of patients and their families. Behavior modification techniques were applied to help patients change selected behaviors so as to improve function rather than to treat pain directly. That large numbers of patients began to report decreasing pain following the application of these methods was not surprising, but decreased pain per se was never a primary goal for these rehabilitation methods.

Currently, behavioral methods are used in virtually every legitimate pain treatment program in the United States (Fordyce, 1983). Almost all of these programs have, as a core element of treatment, an assumption that audible and visible communications of pain, together with impairments associated with these indicators, are behaviors. As with any behavior they may come under the control of conditioning effects. The behavioral methods for the treatment of chronic pain, as well as the effectiveness of these techniques, is now well documented (cf. Fordyce, 1976; Roberts, 1981; Roberts & Reinhardt, 1980).

As published reports of these methods and the results of their applications have proliferated in the literature, they have been followed by critical articles and reviews (cf. Block, 1982; Latimer, 1982; Turner & Chapman, 1982; Turk, Meichenbaum, & Genest, 1983). In general, criticisms fall into two categories. The first questions the methodological adequacy of studies attempting to assess the efficacy of behavior management in the treatment of chronic pain. This observation is, in general, accurate. The difficulties of designing prospective experimental studies in an area like this one are formidable and none have been reported to date. The consistency of positive clinical reports from a variety of settings over a long period of time does, however, argue for effectiveness (cf. Carins, Thomas, Mooney, & Pace, 1976; Follick, Zitter, & Kublich, 1981; Fordyce, 1976; Roberts & Reinhardt, 1980; Seres & Newman, 1976; Sternbach, 1974). This argument is strengthened when it is considered that these treatment methods are usually applied to patients who have not improved for long periods of time despite interventions by traditional medical and surgical treatment methods. When people remain disabled despite a variety of treatments and the disability diminishes when a new method is tried, the inference may be drawn that the new treatment is more effective than previous interventions. In a complex treatment program, however, it is difficult to determine what the "active ingredients" might be.

A second group of criticisms is concerned with whether or not these treatment methods, when applied, actually alter the patient's pain. This criticism asks whether or not behavioral management methods alleviate the patient's pain or whether these methods simply teach patients to be more stoical about the pain they continue to have.

In a recent paper Fordyce (1983) responds to both of these criticisms. It is sufficient here to point out that these methods were never intended to "cure" pain; they were devised to reduce the disability. The interventions are intended to modify social feedback to the patients' pain-associated behaviors, and thus alter these behaviors so that the patient can function more efficiently.

The concept of excess disability helps to emphasize that the focus is upon the disability rather than upon the presumed underlying causes of this disability. At the same time it extends behavioral methods to a wider variety of problems ranging from decreased physical activity accompanying increasing age, to more severe disability associated with chronic illness and disease. Excess disability refers to an inability to lead a full independent life for reasons other than those that can be attributed to irreversible organic disease. Thus, excess disability may include disability related to pain, mood disorder, fatigue or tiredness, lack of "motivation," or problems associated with chronic illness. Behavioral methods in this context are intended to increase function in the presence of and despite diagnosed chronic illness.

Physical Activity and Aging

Excess disability is objectively defined primarily in terms of physical activity. From either a preventive medicine perspective or from a rehabilitation medicine perspective, increasing physical activity becomes an important goal of behavioral management programs directed toward elimination of excess disability. Several recent reviews of the research in this area are available (e.g., Bassey, 1978; Cross, 1980; Laerum & Laerum, 1982; Naughton, 1982; Shephard & Sidney, 1978; Taylor & Rowell, 1980). The most comprehensive of these critical reviews is that of Shephard and Sidney (1978).

Since a key element in the treatment of excess disability is the increase of physical activity through exercise, it is important to be aware of the effects of exercise upon the elderly. While many tend to think of exercise in the context of prolonging life, there is certainly no evidence that any kind of exercise will extend the life span, particularly when exercise is started late in life. The exercise is justified on the more pragmatic grounds of increasing function and increasing the quality of life.

In general (Shephard & Sidney, 1978) the health benefits of regular exercise include the ability to increase work load so that the person can work for a longer period of time with less fatigue, increased respiratory function, and decreased incidence of cardiovascular disease. There are also metabolic benefits that may include decreased obesity, decreased osteoporosis and, for those patients where it is a factor, increasing control of diabetes.

Psychological benefits have been demonstrated to result from increased physical activity including decreased depression, decreased aggression and, in some studies, a suggestion of increased mental function (Folkins & Sime, 1981). There have been demonstrations of increased well-being among those who exercise regularly; many regular exercisers do it because it appears to make them feel better (Berger & Owen, 1983; Folkins & Sime, 1981).

It is important to recognize that many of the assertions concerning the relationship between exercise and improved psychological function are subject to continuing controversy on empirical grounds and that in many instances, these conclusions are based on poorly controlled studies. The weight of the evidence from the studies that have been reported (cf. Folkins & Sime, 1981) appears to justify the routine use of physical fitness training in programs designed to manage excess disability.

A recent study by Morris, Vaccaro, and Harris (1983) compared four groups on "quality-of-life" measures. Prior to their study, all groups evaluated were comparable on the quality-of-life measures they used. Sixty older adults were assigned to interventions which included ballroom dancing, ballet, aerobic dancing, and dollmaking for 12 weeks. At the end of the study, the ballet and aerobic dance groups were significantly more improved on the quality-of-life measures and the increases on these measures were proportional to the amount of physical activity in which each group participated.

In their critical review of the effects of exercise in aging people, Shephard and Sidney (1978) concluded that aged persons do benefit from appropriate programs of regular vigorous exercise. They pointed out that physical performance is improved by gains of aerobic power and appropriate adaptations of the cardiorespiratory system to muscular effort. They also concluded that beneficial changes in the electrocardiogram, body composition, strength, hormonal response, and psychological test scores may result from programs of physical exercise. There are reports of increases in agility, muscular endurance, and flexibility with exercise. Shephard and Sidney (1978) felt that the extent of physiological gains with physical fitness training in the elderly probably depends upon personal factors, such as motivation and attitudes, as well as programmatic factors, such as intensity, frequency, and duration of effort.

Assessment Procedures

Identification of the Problem

The management of excess disability depends first of all upon its identification. While this is not a problem in the area of prevention, it appears to be the major stumbling block to the application of behavioral procedures to those who are already experiencing decreased function. For persons already in the health care system and suffering from severe chronic illness or disease, there is considerable reluctance to make a judgment that the person should be functioning at higher than current levels. There is resistance among health care professionals to asking the sick and the elderly to exercise. It is necessary as a first step for a physician to identify the disability as excessive and to provide medical sanction and support for a program to decrease the disability. Medical involvement and sanction form a necessary requisite for both initiation and maintenance of programs to manage excess disability.

Evaluation

Once the problem is identified and a person is referred for evaluation and treatment, the next step is a functional behavioral analysis. The purpose of this analysis is to determine what social and environmental reinforcers are responsible for the development and maintenance of the excess disability. The medical diagnoses of these patients may range from physical deconditioning—with the patient complaining of such things as fatigue, weakness, tiredness, dizziness, or shortness of breath—to severe debilitating chronic disease.

The most common presenting complaint is that of pain. Sometimes the pain has a diagnosable but untreatable physiological etiology. At other times the origin of the pain is unknown. *It is important in assessment to focus not on the presumed medical problem responsible for the complaints and symptoms but rather upon their behavioral consequences.* The common thread is inability to function physically at optimum levels.

Many patients do not perceive their disability to be excessive. To be effective the evaluation must often include an element of confrontation and education before the patient and family members can accept a treatment program designed to increase the level of function. A bedridden, medication-dependent person suffering from severe and intractable pain has great difficulty in accepting the notion that he or she can learn to live a normal life even though the pain might continue. A program that is presented inaccurately as intending to cure or alleviate the presenting complaint might persuade the patient to participate in a treatment program but is almost certain to fail when the presenting symptom persists.

It is during the evaluation that new expectations in the form of new information are communicated to the patient and the family. This intervention is aimed at education and is designed to change beliefs and perceptions in order to prepare the patient and family to set new goals. This aspect of treatment does not itself change behavior but does prepare the patient and family to accept a behavioral program.

During the course of chronic illness the patient has come to accept certain misinformation and misperceptions. These must be corrected in order for the patient to accept a treatment program. Some of these incorrect beliefs directly support disability and may be an underlying cause of some of the patient's problems.

An example is the medical advice commonly provided to patients with musculoskeletal pain: "If it hurts, don't do it." Such advice, if taken literally for other than brief periods of time, may lead to progressive physical deconditioning. The common misperception is that the best treatment for pain is rest. While this may be good advice for short periods of time, decreased activity may cause more pain as time passes. As muscles become weak and tight from misuse or disuse, there is increasing pain and, frequently, muscle spasm when these muscle groups are activated. Patients are often surprised to learn that a graded program to increase exercise and activity will decrease rather than increase pain.

The fact that prescription analgesics when used for long periods of time may exacerbate pain rather than relieve it is almost always surprising to patients (Roberts, 1981, 1983). While many patients do not like to use analgesics, it is their belief that their pain will become increasingly unbearable if they stop using them. It is important to inform patients and families that pain will decrease when they are weaned from analgesics, that their sleep will improve without sleeping pills, and that their muscle spasms will decrease without tranquilizers and muscle relaxants.

The rationale and the supporting data for these assertions have been discussed by Fordyce (1976), Roberts (1981, 1983) and others. Treatments which are appropriate for acute pain generally tend to make chronic pain worse. While this is now generally accepted, convincing patients is sometimes difficult. It is, however, always necessary.

Further preparations of patients for treatment requires education concerning the general idea that pain behaviors can be learned and unlearned. This assumption underlies many of the behavioral techniques used in a treatment program. If patients understand this they will understand partly why some of these techniques are used in their treatment. Even if they do not believe the assumption, this knowledge provides some rationale for the seemingly odd things that are done during treatment, such as ignoring their complaints or other pain behaviors.

It is not necessary that patients believe or agree with any of the underlying assumptions about the treatment program. Patients do need to have some understanding about why these methods are being used if they are to accept a treatment program and behave in ways consistent with that program. Even if informed patients and families are skeptical, many will go along with a treatment program as "an experiment." Most often they understand that they have few other options.

The participation of the family in both the assessment and treatment of excess disability problems is extremely useful and in most cases mandatory. It has become increasingly evident that family members are primary reinforcers of disability and of activity.

Data suggest that treatment programs are much more likely to be successful when family members are involved and cooperative (Hudgens, 1977; Roberts, 1983; Roberts & Reinhardt, 1980). When behavior modification programs fail, it is most often because significant operant contingencies have not been fully controlled. Involvement of the family at all levels of assessment and treatment increases the likelihood that these contingencies can be managed more effectively and more broadly. A treatment program that is primarily an outpatient program must be supported at home as well as in the clinic both during and after the treatment program.

Since patients with a wide variety of presenting complaints are seen in the clinic, it is difficult to specify precisely each of the components that must be covered in an assessment. In general the following areas are usually covered.

Psychological Testing. Usually an MMPI is administered to both the patient and his/her spouse prior to the evaluation. This allows for the screening of psychopathology, levels of depression and anxiety, the degree to which the patient and his/her spouse are focusing on somatic concerns, perceived energy levels, ego strength, dependency, and similar variables. It is possible, in comparing the MMPI of a patient and spouse, to make some predictions about the way the two will interact. There are data suggesting that elevations on certain MMPI scales of the spouses of patients are better predictors of treatment outcome than the MMPI scores of the patients themselves (Roberts & Reinhardt, 1980).

A common use of the MMPI is to evaluate whether or not the patient's complaint is organic or functional. The use of the MMPI to make this kind of determination is ill-advised and misleading (Roberts, 1983). People with acute organic pain frequently have many of the same psychological symptoms found in people with chronic pain (e.g., dysphoria, anxiety, autonomic arousal, or cognitive impairment). Similarly the psychological problems of patients with chronic pain (e.g., depression, anxiety, sleeplessness, the excessive use of repression and denial, somatic overconcern, or passive-aggressive behaviors to name only the more prominent ones) are no different in kind or degree from those of many patients with any chronic disabling disease or people who become dependent upon drugs or medications obtained from either the street or the pharmacy. Thus attempts to use the MMPI to try to determine whether the patient's presenting problem is "real" are bound to mislead and ultimately fail (Roberts, 1983).

The purpose of the MMPI or any other psychological test in this context should be to evaluate current emotional status, prominent defense mechanisms, and likely modes of interactions with others. A particularly useful contribution of the MMPI is to detect depression in patients or spouses that might not otherwise be clinically evident. The use of the MMPI for this purpose, however, does not imply any cause or effect determination. Depression might be either a cause or an effect of the illness and disability.

Medications and Drugs. The misuse or abuse of medications, alcohol, or "recreational" drugs is frequently found to provide a significant contribution to excess disability. Our experience is that street and recreational drugs are less commonly a factor in excess disability among the elderly than among younger adults. Medications, particularly analgesics, tranquilizers, and muscle relaxants, have been amply documented as reinforcers for pain and disability (Fordyce, 1976; Roberts, 1981, 1983). A primary goal in the management of excess disability is to have patients discontinue all unnecessary medications.

Among the most prevalent of these are the prescription analgesics and anti-anxiety or muscle relaxant medications, such as Valium. These medications may serve to reinforce pain behaviors or they may increase dysphoria. In either case they contribute to the increasing disability. The inappropriate use of medications is both a cause and a consequence of disability.

Other abused substances are frequently found associated with disability in the elderly, caffeine and alcohol being the most obvious ones. The excessive use of caffeine is frequently noted in patients with chronic headaches, some of which are severely disabling. Chronic pains attributable to muscle spasms or muscle tension are also exacerbated by caffeine.

The elderly appear to be at special risk for the abuse of alcohol as well as unnecessary medications. A recent survey of 350 elderly inpatients (Dalessio, Orler, Trygstad, & Anderson, 1983) found mean corpuscular volumes above normal at values suggesting alcohol abuse in 23 percent of the patients surveyed. Fifty percent were on tranquilizers or sleeping pills. For this group of patients, activity levels and measures of depression correlated −.44 while activity levels and estimates of brain function correlated .28.

An evaluation of drug and alcohol use requires the participation of family members since those who are abusing substances frequently deny that they are to themselves and others. We frequently find patients who are surprised when told that they are overusing a particular medication or group of medications. In our experience, the elderly are much more willing to reduce voluntarily prescribed medications when asked to do so than are younger patients. An appropriate evaluation should include data about past use of alcohol, family histories for alcohol abuse or emotional disturbance, and the past use of other medications or drugs.

Depression. Depression constitutes another area of inquiry. Even in patients who deny being depressed there are frequently disturbances of sleep and appetite that may be symptomatic of depression. These may be the only significant clinical indicators of depression present other than the disability itself or psychological test findings. Many patients will complain of pain and sleep disturbance but at the same time deny being depressed. If they admit to being depressed, they may attribute it only to their medical problems.

Depression is often associated with physical disease in older patients and may arise in several ways. It may be a response to physical illness, it may be part of the syndrome of the physical disease, it may be caused by the treatment for the illness (usually medications), or it may appear as a variety of physical complaints (i.e., the illness itself) (Salzman, 1983).

It is important to determine whether or not the patient has sleep-onset disturbance, early awakening, or multiple awakenings. It is also important to inquire about whether a patient finds his/her sleep restful.

Depression rarely becomes a major focus of treatment for excess disability, nor does it directly influence the decision about whether a patient can or should be treated. Unless the patient has a major depressive disorder or is psychotic, it is reasonable to assume that the depression is secondary to the disability rather than primary since the depression should respond to treatment aimed at increasing function (Folkins & Sime, 1981).

Sometimes patients who are depressed and anxious enough to have sleep disturbances benefit from small doses of tricyclic antidepressant medications. Administered by the physician in doses just high enough to promote sleep but low enough to avoid daytime drowsiness or significant side effects, these nonaddictive medications often provide acceptable substitutes for sleeping medication, tranquilizers, muscle relaxants, or even analgesics. Careful medical supervision is necessary since older patients are more likely than younger adults to develop adverse side effects (DiGiacomo & Prien, 1983).

Functional Disability. This part of the assessment covers the disability itself, with the degree of dysfunction and the reinforcers for disability being the primary foci of attention. Inquiry is directed at how long the person has been having problems, how many health care professionals have been consulted, the number of hospitalizations, and the particular kinds of treatments that have been tried and have failed.

Many leads concerning reinforcement for pain and disability may be obtained by asking the patient what kinds of things help the pain and what things seem to make it worse. We often ask the patient what he or she would do if the medical problems or the pain were "magically" taken away. A question such as "If your pain were gone, what would you do that you're not able to do now?" frequently provides data about the degree and nature of the diability. For example, the patient might reply that he/she would do his/her homemaking chores, drive a car, travel more, or return to employment outside the home if the pain were gone. These answers provide clues to both the areas and amount of disability.

Decision to Treat

The decision to treat a disabled patient is based on the judgment that the patient will improve functionally if treated. If a major complaint is pain, one must decide whether the patient will maintain improvements even if the pain continues after treatment. While most patients are willing to "live with pain" as long as they can improve function, a few insist that the pain must be alleviated by the treatment program. We generally decide not to treat patients who insist on a "cure" for their pain since they are very likely to regress once treatment is completed.

Other variables that predict poor outcome include severe mental illness, pending litigation, relatively high levels of compensation that will be lost if the patient improves, or families unwilling to participate in and cooperate with the treatment program and its goals (Roberts & Reinhardt, 1980). Each of these variables must be weighed before embarking upon an arduous, extended, and relatively expensive treatment program.

Severe mental illness makes it more difficult to treat patients. Sometimes a severe emotional disturbance (e.g., agitation, paranoia, hostility) makes it more difficult for the staff to work with the patients.

Some clinical judgment must always be made concerning whether or not to proceed. We have, however, successfully worked with patients retarded by depression and with a few who have had brief, intermittent psychotic episodes while they were being treated. Inability to focus or concentrate, or severe memory loss, certainly makes it more difficult to work with the patient and increases the likelihood that the program will not be maintained following treatment.

Pending litigation, the outcome of which may be influenced by the results of treatment, is a serious limiting factor. We have worked successfully with patients whose litigation is still pending, but this tends to be effective only when the outcome of litigation is independent of the outcome of the treatment program. One way to assess this is to ask the patient to have his/her attorney send a letter stating that a good treatment outcome will not significantly change the outcome of litigation. If the attorney is unwilling to make a statement to that effect in writing, our decision has usually been to defer treatment until the litigation is settled.

The family's willingness to support a program and to cooperate in the treatment is a major determinant of both short-term and long-term outcome. Families who subvert the program, or who will not withhold reinforcement for disability or who will not provide reinforcement for activity make it extremely unlikely that the patient can be successfully treated (Hudgens, 1977).

Summary

The data gathered in the assessment provide the basis for making a decision about whether or not to treat a patient and also help to determine the appropriate components of a behavioral management program. How disabled is the patient? How much time, effort, and expense is the patient and his/her family willing to put into a treatment program? What components of a management program are necessary to increase function and which can be dispensed with? How long should a treatment program continue? How much follow-up is needed?

Will the patient need special treatment or attention for depression? In addition to the withdrawal of medications and focus on increasing activity and function, what special problems such as alcohol or weight need to be addressed? If the patient has a weight problem that is medically significant, will diet need to be a component of the program or can it be managed by exercise alone? What are the marital and family relationships contributing to the disability? Can intervention change these sufficiently to reasonably assure that the patient will not only increase his/her activity but also maintain these changes? If marital stress is involved, are interventions possible or appropriate to reduce these stresses?

The answers to these questions generally flow from the assessment and determine, not only whether or not the patient will be treated, but also the outlines of specific programs for individual patients.

Intervention

The most typical components of a program to decrease excess disability include obtaining medical sanction and support from a physician, discontinuing all unnecessary medications, increasing physical activity, and involving family members in reinforcing physical activity and discontinuing the reinforcement of disability. Other components and goals may become relevant based upon the assessment, but these four aspects are most generally applicable to elderly patients with this problem. It goes without saying that the informed consent of the patient is needed. If patients or their families are unwilling to participate in a treatment program, then I know of no other way to involve them.

Many times patients are extremely skeptical but agree to participate on a wait-and-see basis. Skepticism per se does not contraindicate treatment, and my impression is that these patients do as well as those who enter into the programs wholeheartedly, assuming family involvement and support are available.

General Considerations

The outpatient treatment team typically consists of a physician, a psychologist, a physical therapist and, sometimes, an occupational therapist. The techniques of behavior modification used in an outpatient program to treat excess disability include contingency contracting, positive reinforcement, shaping, and modeling.

All members of the treatment team are concerned with issues of positive reinforcement throughout the treatment program. A wide variety of reinforcements are used for behaviors that we wish to strengthen. A conscious attempt is made to avoid using reinforcers that are not fully under the control of the treatment team. Cigarettes and television watching, for example, are avoided because the patient clearly has access to these from sources other than those controlled by the staff. Most often, reinforcers are kept as simple as possible.

The most common reinforcer is praise and attention from members of the health care team and family. Since patients typically have a long history of using the health care system, this kind of attention is almost always reinforcing to the patients.

Graphs, particularly bar graphs, are used to record the patient's progress on a day-to-day basis. The increases in exercise levels and activity shown on the graphs as the program progresses are highly reinforcing for the majority of patients treated (Cairns & Pasino, 1977). In addition, the graphs can be used to positively reinforce the patient by team members who are not present when the exercises and activities are performed. The physician or the psychologist seeing the patient and spouse in his/her office will typically ask to see the graphs that the patient carries around with him/her throughout the program. Going through the graphs, the team member can point out the progress that has been made and praise the patient for what he/she is doing.

Occasionally additional reinforcers may be chosen, such as soft drinks following the completion of exercises in the therapeutic area if the patient might find this reinforcing. Activities that the patient likes to do are often used by the occupational therapist to reinforce the patient, especially during another activity that, in itself, may not be pleasurable but requires positive reinforcement. An example of this might be requiring the patient to sit, rather than lie down, for progressively longer periods each day; the therapist might provide a task that the patient enjoys for the period when he or she is required to be sitting.

Since the patient is disabled and thus inactive, fatigued, and often in pain, rest is a very common reinforcement used to reward the completion of activities. In this instance, rest is used as a reinforcement for exercise, allowing the patient to perform the activity we want to decrease (rest) as a reinforcement for the behaviors we wish to increase (activity).

Shaping is an integral part of the strategy of treatment. The desired behaviors are divided into successive gradual steps that are taught sequentially. Each of these steps is rewarded, and the patient moves on to the next step after he/she has completed the previous one. In this way, a new behavior is learned slowly as the patient comes closer and closer to approximating normal levels of activity.

Modeling is used both consciously and unconsciously by the treatment team. Therapists participate in exercises and activities with the patients. Sometimes treatment team members who are not usually present during therapy attend therapy sessions and participate in the exercise programs with the patients at those times. Family members often attend therapy and exercise with the patients. They are also encouraged to do so at home.

The withdrawal of positive reinforcements for behaviors that we wish to decrease is an important aspect of treatment. At the same time we begin reinforcing behaviors that are incompatible with those that are to be decreased. During the treatment program, all identifiable pain behaviors are ignored by all members of the treatment team. During exercise if the patient winces, complains, screams, or talks about pain, the therapist ignores these behaviors, acting as if he/she had not heard. Therapists will change the subject or, if absolutely necessary, walk away from the patient. The treatment team must be made aware of the fact that ignoring a well-established response will tend to increase that response initially rather than decrease it. Only later will it decrease.

It is important that therapists working with patients in programs like this make continuous efforts to discriminate between what the person says about his or her pain and disability and what the patient actually does about it. The focus of the program is entirely upon behavior change. The amount of pain or fatigue that is described by the patient may change very little during the course of a treatment program, but what the patient does in terms of increasing activity level and reducing disability will change significantly. Patients' verbal complaints are not themselves measures of success or failure in a treatment program like this. It is the objective measures of decreasing disability and increasing function that are the criteria for success.

Treatment Contract

The issue of informed consent should not be ignored and is relevant to patient and family trust and cooperation. Typically a treatment program included a contingency contract signed by the patient, by the spouse, and by a key member of the treatment staff. A treatment contract properly written and executed serves to set appropriate levels of expectations for the patient and his/her family; specifies the contributions of the patient, the family, and the treatment team; and provides contingencies for failure to perform. A well-written treatment contract should meet all requirements for fully informed consent. An example of a contingency contract for an inpatient program may be found in Roberts (1981).

Inpatient or Outpatient Treatment

The majority of treatment programs for elderly patients can be done on an outpatient basis. Occasionally, patients can be expected to benefit from an inpatient treatment program and not from a program conducted on an outpatient basis. Usually these are patients so heavily dependent upon medications that, for either psychological or medical reasons, they cannot be expected to withdraw from them on their own. Some patients are so totally disabled that they are unable to travel back and forth from home to an outpatient clinic and their programs must at least be started on an inpatient service.

Inpatient programs for the management of excess disability are extremely expensive compared to outpatient programs and should be avoided whenever possible. At one time it was thought that programs could be accomplished only on an inpatient basis, but our experience over the past four years contradicts that position. The details of inpatient programs have been fully described by Fordyce (1976), Roberts (1981), and others. Essentially, an inpatient program is a more complicated and more intensive extension of the outpatient program described here. In general, inpatient programs are appropriate when the more significant contingencies reinforcing disability cannot be manipulated and controlled on an outpatient basis.

Medical Sanction and Support

The importance of medical sanction and support for these programs cannot be overestimated. The majority of the patients requiring treatment programs like this see themselves as physically ill, disabled, and incapable of performing the general tasks of day-to-day living. They perceive considerable potential for exercise and activity to increase their pain or make them sicker. They have received substantial positive and negative reinforcement from physicians in the past and have come to depend heavily upon them, not only for basic medical care but for emotional support as well.

Perhaps the most important statement a physician can make to a patient about to embark on a behavioral management program is that the exercise will not make the patient's medical problem worse. Spoken or unspoken, there is an almost universal fear among the chronically ill and disabled that exercise and activity will injure them or increase their symptoms of pain and fatigue. Unless this assurance is provided loudly and clearly, without ambivalence, many patients will suffer unnecessary fear and anxiety and produce less than optimum effort.

Medication Management

Fortunately, the elderly seem to have a much easier time than younger people in withdrawing from prescribed medications upon which they have become dependent. In the majority of outpatient programs, patients need only to be told of the necessity of withdrawing from these medications after pointing out to them how they have become dependent upon the medications. Many elderly patients are genuinely surprised when told that they are dependent upon the drugs. They are even more surprised when it is explained to them that these medications when used for more than brief periods of time tend to make the pain worse rather than better. Generally, these patients do adhere to a progressive withdrawal schedule for these medications, if the schedule is slow enough to minimize withdrawal symptoms. Patients unable or unwilling to withdraw from their unnecessary medications are typically candidates for an inpatient treatment program.

Medication that should be withdrawn include all prescribed medications not deemed necessary for the treatment of a diagnosed medical problem. These include all prescription analgesics, tranquilizers and muscle relaxants. Antidepressant medications are generally continued when they are judged to be appropriate; in some instances they are added as part of the treatment regimen for excess disability.

Alternatives to prescription analgesics, tranquilizers, and muscle relaxants are primarily plain aspirin or plain acetaminophen and occasionally relatively low doses of tricyclic antidepressant medications. It is explained to the patient that these medications are the most effective analgesics that can be used on a long-term basis without increasing pain. As the other medications are gradually withdrawn, plain aspirin or plain acetaminophen is gradually added to the regimen on a time-contingent rather than a pain-contingent basis. That is, the medication is administered according to prearranged time intervals, not according to the patient's perception of pain. It is explained that if the patient waits until the pain becomes strong before taking aspirin or acetominophen, these nonprescription analgesics are not nearly as effective as they will be if the blood levels of the medications are raised to optimum levels and maintained. Thus, two aspirin or two regular-strength acetaminophen every four hours constitutes an appropriate maintenance dose for the management of pain. Possible problems and side effects from these medications should be carefully explained even though they may be obtained without a prescription.

Components of Treatment

Physical and occupational therapy programs to increase activity levels and exercise are primary components of a treatment program for excess disability. These exercise programs must be designed so as not to excessively stress the patient physically. As in all aspects of the program, medical sanction and support are necessary so that patients can be assured that nothing they are asked to do will make their problems worse. The program must be designed so as to promote adherence during treatment as well as promote adherence after the program has been formally completed.

Physical and occupational therapies must offer programs individualized for each patient. A typical program for outpatients lasts from six to eight weeks and includes from 10 to 12 exercises and activities designed to promote strength, endurance, stretching, posture, body mechanics, and ADL (Activities of Daily Living) activities. For more information about these exercise programs, the reader is referred to Fordyce (1976) and Roberts (1977, 1981).

Aerobic exercises are designed to promote cardiovascular fitness as well as to assist patients in the management of stress and tension and to relieve fatigue and tiredness. Therapists are specifically asked to focus on exercises and activities that the patient has particular difficulty performing. If patients are unable to stand, for example, exercises designed to increase standing are included in the program. If they are unable to bend, then stretching and bending exercises are given special attention. Patients who state that they are unable to sit for long periods of time because of pain are provided with "sitting exercises."

A typical prescription for an outpatient program might state that the patient be seen in therapy once a day, five days a week for two weeks; once a day, three days a week for two weeks; and once a day, one day a week for two weeks. Follow-up visits may then be scheduled as necessary. This kind of a six-to-eight-week program seems to provide enough time to evaluate a patient, prescribe a program, and reinforce significant progress in that program to the point where the patient should be able to continue it on his or her own and maintain the program when specific goals have been reached. Usually, the patient is expected to do the prescribed exercises and activities twice a day, every day, whether seen that day in therapy or not.

Establishing Baselines

The first three to five days of therapy are spent evaluating the patient. The patient is asked to do a large variety of exercises covering the areas noted above, doing each of these exercises and activities to tolerance. For example, the patient might be asked to do as many partial sit-ups as possible each day for three to five days in a row, or to do a particular stretching or strengthening exercise as many times as possible. He/she may be asked to ride an exercise bicycle for as many minutes as can be tolerated. The patient will walk with the therapist, and minutes of walking and heart rate are recorded. He/she may be asked to sit in a standard chair for as long as possible.

If homemaking tasks are a problem, the patient will be evaluated by an occupational therapist in the same way. Tolerance of the usual homemaking responsibilities will be evaluated by asking the persons to actually sweep, do dishes, launder, make beds, get up and down from low places, and perform similar tasks. Homemaking is promoted only when the patient states that these are problems for him/her and that he/she would like to be able to do these tasks. Activities outside the house are always encouraged. The patient is clearly informed that it is perfectly all right for a spouse to do these tasks or share them after treatment is concluded but *not* because the patient hurts or is too fatigued. Sharing of responsibilities within the family is encouraged, but not in ways that reinforce inactivity or disability.

After several days of performing each exercise to tolerance, a baseline is obtained that tells the therapist precisely how much of each exercise the patient is capable of doing on the average. This baseline provides a data base for prescribing exercise and activity to carefully chosen criteria levels instead of performing to tolerance.

The Exercise Program

Once the data base has been compiled in both occupational and physical therapy, a number of exercises and activities are chosen. The patient will than be expected to do these chosen exercises twice a day at a slowly increasing rate throughout the program. It is important that repetition levels start at no greater than one-third to one-half of the average baseline level from the baseline data obtained during the evaluation period. During that evaluation period, the patient will have done these activities to tolerance and he/she will now be required to do them to selected criteria levels that begin low and increase slowly to the point where the patient is functioning at "normal" levels for his/her sex and age for each exercise and activity.

Both the beginning level and the rate of increase are chosen to ensure that the patient never fails an assignment throughout the program. *It is more important that the patient do the exercise at a low level and succeed each time than it is that he/she do it at a higher level and sometimes fail.* Failure is never reinforcing.

It is also more important that the patient succeed in doing an exercise each day than that the exercise be increased to high levels at a rapid rate. The most common error made by therapists is to set criterion levels too high or to raise them too rapidly. Whenever there is a question about this, therapists are encouraged to be extremely conservative. Each time the patient reaches his/her quota of exercise, the therapist provides rest, praise, attention, and other selected reinforcers.

Failure to do an exercise must be managed so as to minimize both negative and positive reinforcement from the failure experience. Patients sometimes refuse to come to therapy or else come to therapy and refuse to do one or more of the prescribed exercises or activities. The contingencies for managing this should be specified in the treatment contract.

If the patient does not meet his/her performance criterion for any particular exercise on any given day, the therapist simply ignores this and goes on to the next exercise. If the patient fails a particular exercise for three days in a row, however, the criterion is dropped one level. If the patient is unable to meet the criterion after it has been lowered for an additional three days in a row, the patient is discharged from the program.

Only rarely, if at all, will renegotiating the contract improve the situation. There is no way to be coercive in treating patients. If the patient cannot meet exercise criteria that are selected to ensure that he/she will not fail, then we clearly are not able to help that particular patient. In this context it is important that the therapist ignore failures when they do occur and not coax or coerce the patient, other than to remind him/her about the contingencies written into the contract.

Graphs and Charts

All exercises and activities required of the patient are graphed. These include regular exercises and activities or special prescribed activities, such as increasing standing or sitting time. The patient is asked to carry all the graphs in a folder whenever in the clinic. These graphs are self-reinforcing; when the patient plots the required data, he/she sees immediately that progress has been made. These graphs also provide a basis for reinforcement from other team members. When physicians or others who are not present when the exercises are being done talk with the patient, the team member can look at the graphs and provide verbal reinforcement for what has been occurring.

Working with Family

In the outpatient program, a member of the team meets with the patient and spouse at least once or twice a week. The details of the kinds of work that are done with the family members have been described by Hudgens (1977).

In general, the family members of chronically disabled patients either allow the disability to continue through various forms of reinforcement, or fail to reward healthier kinds of behavior. The team member working with the family helps the family change this pattern of reinforcement. Family members are provided help in identifying pain behaviors, and these observations are discussed. Spouses are also asked to observe their own behaviors in the presence of the patient and to become alert to ways in which they have been responding when the patient complains of pain or acts in other ways communicating illness or disability.

The professional working with the patient and spouse teaches the spouse and others to behave appropriately by modeling and role-playing ways in which spouses can ignore sick behavior and reward healthy behavior. Family members are taught that negative attention, fussing, nagging, and similar behaviors are all forms of attention that may reinforce pain behavior and disability. It is also critical that spouses learn that ignoring sick behavior is not enough. Healthy, active behaviors must be attended to and reinforced systemically.

Generalization of the Treatment Program

An outpatient treatment program has an advantage over inpatient treatment programs for excess disability. Patients in outpatient programs spend more time at home than they spend in the clinic. Therefore, there is a built-in opportunity for generalization. Exercises and activities are done where they will continue to be done after treatment. Requiring exercises to be done twice a day ensures that the exercises will be done at least once at home even on days patients visit the clinic.

Working with the families is essential to ensure the generalization of newly learned healthy behaviors. If the patient returns home to the same setting with the same reinforcements for sick behavior, the learning that is achieved during the clinic visits will invariably deteriorate. The family is always taught to allow the patient to assume full responsibility for the management of his/her own body, medical problems, and medications.

Often the patient is returning to a physician for primary care who is not associated with the clinic where the treatment program is located.

It is necessary to explain to the referring or primary physician what has occurred and the need for a different kind of patient–physician relationship. This must be done in ways that will enhance understanding, cooperation, and support. Health care professionals often have been unwittingly reinforcing the patient's disability with high levels of caring, concern, and sympathy. Many physicians are unfamiliar with the behavioral model and they conceptualize the patient's problems entirely within the disease model. It is difficult for a physician who has been treating a chronically disabled patient for a long period of time to refrain from represcribing medications when a patient asks for them.

Sometimes a verbal or written contingency contract can be negotiated between the patient and the primary physician that defines more appropriately their future relationship. For some patients it is helpful if the primary physician agrees to regular visits by the patient at prescribed intervals, contingent upon the patient not using pain or sickness as an excuse for these visits, and this can be agreed upon in writing through the use of a brief contingency contract signed by both the patient and the physician.

Case Illustrations

A Case of Connective Tissue Disease

Mrs. S. is a 63-year-old homemaker from northern California. She was in generally good health until the summer of 1970. At that time, her mother died. During the activities attending her mother's funeral, Mrs. S. noted that she became easily fatigued, weak, and exhausted. There was not, however, any loss of muscle strength.

Her symptoms progressed throughout the fall of that year and in December she developed a fever; arthralgias of her hands, wrists, elbows, hips, and knees; and signs of congestive heart failure. In January 1971, she was hospitalized and was diagnosed as having a connective tissue disorder. She was treated with high doses of prednisone, and by April she had considerable subjective improvement with a return of some strength and stamina.

In the following years, Mrs. S. continued to have active disease with pain, soreness, weakness, fatigue, and dyspnea. She was able to do only light household chores. She had intermittent fevers.

She was first seen in the Behavioral Medicine Clinic in June 1980. At that time, she was a hospital patient with medical diagnoses of polymyositis-pulmonary fibrosis, exogenous Cushing's syndrome, and a depressive reaction. She was seen together with her husband for excess disability associated with these medical problems. They reported that during the past several years, Mrs. S. had continued to have pain and weakness and that she had become progressively disabled. When asked why she was seeing me, she said that she had muscle pain from her feet to her head and that she was weak. She and her husband agreed that she spent less than two or three hours a day on her feet. The rest of her time was spent lying around, either in bed or on the couch.

Her husband turned out to be an extraordinarily loving, supportive, and reinforcing person who was very concerned for his wife. At home, he cooked, performed the housework, and did just about everything for his wife that he possibly could. At the same time, he sincerely wished that she could be more active, not realizing that his caring behaviors were discouraging her from being more active.

After careful medical evaluation, it was decided that the primary focus of treatment would be her invalidism. There was no reason to believe that the disability directly resulted from medical limitations imposed by her illness. She did have a sleep disturbance, and it was recommended that she begin a course of amitriptyline, 25 mg at bedtime, and this was gradually increased as she was able to tolerate it. It was also recommended that Dalmane, a sedative depressant drug, be discontinued.

Her physician strongly supported a physical therapy program, including mobilization and muscle-strengthening exercises, and a behavioral physical therapy program was proposed. This program had to take into account medical limitations, especially osteoporosis and possible compression fractures. Questions were raised about whether or not Mr. S. had the ability to refrain from continuing to reinforce his wife's disability or to wholeheartedly encourage and reinforce activity.

Physical therapy orders requested a behavioral evaluation and the initiation of a gradual program to increase both strength and endurance. Graphs and charts were to be taken home with the patient when she was discharged from the hospital and she was to be followed by a physical therapist near her home.

While hospitalized, the patient was seen twice a day in physical therapy for five days. Strengthening and stretching exercises were prescribed. She was also evaluated for walking and stationary bicycle. At the beginning of the program, she was able to do only between three and five of each of the prescribed stretching and strengthening exercises. She was able to walk approximately 200 feet. On a stationary bicycle she could ride for only 2 minutes. Goals for most of the exercises were set at 20 repetitions. Her walking goal was set at 20 minutes and her bicycle-riding goal was set at 10 minutes. She was then discharged from the hospital to be followed by the physical therapist near her home. Just prior to Mrs. S.'s discharge the therapist working with her phoned her new physical therapist and explained the program to him. The patient and her husband agreed to return for periodic visits for evaluation and follow-up.

One month later, she and her husband returned for a follow-up visit and brought with them a letter from her local physical therapist together with her graphs. She was walking, smiling, and without any apparent depression. She was doing all of the assigned exercises in physical therapy and at home. In addition, she had begun working with weights and was doing a timed progressive, resistive exercise program. She was making her bed, preparing most of the meals, and cleaning up afterwards. She was walking daily and riding the stationary bicycle. She was doing all of her laundry. Her mood was good. She was sleeping well and her appetite had improved. She had no major complaints of pain.

Mrs. S. has been followed periodically since that time. There has been no evidence of depression since she was first seen. She has been hospitalized for the removal of cataracts and for treatment of a nephrotic syndrome, but after each hospitalization she has returned to optimum activity at home. Each time she has been reevaluated in physical therapy it has been her desire to continue exercises which will increase her strength and endurance.

A Case of Chronic Back Pain

Mrs. T. is a 68-year-old woman with a seven-year history of chronic back pain. The problem began when she twisted her back getting out of her automobile. She recalls that the same day this happened she had been lifting heavy flagstones in a wheelbarrow. Despite numerous medical evaluations and tests, all findings have been negative.

The back pain has been continuous since she first twisted her back. She describes the pain as "twisting and tearing." On some occasions she feels as though she is "sitting on a piece of lead pipe which is going up my spine." She says she has no pain in bed, but that the pain returns almost immediately when she arises from bed and tries to perform daily activities.

It is obvious that the relationship between perceived pain and rest or activity is highly reinforcing of bedrest. In fact, the pain is severely disabling to her. She reported that if she had no pain she would garden, lift, vacuum, drive a car—all things she was not doing when evaluated. She spends almost the entire day lying down.

At the time of evaluation she was complaining of a sleep disturbance (early awakening) and poor appetite. She denied being depressed and denied any significant stress in her life other than her medical problem. The MMPI suggested moderate to severe levels of anxiety and depression.

She appeared not to be dependent on medications. She was using Darvon once a day only two or three times a week. She found medications generally distasteful.

Mrs. T. and her husband had been married for 48 years and both are retired. He is almost 80 years old. His health is generally good except for a cardiac arrythmia. Mr. T. had been routinely responsive to her pain complaints throughout the seven-year history. He did all the homemaking chores, rubbing her back, fetching things for her, and generally being considerate and helpful. Her back pain was the major focus of both their lives at the time she was seen, and they spoke to each other of little else.

The patient was started on low doses of an anxiolytic antidepressant medication with instruction to slowly increase the dose until she was sleeping well but not to take so much that she was drowsy during the day. Plain aspirin on a time-contingent basis (two every four hours) was substituted for the Darvon she had been taking on a pain-contingent basis.

An outpatient physical and occupational therapy program was prescribed by her physician. This program included a wide variety of exercises to increase strength and endurance. Several stretching exercises were prescribed. Aerobic walking and stationary bicycle exercises were started. She was instructed in posture and body mechanics. The occupational therapist worked with her in increasing functional ability in ADLs including vacuuming, dusting, bed making, gardening, and sitting for increasing periods of time.

She was seen once a day, five day a week for two weeks; once a day, three days a week for two weeks; and once a day, one day a week for two weeks. She was seen by the psychologist, together with her husband, once a week during this six-week period. In therapy the therapists studiously avoided responding to her pain complaints and behaviors. In office visits her husband was instructed in ways of doing this. He was also taught to be more attentive to his wife when she was being active. The patient was expected to do all exercises twice a day every day, and she kept accurate bar graphs for each exercise and activity.

The course of both physical and occupational therapy was stormy with the patient appearing in slippers and refusing to wear shoes. On one occasion she complained of having "sprained my ankle" because of wearing weights on her legs while doing low-grade exercises that had been prescribed for her. She almost always appeared angry. In office visits she vacillated between pain complaints (which were ignored) and talking about how much better she felt and how much more she was accomplishing. She always followed the exercise program despite her complaints.

At the end of six weeks she was well on her way to reaching all of her exercise and activity goals. She was walking briskly 20 minutes twice a day with an intended goal of 30 minutes once a day. She was able to sit up for 30 minutes or longer. She was able to get down and up from the floor. She could dust for 25 minutes reaching and stretching, and she was carrying five pounds.

When seen in follow-up several months later she had discontinued all medications, she was still exercising once each day, and she was leading a normal life except that she was still refusing to drive a car. On a follow-up questionnaire she remarked that her pain was no better or worse than it had been when she started treatment.

A Case of Physical Deconditioning

Mr. U. is a 73-year-old gentleman with complaints of "total body pain." He has been diagnosed as having arthritis and for the past 11 years has been taking aspirin on a regular basis. For the past four years he had complained of increasing pain and had become increasingly inactive.

He gets up in the morning, dresses, eats, and then watches television or reads most of the day. He manages to keep his one-bedroom condominium apartment clean. Once or twice a week he drives to the grocery store and buys what he needs.

Asked about the stress in his life, he talked at length about the pain and soreness in almost all of the muscles and joints in his body. He said that his greatest limitation has been his inability to play golf for the past two and one-half years. For that reason he hardly ever sees his golfing partners. He spoke at length of his loneliness. Finally, he spoke with tears in his eyes about his 11-year-old dog, who was becoming increasingly sick. His veterinarian had recently suggested that his dog be put to sleep.

A three-visit physical therapy program was prescribed for Mr. U. in order to evaluate him and prescribe a behavioral aerobic physical conditioning program. Walking ability was assessed and a series of stretching and strengthening exercises were prescribed. Graphs were provided for a walking program and for each of the stretching and strengthening exercises. All exercises, including walking, were to be done twice a day.

He was seen in follow-up visit in physical therapy and behavioral medicine as well as by his rheumatologist one month later. At that time he was walking briskly 18 minutes twice a day with an additional three minutes of slow walking before and after to warm up and cool down. He was religiously following the stretching and strengthening program. His resting heart rate had decreased 12 percent.

He was particularly elated about his dog. He had started to take his dog walking with him and was surprised to find his dog "revived" and "almost acting like a puppy again." He asked if and when he might return to playing golf again.

Mr. U. was told to begin walking only once a day but for longer periods of time. The other exercises were to continue twice a day until his goals were reached. New graphs were provided.

One month later Mr. U. returned again to report that he and his dog were walking an hour a day. Strength and flexibility were markedly improved. Resting heart rate had decreased another 4 percent. He found his aches and pains to be very tolerable and well controlled by aspirin. Walking, stretching, and strengthening exercises were to be continued once a day five days a week for life. He was instructed to return to playing golf.

Summary and Conclusions

There are prevalent social attitudes which militate against even moderate physical activity in the elderly. When an elderly person has a diagnosed medical problem, these negative attitudes are markedly strengthened. Yet there are good reasons to believe that many people, not living independent lives either at home or in institutions, could be living independently had they maintained reasonable levels of physical condition by maintaining higher levels of physical activity.

The elderly are inhibited from exercise by fears that it will cause injury, exhaustion, or overt illness. They are encouraged to forgo exercise, to play it safe, and this is to their detriment.

It is nevertheless possible for the elderly to arrest or reverse physical deterioration by increasing levels of activity. If the elderly are to remain adapted to independent living, then adequate muscle strength must be maintained. Beyond this simple relationship, the interrelations among age, inactivity, physical condition, work capacity, and attitudes are extremely complex.

We have described behavioral methods for increasing and maintaining strength, endurance, flexibility, and cardiovascular fitness in the elderly. These methods are equally valid for persons without disease as well as for those who are excessively disabled by a medically diagnosed illness. The reduction of habitual activity with age can only hasten or exacerbate deterioration in physical conditioning which, in turn, reduces the capacity for independent living.

Intervention requires, first of all, a shift in the attitudes of health care providers and those providing services to the elderly. Exercise and activity must be seen as a necessary aspect of day-to-day living for the elderly as well as for younger persons. It must be recognized that a considerable part of the physical and emotional deterioration of the inactive elderly person is reversible.

Bozarth (1980) has commented that "age is not a disability nor a physical, mental or social handicap" (p. 51). Many people feel and behave as if it is. The application of the behavioral methods described in this chapter have been demonstrated to alter some of these behaviors. As Fordyce (1971) has pointed out, an expedient way to help disabled people is first to help them change their behaviors. It is possible that attitude and feeling changes will then follow these behavior changes.

References

Bassey, E. J. (1978). Age, inactivity, and some physical responses to exercise. *Gerontology, 24,* 66–77.

Berger, B. G. & Owen, D. R. (1983). Mood alteration with swimming— swimmers really do "feel better." *Psychosomatic Medicine, 45,* 425–433.

Block, A. R. (1982). Multidisciplinary treatment of chronic low back pain: A review. *Rehabilitation Psychology, 27,* 51–63.

Bozarth, J. (1980). Pro/Con: Rehabilitation of the aging. *Journal of Rehabilitation, 46,* 50–51.

Butler, R., & Newacheck, P. W. (1982). Health and social factors relevant to long term care policy. In J. Meltzer (Ed.), *Policy options: Long term care.* Chicago: University of Chicago Press.

Cairns, D., & Pasino, J. (1977). Comparison of verbal reinforcement and feedback in operant treatment of disability due to chronic low back pain. *Behavior Therapy, 8,* 621–630.

Cairns, D., Thomas, L., Mooney, V., & Pace, J. B. (1976). A comprehensive treatment approach to chronic low back pain. *Pain, 2,* 301–308.

Costa, P. T., & McCrae, R. R. (1980). Somatic complaints as a function of age and neuroticism: A longitudinal analysis. *Journal of Behavioral Medicine, 3,* 245–258.

Cross, D. L. (1980). The influence of physical fitness training as a rehabilitation tool. *International Journal of Rehabilitation Research, 3,* 163–175.

Dalessio, D. J., Orler, J., Trygstad, C. W., & Anderson, R. W. (May 1983). *Partway up the hill: A progress report on a study of Scripps Clinic patients over 65.* Paper presented at Grand Rounds, Scripps Clinic and Research Foundation, La Jolla, CA.

DiGiacomo, J., & Prien, R. (1983). Pharmacologic treatment of depression in the elderly. In T. Crook & G. D. Cohen (Eds.), *Physicians' guide to the diagnosis and treatment of depression in the elderly.* New Canaan, CT: Mark Powley Associates.

Folkins, C. H., & Sime, W. E. (1981). Physical fitness training and mental health. *American Psychologist, 36,* 373–389.

Follick, M. J., Zitter, R. E. & Kulich, R. J. (1981). Outpatient management of chronic pain. In T. J. Coates (Ed.), *Behavioral medicine: A practical handbook.* Champaign, IL: Research Press.

Fordyce, W. E. (1971). Behavioral methods in rehabilitation. In W. S. Neff (Ed.), *Rehabilitation psychology* (pp. 74–108). Washington, DC: American Psychological Association.

Fordyce, W. E. (1976). *Behavioral methods for chronic pain and illness.* St. Louis: C. V. Mosby.

Fordyce, W. E. (1983). *Chronic pain and social contingencies.* Unpublished manuscript, University of Washington, School of Medicine, Seattle.

Fordyce, W. E., Fowler, R. S., & DeLateur, B. (1968). An application of behavior modification technique to a problem of chronic pain. *Behavior Research and Therapy, 6,* 105–107.

Fordyce, W. E., Fowler, R. S., Lehmann, J. F., & DeLateur, B. J. (1968). Some implications of learning in problems of chronic pain. *Journal of Chronic Disease, 21,* 179–190.

Holloszy, J. O. (1983). Exercise, health and aging: A need for more information. *Medicine and Science in Sports and Exercise, 15,* 1–5.

Hudgens, A. J. (1977). The social worker's role in a behavioral management approach to chronic pain. *Social Work in Health Care, 3,* 149–157.

Laerum, M., & Laerum, O. D. (1982). Can physical activity counteract aging? *Scandinavian Journal of Social Medicine, 29,* 147–152.

Latimer, P. R. (1982). External contingency management for chronic pain: Critical review of the evidence, *American Journal of Psychiatry, 139,* 1308–1312.

Morris, A. F., Vaccaro, P., & Harris, R. (1983). The quality changes of older adults during various physical activity programs. *Medicine and Science in Sports and Exercise, 15,* 117. (Abstract)

Naughton, J. (1982). Physical activity and aging. *Primary Care, 9,* 231–238.

Perry, B. C. (1982). Exercise patterns of an elderly population. *Journal of Family Practice, 15,* 545–546.

Pilling, L. F., Bronnick, T. L., & Swensen, W. M. (1967). Psychologic characteristics of patients having pain as a presenting symptom. *Canadian Medical Association Journal, 97,* 387–394.

Roberts, A. H. (1977). *The pain clinic and pain treatment program procedure manual* (2nd ed.). Minneapolis: Department of Physical Medicine and Rehabilitation, University of Minnesota.

Roberts, A. H. (1981). The behavioral treatment of pain, In J. M. Ferguson & C. B. Taylor (Eds.), *The comprehensive handbook of behavioral medicine: Vol. 2. Syndromes and special areas* (pp. 171–189). Jamaica, NY: Spectrum Publications.

Roberts, A. H. (1983). Contingency management methods in the treatment of chronic pain. In J. J. Bonica, U. Lindholm, & A. Iggo (Eds.), *Advances in pain research and therapy.* (Vol. 5, pp. 789–794). New York: Raven Press.

Roberts, A. H., & Reinhardt, L. (1980). The behavioral management of chronic pain: Long term follow-up with comparison groups. *Pain, 8,* 151–162.

Salzman, C. (1983). Depression and physical disease. In T. Crook & G. D. Cohen (Eds.), *Physicians' guide to the diagnosis and treatment of depression in the elderly* (pp. 9–17). New Canaan, CT: Mark Powley Associates.

Seres, J. L. & Newman, R. I. (1976). Results of treatment of chronic low back pain at the Portland Pain Center. *Journal of Neurosurgery, 45,* 32–36.

Shephard, R. J., & Sidney, K. H., (1978). Exercise and aging. *Exercise and Sports Reviews, 6,* 1–57.

Sidney, K. H., & Shephard, R. J. (1976). Attitudes towards health and physical activity in the elderly. Effects of a physical training program. *Medicine and Science in Sports, 8,* 246–252.

Sidney, K. H., & Shephard, R. J. (1977). Perception of exertion in the elderly. Effects of aging, mode of exercise and physical training. *Perceptual and Motor Skills, 44,* 999–1010.

Sternbach, R. A. (1974). *Pain patients: Traits and treatment.* New York: Academic Press.

Taylor, H. L. & Rowell, L. B. (1980). Exercise and metabolism. In W. R. Johnson & E. R. Buskirk (Eds.), *Structural and physiological aspects of exercise and sports* (pp. 84–111). Princeton, NJ: Princeton Book Co.

Turk, D. C., Meichenbaum, D., & Genest, M. (1983). *Pain and behavioral medicine: A cognitive-behavioral perspective.* New York: Guilford.

Turner, J. A., & Chapman, C. R. (1982). Operant conditioning, hypnosis and cognitive behavioral therapy. *Pain, 12,* 22–46.

U. S. Department of Health and Human Services. (1979). *Facts about older Americans 1979* (DHHS Publication No. 80-20006) Washington, DC: U. S. Government Printing Office.

U. S. Department of Health and Human Services. (1981). *Statistical notes from the National Clearinghouse on Aging* (DHHS Publication No. 81-20047) Washington, DC: U. S. Government Printing Office.

4

Severe Behavioral Problems

Richard A. Hussian

It has frequently been noted that the elderly show more psychopathology than other age-groups. Depression, hypochondriasis, paranoia, and management problems associated with organic mental disorders are among the most frequently encountered problems. A behavioral approach (see Baltes & Barton, 1977) encourages the targeting of *specific* responses for change, rather than global classifications. Employing specific terminology provides the clinician with observable, quantifiable responses, thus making the choice of intervention and the process of treatment evaluation easier.

A subset of these problems is particularly difficult to manage (or ignore) in institutionalized settings. They tend to cause discomfort for either the client exhibiting them, for the staff observing them, or both. It should be appreciated, however, that most of these problems involve discomfort for the observer, not the client.

A few of these severe management problems, which often lead to restrictive consequences include agitation, combativeness, multiple complaints, multiple demands, yelling, abusive and threatening verbalizations, self-stimulation, noncompliance, wandering, inappropriate voiding, and inappropriate sexual behavior.

The presentation which follows includes a description of the most severe behavior problems encountered in institutions for the elderly, the variables which may contribute to these problems, ways to assess and treat the problems, and a case illustration showing these techniques being utilized.

There are several reasons that behavioral problems occur at relatively high rates in the geriatric population. First, there is a high incidence of organic disturbances among this group and many of these disturbances cause psychological and behavioral dysfunction in addition to the physical symptoms. Some of these disturbances include congestive heart failure, diabetes mellitus, electrolyte imbalances, impactions, infections, and pulmonary dysfunctions. These disturbances may actually manifest themselves in disruptive behavior before any physical manifestations are present.

Second, many elderly individuals have few personal contacts. Because of the deaths or movement of family and friends, the elderly may live for long periods of time without the feedback and social reinforcement necessary for continued adaptive responding.

Third, the elderly often are in situations where there is very little positive response for the exhibition of adaptive behavior even when potential sources of this reinforcement are plentiful. Because of the low expectations of others and the acceptability of dependent behavior, adaptive responses may actually be ignored or prevented in many institutions.

Fourth, the elderly have a higher incidence of sensory and central processing deficits and slowing. Multiple changes across sensory modalities can lead to apparent dysfunctional behavior. Central deficits may be responsible for inappropriate behavior marked by poor judgment and incomplete impulse control.

A combination of these factors, or one factor if sufficiently intense, may lead to inappropriate responding, which may be maintained by the environmental contingencies.

Behavioral Analysis of Management Problems

According to a biobehavioral or operant view of maladaptive responding, behavioral problems can be seen as being maintained by the absence of positive consequences following approprate behavior, the absence of discriminative stimuli to elicit appropriate behavior, the presence of aversive consequences following appropriate behavior, the presence of positive consequences following inappropriate, dependent behavior (see Baltes, Honn, Barton, Orzech, & Lago, 1983), or the presence of inhibitory discriminative stimuli. These contingencies and environmental events shape geriatric response rates and thereby lead to excessive, deficient, or "out-of-context" behaviors (Hussian, 1984).

The focus of this chapter is those behaviors that tend to disrupt ongoing activity within an institutional setting. Therefore we shall be concentrating on those responses that are best viewed as behavioral excesses or those that, though they do not occur at higher than acceptable rates, occur independently of normal discriminative stimuli (e.g., inappropriate voiding or sexual behavior, wandering). Both types of behavior often lead to excessive attention from observers and cause major disruptions within the institution.

This behavioral or functional analysis can be applied to any target behavior exhibited by an elderly client if it is expanded somewhat over traditional behavioral analysis to include organic variables. These organic causes are important to consider, and it would be potentially harmful if the mental health professional ignored or minimized the impact of electrolyte imbalances; variable circulation in the brain; the presence of physical illness, viral or bacterial infection, fractures, impactions, impaired sensation, hormonal imbalances, metabolic disturbances, tumors, metastasis; and drug toxicity and idiosyncratic drug responses.

Though these causative factors are seldom considered by behavioral psychologists, the frequency with which they are implicated demands our attention. We must emphasize these variables in order to lead to a more complete evaluation, more useful treatment planning and evaluation, more accurate expectations with regard to prognosis, better allocation of staff time, and prevention of the worsening of cognitive and physical functioning caused by an untreated physical disturbance.

It should be clear that in order to conduct a comprehensive assessment the psychologist should have knowledge of laboratory values, physical symptoms of diseases, drug effects and interactions, and neurologic signs. If this knowledge is wanting, it is extremely important to establish a good relationship with a physician, a psychiatrist, and/or a neurologist.

The mental health professional who works with geriatric clients will find that he/she will need to consider these organic variables more than when dealing with any other client population. However, it is equally important to evaluate functional components of the behavioral disturbance even when a physical etiology is present. Most severe management problems represent the interaction between these organic influences and maladaptive learning. For example, even when a client has been correctly diagnosed as having Alzheimer's disease, the depression or anxiety which may result from the unfortunate deficits present is due to poor coping behavior and can be treated with behavioral methods. Though the underlying dementia will continue to be present and cause management difficulties, the depression or anxiety can be managed. The client, therefore, may be able to live a more comfortable life.

Rationale for Addressing Management Problems

The reasons for attempting to deal with severe management problems as exhibited by the elderly are presented below.

1. Many of the management crises are directly and indirectly damaging to the lives, health, and safety of the clients exhibiting the behavior as well as for other clients and staff in the vicinity. Also, the exhibition of some of these behaviors (e.g., wandering) can lead to punitive measures by other clients (e.g., physical aggression).

2. Many of these behaviors interrupt the daily activities and therapies occuring on the ward and deprive the client and other clients from benefiting from the therapeutic milieu.

3. The client not only cannot benefit from therapeutic programs during the exhibition of these types of responses, but he/she also may not be able to benefit from therapy even after the behavioral problem has been temporarily resolved. This is because of the interventions which often follow such behavior. For example, medication given on a p.r.n. basis often slows general responsivity, time-out and seclusion further deprive the client of access to new learning experiences, and contingent restraint of movement or restrictions further reduces access to appropriate stimulation and training programs.

4. Much staff time is involved in correcting the effects of such behavior and therefore cannot be utilized in more constructive and therapeutic pursuits. Social interaction between clients and staff is severely limited by routine tasks on the ward as it is, but these valuable interactions become even more difficult when crisis intervention or self-preservation is continually required.

5. The continual presence of management difficulties may limit visitation and constructive interactions with friends and family from outside the institution. The frequency and duration of such interactions may be severely curtailed if these visitors find such behavior threatening, disruptive, or embarrassing.

6. The results of such behavior include damage to property such as linen and other supplies, which raises health care costs and limits the availability of these articles to others.

7. Some of these behaviors lead to avoidance of the client by staff at *all* times, not just when the undesirable behavior is occurring. This deprives the client of important interactions, reinforcement for neutral or appropriate behavior, feedback, and medical monitoring.

8. The exhibition of such behavior may prevent discharge to less restrictive settings despite the fact that the client could otherwise function quite well there. If these behaviors are exhibited in the community, placement in a more restrictive setting might be indicated.

9. If these problems become frequent or intense enough, staff morale can suffer and staff turnover rates can increase. Noise level, distraction, and malodorous conditions can lead to poor morale.

Having established the ecological validity for intervention, considerations in the assessment and treatment follow.

Assessment

Though a variety of assessment devices have been generated to supplant traditional methods, they all show significant false positive rates (Hussian, 1981). Standardized intelligence tests and neuropsychology batteries tend to use norms which do not include a sufficient number of healthy elderly individuals. As a result, elderly intelligence scores tend to be higher than the level of adaptive skills would indicate, while results on most standard neuropsychological batteries indicate more dysfunction than is supported by other means of assessment.

Given these deficiencies of standardized testing, the mental health professional will probably find other means of assessment more reliable and revealing. For management problems a frequency count is the most effective sampling technique. Other measures such as intensity and duration may also be included. By measuring the rates of occurrence of the targeted behavior, the professional has a clear indication of the severity of the problem that is based upon the individual's rate, not group norms. This provides a convenient method to evaluate the effectiveness of the intervention procedure(s).

In addition to simple frequency counts, the assessor should consider the relationship between environmental variables and the differential rates of response. This analysis should provide the assessor with a possible cause of the behavior of interest. For example, if, through time-sampling and naturalistic observation, it is revealed that the rate of physical aggression as exhibited by a given client increases immediately after a family visit, it may be assumed that something occurs during these visits to cause the aggression, thus suggesting an intervention.

We now turn to a description of the most frequently encountered management problems found in geriatric facilities. Methods of assessment and possible causal factors will be presented for each behavior. In the following section, treatment strategies to reduce these management problems will be offered.

Agitation and Combativeness. Extreme agitation and aggressive physical contacts are among the most dangerous behavior management problems encountered in inpatient settings. Not only may this behavior result in harm to others or property damage, but the client may also be harmed while being subdued or when another client attempts to avoid harm. This behavior also often results in the application of restraint, medication delivery, or other restrictive measures. In many nursing, rest, and personal care homes, physically debilitated elderly clients reside alongside recently discharged psychiatric clients. Some of these psychiatric clients experience fluctuations in behavior and may harm the frail elderly clients.

Agitation and physical aggression may result from three sources. It is important to determine which of these is leading to the problem.

First, agitation and physical aggression are frequently observed in the early stages of Alzheimer's disease and related disorders. It appears that this behavior is in response to misperceptions of the actions of others, as when the client does not recognize a family member living in his/her house, or when the client misplaces keys, glasses, or money and blames the spouse or child for hiding the item. Often, these confrontations are the basis for the first contact between the client's family and a health professional.

Second, agitation, startle, and striking out can occur in the later stages of dementia. This agitation, if one may be allowed an inference, seems to be secondary to misperceptions, distortion, or hallucinatory processes. "Strangers in my house," "People in the attic," and the like are statements frequently encountered in conjunction with the combativeness.

Third, agitation and combativeness may arise in institutions where elderly with lengthy hospitalization reside. This combativeness appears to be a method to either gain attention or gain a favored item or position on the ward. This type of behavior, of course, is not confined to the elderly institutionalized population and may be seen in younger chronic populations as well.

Fourth, agitation may be secondary to an acute organic process. Physical aggression can coincide with elevated blood glucose level, active congestive heart failure, elevated BUN, and mild myocardial infarction. The agitation subsides when the underlying physical cause is successfully treated.

In order to differentiate among these causes one needs to take into consideration other responses and the context in which the agitation/combativeness occurs. If there are no signs of global organic dysfunction such as aphasia, ataxia, dyspraxia, self-stimulation, extreme memory loss, confusion, disorientation, or incontinence, the cause is probably attention seeking or reinforcement seeking. If the cognitive impairment is mild, with some anomia, it may be early senile dementia and the cause would be misperceptions or frustration secondary to memory impairment. If the cognitive involvement is drastic with a chronic onset, the clinician should consider later stages of senile dementia and look for hallucinatory processes as a cause. If the cognitive impairment is significant and the onset is acute, the clinician should suspect delirium.

Multiple Complaints and Demands. Another form of excessive responding that can become a severe management problem is multiple somatic complaints or multiple requests for pain medication *in the absence of organic etiology*. This behavior is a legitimate target for intervention since these requests can lead to overuse of medication, staff annoyance, and/or staff avoidance. It is also possible that a history of unfounded complaints may lead health care professionals to ignore a legitimate symptom.

It is extremely important to rule out an organic cause prior to a behavioral intervention such as extinction. It should be noted that the classic symptomatology of a disease process or syndrome may be absent or different among the elderly than with other age-groups. Therefore, one should consider that the requests or complaints stem from an organic dysfunction first until it becomes clear that one can pinpoint hypochondriasis. If the frequency is extremely high, there is no evidence of any physical source, the client also complains frequently about nonsomatic issues (e.g., the food, the temperature, roommates), and there is a history of similar behavior (e.g., multiple physicians, multiple prescriptions), the clinician should suspect hypochondriasis and intervene behaviorally.

Shouting. Continual high-intensity vocalizations are another form of excessive behavior which can interfere with ongoing institutional activities. Incessant yelling can lead to such undesirable consequences as retaliation by other clients, relocation to a less stimulating area, increased medication, and employee dissatisfaction. The analysis of shouting must take into account several points.

First, the content of the vocalizations should be considered. If the content is threatening or abusive, the clinician should consider either some focal cerebral damage or an attempt to receive attention.

Second, if the behavior is primarily non-verbal and repetitive, the cause is probably global cerebral deterioration. This form of self-stimulation is sometimes observed in advanced Alzheimer's disease (Hussian & Hill, 1980).

Third, if the target behavior appears to be accompanied by other signs of discomfort (e.g., grimacing, rubbing), one should suspect a physical cause. Likely physical causes include arthritis, fractures, and impactions. In nonverbal or retarded elderly persons, self-report cannot be relied upon. If a recent fall has been observed or if a history of constipation and impaction is present, these should be assessed by x-ray or rectal examination, respectively.

It is important to note that in the case of the maintenance of shouting behavior by staff's attention that this attention need not be "positive" in nature. Shouts to quiet down or threats of restriction can serve as positive reinforcement for the behavior of some clients. In some institutions this type of behavior may be the only response which receives attention, and therefore it will continue to occur at high frequency. This is an example of the powerful partial reinforcement effect.

Noncompliance. Another major management problem is the failure to comply with medical, educational, or psychosocial regimens. Noncompliance is often the reason for readmission *to* mental institutions and may deter discharge *from* mental institutions. Noncompliance within the inpatient setting can lead to forced compliance, physical aggression or resistance, worsening of medical or psychiatric conditions, and a change to more intrusive forms of therapy (i.e., injections).

Two factors must be considered in the assessment of noncompliance. The failure to conform to therapeutic regimens may be due to poor memory or to pure refusal.

It is relatively easy to differentiate these two causes by assessing memory functioning. One also should consider memory deficits as a cause of noncompliance in Alzheimer's clients. For some reason, clients with middle- to late- stage dementia periodically refuse food or medication. Their impaired judgment makes verbal intervention useless.

The management problems discussed above can occur in any client population. There are three sets of behavior, however, which are confined primarily to geriatric populations. Poor stimulus control plays a large role in the maintenance of these behaviors. The problem behaviors are wandering, inappropriate voiding, and inappropriate sexual behavior.

Wandering. Ambulation, in and of itself, usually presents few [*moving, shifting, walking*] management problems. The behavior involved is not usually excessive and certainly should not be met with the same consequences designed to reduce rates of response. However, sometimes ambulation can result in harm to the ambulator. This may happen when the ambulation results in access to potentially dangerous areas or items such as highly trafficked roadways, forests, exposed water, kitchens, stairwells, and slippery ground. When the danger inherent in these areas does not appear to alter the ambulation pattern because the stimulus control is no longer viable, accidents and exposure may occur.

It is clear that the clinician should not attempt to assess the *rate* of ambulation but should, instead, evaluate the impact that the context of setting has on the behavior. The assessor should observe the pattern and route of ambulation as well as the nature of the point at which the ambulation terminates.

It is important to differentiate the causes of ambulation. One analysis of ambulatory patterns in institutionalized geriatric clients (Hussian & Davis, 1983) revealed four possible causes for the behavior, which suggest different treatment strategies. These behavioral patterns are as follows.

1. *Akathisia-induced ambulation.* This behavior is usually caused by long-term use of neuroleptics. The motor restlessness results in non-goal-directed ambulation and is associated with other signs of akathisia such as reports of inability to sit still, repetitive movements while stationary, and other extrapyramidal symptoms. [*frontal cerebral cortex motor center*]

2. *Exit-seeking.* This behavior is usually observed in recently admitted clients on locked wards. This behavior is also associated with statements reflecting a desire to leave and return home. The doors that are tried by these clients are usually doors with access to the outside.

3. *Self-stimulatory behavior.* This takes the form of ambulation. This type of ambulation is usually seen only with advanced progressive dementia and is associated with other forms of stereotypy such as furniture rubbing, clothing manipulation, hand clapping, and repetitive vocalizations. These clients are less interested in the door as a means to exit than they are the sensory stimulation received from the turning knob.

4. *Modeling.* This may occur when a client shadows an ambulator who belongs in one of the other three classes. These clients are usually severely demented and will ambulate only in the presence of another client. This shadowing behavior can be dangerous if the other client enters a hazardous area.

Inappropriate Voiding. Another behavior that can result in time-consuming management is voiding in areas other than the toilet. The results of such voiding are the same whether the client is mistakenly voiding in these areas or purposively voiding there. The behavior can result in large amounts of staff time involved in unpleasant tasks, increased linen bills, lower employee morale, hazardous conditions on the ward, and catheterization.

There are several causes of inappropriate voiding to be considered prior to choosing an intervention. First, it may be a consequence of increased attention received from the staff. This attention may involve tactile stimulation as well as verbal interactions.

Second, the client may urinate inappropriately simply because it is more convenient than urinating in the appropriate receptacle. If there are no physical reasons for the behavior (i.e., lack of ambulation, poor sphincter control, insufficient bladder feedback) and no barriers to access are present, convenience should be suspected. It is often associated with other signs of insufficient motivation such as the lack of independent grooming, poor personal hygiene, and a low activity level.

Third, the behavior may result from insufficient stimulus control. In this case, the urination is usually preceded by the appropriate precursor responses such as the exposure of the genitals. The behavior often occurs around objects which apparently seem like a toilet and may occur, unlike the voiding of the attention seeker, in areas not under direct observation. This is seen in progressive dementia and is frequently the referring problem.

Inappropriate Sexual Behavior. Masturbation and sexual contact with others become problematic when they occur in inappropriate settings. Masturbating, for example, in the lobby of an institution is inappropriate, not because the act is inherently wrong, but rather because it is occurring in the wrong place. Assessment, therefore, should include environmental variables that contribute to the exhibition of the sexual behavior such as the location of occurrence, the recipient, and any identifiable antecedents.

Inappropriate sexual behavior may be caused by several factors. First, the behavior may occur because it has been followed in the past by positive consequences (e.g., orgasm, attention from others). Second, the behavior can result from decreased inhibitory control due to brain damage. Some stroke patients show this loss of inhibition. Third, the behavior can result as a consequence of inappropriate stimulus control.

The following considerations should be made prior to intervention.

1. It is important to determine whether intervention is warranted. Decisions regarding the inappropriateness of a certain behavior must be made with multiple inputs and should consider the dangerousness of the behavior, whether it violates the rights of other clients, whether it is severely disrupting ward routine, whether the exhibitor is competent, and whether the recipient of the sexual behavior is competent or requires protection.

2. Is the behavior sexual in nature, or does the functional analysis reveal that it involves contact but without sexual intent? This is frequently the case when confused clients climb into bed with one another.

3. Is the sexual behavior itself inappropriate or is it simply occurring at inopportune places or times?

These are but a few of the severe management problems likely to be encountered in institutions housing geropsychiatric clients. Other management problems include pica, stripping, drooling, spitting, low activity level, deficient independent behavior, and furniture movement. Many of the techniques discussed in the next section can be used in the treatment of these behaviors as well.

The previous discussion should point out the extreme difficulty in the determination of etiology when behaviors are similar. It is necessary, therefore, to observe the behavior in the situational context across time. For the behaviorist, it is also extremely important to become familiar with medical and laboratory assessments and the importance of neuropsychological testing.

Intervention

Having determined the target behavior to be changed and the nature of
the maintaining variables involved (i.e., poor stimulus control, electrolyte disturbance, noncontingent reinforcement, paucity of reinforcers),
the appropriate intervention(s) should be chosen (see Table 4.1). Despite
the magnitude of the assessment problem with the elderly, intervention
techniques require little modification or special consideration. The techniques used with similar problems in other age-groups are useful here.

Table 4.1 Outline of management problems and interventions

Management Problem/Cause	*Intervention of Choice*
Verbal abuse or threats	Extinction, then corner time-out
Physical aggression	Room time-out
Multiple complaints or demands	Extinction, then response cost and/or corner time-out
Shouting	
Self-stimulation	Sensory extinction
Attention seeking	Extinction, then corner time-out
Noncompliance	
Memory impairment	External cues
Refusal	Response cost or restriction
Wandering	
Akathisia	Medicine adjustment
Exit seeking	Extinction
Self-stimulation	Sensory extinction or DRO
Modeling	DRO
Inappropriate voiding	
Attention seeking	Correction, then response-cost/restriction
Poor motivation	DRO
Poor stimulus control	Stimulus enhancement or stimulus control
Inappropriate sexual behavior	
Gratification	Prevention, then time-out, then response-cost/restriction
Decreased inhibitory control	Prevention, then extinction
Poor stimulus control	Stimulus enhancement or control

Agitation and Combativeness. The source of the agitation/combativeness determines the appropriate behavioral intervention. The agitation due to memory impairment and frustration in early Alzheimer's disease may be prevented through certain environmental modifications.

1. Minimize the number of persons visiting the client, whether at home or in the institution. Introduce visitors and family members on each meeting.
2. Minimize change and establish a routine in the daily activity schedule and keep a constant environment. Well-learned patterns often remain to control current behavior and should not be disrupted.
3. Color code places which require specific responses and train the client to exhibit those responses only in the presence of those cues. Bathrooms, storage areas for personal items, and hazardous areas should be highlighted by such stimulus enhancement methods as bright colors, textures, and so on.

Hallucinatory behavior, often accompanied by startle responses, which occurs in later stages of senile dementia, is more difficult to control since the stimulus control is not as readily accessible to the therapist. Again, prophylaxis is the optimal management technique. This approach attempts to reduce the likelihood that visual and auditory information will be misinterpreted by the client. The following suggestions may achieve this goal.

1. Move slowly into the visual field of these clients. Interact from the front of the client and move slowly. Movement in the periphery seems to cause startle responses and combativeness.
2. Reduce the amount of stimulation in order to prevent information overload and misinterpretation. Check for possible sources of misinterpretations such as other clients wandering through the sleeping area, animals or unattached objects moving in the attic, basement, or between the walls, or neighborhood children playing pranks on the client.
3. Assure adequate amounts of sleep at night. Agitation is frequently related to sleep–wake reversal or sleep deprivation.
4. Within the institution, working with a physician who can order medication as needed is extremely important. Infrequent p.r.n. dosing might be preferable to routine neuroleptic usage in the control of startle agitation.

Agitation and combativeness which occur because of a history of reinforcement can be reduced with standard behavioral interventions. For example, Rosberger and MacLean (1983) reduced the number of agitated responses (i.e., kicking, tripping, throwing objects, and shoving objects at others) in a 79-year-old nursing home client through the use of differential reinforcement (ignoring the inappropriate behavior while providing positive reinforcement following appropriate behavior).

At the author's institution, time-out, restrictions from favored activities, extinction, response cost, and differential reinforcement of alternative behavior are used to reduce these behaviors. Extinction, ignoring the client during exhibition of the behavior, is generally used following verbal aggression or shouting. Then, more restrictive interventions are used such as corner time-out (i.e., the client is prompted to stand or sit in a quiet corner for five minutes).

An episode of physical aggression results in placement in a time-out room with the same criteria for approved exit. The time-out room is not locked at this point. Early exit from the time-out room results in placement in seclusion where the door is locked. Seclusion is a medical, not a behavioral, procedure.

Strict procedural guidelines should be followed during the implementation of the time-out intervention. The following suggestions may be helpful in designing an acceptable time-out program.

1. Less restrictive alternatives such as extinction, response cost, or restriction should be used prior to time-out unless a physically aggressive act occurs.

2. The prompt for the client to enter into time-out should be short and direct, thus minimizing unwanted reinforcement.

3. The criteria for release should be given on the entry into the time-out area. A simple statement such as "You must be calm and quiet for five minutes," should be sufficient.

4. The client should not be disturbed while in the time-out area except for periodic checks as to physical functioning. These checks should involve as little positive reinforcement (attention) as possible.

5. The client should be prompted to leave the time-out area promptly when the criteria are met.

Agitation secondary to a delirium process requires no extensive behavioral treatment if the etiology can be identified and treated effectively. However, continual monitoring of the incidence of the target behavior, drug type and dosage changes, and laboratory abnormalities can pinpoint reliable correlations between intervention and behavior change.

Multiple Complaints and Demands. Once an organic etiology has been ruled out as the cause for complaining, behavioral intervention can begin. Extinction is the preferable intervention though its successful application requires consistent adherence across staff, shifts, and situations. It should be reiterated that intermittent reinforcement serves to strengthen the inappropriate behavior and ultimately makes it more difficult to eliminate.

In order to ensure that inadvertent positive reinforcement is not provided following the excessive complaints or demands, the observer may incorporate the following.

1. Fixate on a point away from the client who is exhibiting the behavior. Do not turn toward the client or in any way show that you are aware of the verbalization. Frowning, smiling, laughing, or any other change in facial expression may serve as a reinforcer.

2. If the behavior becomes too annoying for the observer to remain in the area without showing some form of attention toward the client, the observer should leave the area. Turning the back toward the client and leaving the area is an effective method of extinction and may reduce the frustration or anger of the observer.

Response cost or dorm/corner time-out may be necessary if extinction fails and the behavior continues at a high rate. Response cost is similar to a fine in that a token or favored item is removed from the client subsequent to the exhibition of an inappropriate target behavior. The response cost should occur immediately and should "fit the offense." Items which the client has a right to have (e.g., regular meals, privacy, bed) are not to be withdrawn under any circumstances.

Shouting. High-intensity vocalizations may arise from organic causes (cerebral, systemic, or peripheral) or may result from the nature of the reinforcement received in the client's history or from a combination of the two (i.e., secondary gain).

Alleviation of the systemic or peripheral-focal disorder should eliminate the shouting if the staff also provide reinforcement contingent upon nonshouting during the resolution of the physical disorder. Shouting can become the preferred mode of response in the absence of reinforcement for more constructive behavior.

Repetitive self-stimulatory shouting, often associated with Alzheimer's disease, is difficult to treat with traditional methods. Work with small numbers of clients (Hussian, 1982) suggests that the prevention of sensory stimulation may result in the reduction of shouting. Ear muffs should provide the sufficient treatment by reducing the feedback.

If it is determined that the shouting is being maintained by consequences provided by others, extinction, time-out, and/or response cost may be useful if it is applied consistently.

Noncompliance. When one is confronted with clients who do not comply with program or medical regimens it should be determined whether memory function might be the cause. If so, prompts and external cues might be employed to "encourage" compliance.

By associating simple color cues or markers with a practiced behavior such as medication consumption, toileting, dressing, or activity participation and then using these prompts when compliance is desired, the desired outcome may be forthcoming. The clients, in essence, learn to respond in the appropriate manner in the presence of the trained stimulus. Work is currently underway at the author's facility to encourage participation in ward activities through the use of a supernormal stimulus and verbal prompts. When the colored stimulus is presented, clients in the area of the activity materials will be rewarded with bonus tokens if a minimum number of clients are participating. It is hypothesized that this movable stimulus could then be used to encourage participation in other activities on and off the ward and for routine therapeutic regimens. This supernormal cue not only serves as an easily discriminable prompt but also is rudimentary enough to prompt behavior through prior associations and contains a group contingency. It is also movable and, therefore, increases generalization.

External prompts are not as likely to improve compliance in those clients who do not exhibit significant memory impairment. When memory impairment is ruled out, intervention similar to that used with the aforementioned target behaviors should be successful. Refusal to comply with reasonable requests should be followed by immediate response cost or restrictions. It is important that the consequence should match the seriousness of the noncompliant act and should not be used as a threat. For example, if a client refuses to take his/her morning medication, it would be appropriate to restrict that client from one token store opening or from one special activity. It would not be appropriate, however, to cancel a weekend pass or deprive the client of a meal until compliance is achieved.

Noncompliance can be dealt with most easily within a token or point system. Points can be awarded in a graduated fashion, with more points given for a lesser degree of prompt. Physical prompting would result in the fewest number of points. Clients with impaired memory would be excluded from this intervention.

Wandering. Once a careful analysis of the ambulation pattern of a particular client has been completed and the client has been identified in the appropriate category, intervention should be considered. It should be noted that wandering in many settings may not lead to dangerous situations and, if discharge is unlikely, intervention is probably not warranted.

The following suggestions are based on only observational data and the logical hypotheses derived from these observations.

1. *Akathisia.* Anti-Parkinson medication may be indicated to reduce motor restlessness and the constant pacing typical in drug-induced wandering. Usually these individuals will not attempt to enter dangerous areas or to exit if they are made aware of the hazard. Clearly marking these doors would limit inappropriate entries.

2. *Exit seekers.* There is little that can be done to limit this type of ambulation on open wards. However, those clients who exhibit such behavior shortly after admission generally discontinue exit seeking with time (extinction). Clients with Alzheimer's disease who exhibit this behavior will also cease looking for an exit with time and tend to ambulate in another category. In the meantime, one can only provide distracting, incompatible activities.

3. *Self-stimulators.* Little research has been conducted on the elimination or reduction of stereotypy with geriatric clients. It may be assumed, however, that some of the techniques effectively employed with other populations (e.g., severely and profoundly retarded, autistic, chronic schizophrenia) might be employed, with modifications, to this population. For example, a form of sensory extinction has been used with some success at this author's facility by simply tightening loose door knobs, thus reducing auditory and tactile feedback and reducing knob turning. Usually, other less problematic forms of self-stimulation will take the place of the knob turning.

Hussian (1982) has shown that stimulus control procedures can reduce entries into potentially dangerous areas. By pairing a noxious stimulus with a colored symbol and then placing this symbol on the door leading to the hazardous area, entries are reduced. Ambulation continues but is confined to acceptable areas.

It may also be useful to provide opportunities to engage in other forms of stimulation. Cloth, paper, noise-producing toys, and the like might be provided to serve this purpose. Also, the doors leading to hazardous areas might be modified in order to provide as little sensory feedback as possible either by tightening the hardware, fitting the door more snugly, or using handles rather than knobs. It also should be noted that continual self-stimulation might suggest the lack of external sensory stimulation in the milieu.

4. *Modelers.* Modeling behavior should decrease if the wandering of the clients in the other three categories is reduced. Engagement in other activities as well as reinforcement by differential reinforcement of other behavior (DRO), should also prove useful in reducing time spent in ambulation.

Inappropriate Voiding. Intervention following inappropriate voiding depends upon the results of the functional analysis. For example, if it can be determined that the inappropriate voiding is being maintained by the attention that follows the behavior, the target for modification is the staff's behavior. The staff should be instructed to interact with the client following this behavior in a straightforward manner, showing neither disgust nor condescension. The client should be prompted to clean the area of urine and change clothes. If this correction procedure is not effective, it can be combined with response cost or restriction. Prompting rehearsal of the correct toileting procedure after the correction procedure is beneficial in other cases of inappropriate voiding but probably provides too much reinforcement for attention seekers.

If a lack of motivation (reinforcement is stronger for inappropriate rather than appropriate voiding) is present, differential reinforcement should be applied. A reinforcer is given for appropriate toileting or dry clothing while response cost and correction are utilized following inappropriate voiding.

If it has been determined that the behavior is a result of insufficient stimulus control, it would be a serious mistake to invoke correction or response cost procedures. This would be equivalent to docking a sightless client of tokens for spilling food in the dining room. At this author's facility, a stimulus enhancement is used on the geriatric unit. Brightly colored symbols are placed on restroom doors. Sometimes a simple prompt to associate the symbol with urination is sufficient. With some clients, however, stimulus control procedures may have to be attempted, where a symbol is paired with the delivery of a positive event and then is placed on the restroom door. The process can be quite slow and usually must be repeated periodically with clients who have progressive dementia.

Inappropriate Sexual Behavior. If it has been decided that a sexual behavior requires attention, it should be determined whether the behavior is due to the consequences which are naturally derived, poor inhibitory control, or poor stimulus control. In the first case, the simplest intervention may be the separation of the instigator and his or her target or audience. A change in rooms or wards, if possible, may prevent an alert client from taking sexual liberties with a functionally incompetent client. If this is not feasible, standard behavior interventions as discussed above such as time-out, response cost, or restrictions may be applied. It is imperative that staff act quickly to protect clients who are incapable of providing consent to these sexual encounters.

In rare cases, cerebrovascular accidents may lead to decreased inhibitory control expressed as sexual behavior. Usually, because of other limitations imposed by the stroke, these advances are merely brief touches or grabs and not an attempt to achieve sexual gratification. These touches can be quite bothersome to staff members, however. Intervention after the advances has met with little success. Prophylactic methods and extinction may be the only viable alternatives.

Inappropriate sexual behavior, like inappropriate voiding, may result from insufficient stimulus control. This is often the case in the late stages of a progressive dementia and involves the exposure of the genitals, stripping, and/or masturbation. In these cases the behavior itself is not the target for change but it is rather the location or the target of the behavior which requires alteration. This can be done by employing stimulus control techniques and differential reinforcement.

Hussian (1982) eliminated public masturbation while increasing masturbation in private, as exhibited by an elderly male resident of a long-term care facility, through differential reinforcement. The client's masturbatory behavior was interrupted when it occurred in public areas while the client was allowed to reach orgasm when masturbating in the privacy of his room. A large, brightly colored symbol was placed in his room and the client was reinforced naturally (via orgasm) for masturbation in the presence of this stimulus. The orange stimulus, in essence, came to control the behavior. That the behavior was shaped to occur in private was essentially an incidental consequence of fixing the stimulus in the private setting only.

This use of differential reinforcement coupled with a supernormal stimulus can change the relative frequencies of responding when rules, natural contingencies, warning signs, or verbal intervention fail.

These are but a few of the management problems faced in settings which house psychogeriatric clients. They are not confined to geriatric clients, of course, but seem to occur more frequently with this age-group. Correct identification and definition of these problems and the correct and timely intervention can result in a better quality of life, less restrictive surroundings, availability for educational and therapeutic interventions, and more acceptance on the part of their caregivers.

Case Illustration

A 67-year-old man was admitted to a long-term care facility accompanied by his wife, who gave the history. Mr. RT. was a high school graduate who had recently retired from an insurance business. He had no prior history of psychiatric illness but had been under a physician's care for several years for congestive heart failure.

Approximately three years prior to the admission, the client had retired and began staying at home. It was at about this time that his wife noticed forgetfulness, lack of spontaneity, low activity level, and accusations that she had hidden certain objects from him. Mrs. RT. initially thought that her husband was depressed because of the recent retirement. However, he also began to get angry with visitors, claiming that he did not know them and that his wife was inviting strangers over for some unknown, but devious, reason. Frequently after going out alone for walks and drives, he had to be brought home by police for erratic behavior and an inability to inform them of his destination. Neighbors complained that he was often abusive with them, their children, and their pets.

Mrs. RT. had the most difficulty coping with his day–night reversal and his constantly shadowing her around the house. He became agitated when she left his sight and would accuse her of trying to have him "put away" or of seeing another man. He began to refuse to eat, stating that he had just eaten, and he became careless with smoking materials and kitchen utensils.

Shortly after admission to the long-term care facility, the client showed exit seeking, verbal abuse aimed at his caregivers, agitation when asked to return to his room, and verbalizations that his roommate was trying to kill him or have him killed; he slept only three or four hours during the day and almost none at night and was incontinent of urine and (periodically) feces. A mental status examination revealed very little due to the lack of cooperation of the client, though severe deficits in short-term memory processes were evident. The client also showed some word search difficulty, speaking in a circular manner in an attempt to avoid certain words.

Several months after admission, the client began to show some stereotypy in the form of clothing manipulation and wall rubbing. The clothing manipulation included continually rolling his pants legs up and down while seated, and placing his slippers on his hands and then back on his feet. He frequently placed his robe on his legs, placing his feet through the sleeves. He would turn his head and respond to loud-speaker announcements as if these announcements were directed to him. He would grimace and begin to cry, independent of the external stimuli or content of the conversation, although these episodes rarely resulted in tearing or sobbing for more than a few seconds.

At about this time, he no longer verbalized desires to leave the facility and the doors which he would touch while wandering were no longer limited to exit doors. The nature of these touches changed dramatically as well. The number of turns per contact went from an average of 3 to approximately 17.

On two occasions the client became extremely agitated and con-fused. He attempted to strike his roommate and other clients ambulat-ing near his geri-chair. He also would throw his tray at passers-by and would attempt to strike night shift personnel when they came to check his vital signs during the night.

The physician diagnosed active congestive heart failure on both of these occasions and the client was started on an antihypertensive and a diuretic. Shortly after the instigation or increase in this regimen, the client showed significant motoric slowing, and the agitation and confusion returned to baseline levels.

It was decided by the treatment team that, in addition to the management of the congestive heart failure, attention should be paid to the crying, agitation and combativeness, wandering, urinary inconti-nence, and general cognitive decline. The noncompliance partially re-solved itself and then was remedied completely, by crushing medica-tion and mixing it with applesauce. An antihistamine ordered for the periodic agitation was changed to a liquid form.

Because of the lack of an external source of stimulus control over the crying, it was thought that it was probably secondary to the brain damage. The motoric slowing was treated with a potassium supplement when it was discovered that the client was hypokalemic (possibly sec-ondary to the antihypertensive-diuretic interaction). Time spent out of bed and in the commons area increased by approximately 50 percent. The crying episodes, as measured by time-sampling and frequency count, also were reduced, by about 30 percent.

The staff was instructed to approach the client, particularly dur-ing future delirium episodes, from the front, and to minimize distracting ward noises or movements. The number of aggressive attacks directed toward the staff was decreased from an average of four per week to one per month. The antihistamine was administered only twice and was subsequently discontinued. No neuroleptic was attempted.

Time spent in self-stimulation was reduced from 62 percent of the intervals observed to 14 percent by supplying the client with modeling clay, magazines, cloth remnants, and other objects.

Corner time-out was used to reduce the grabbing and shouting which occurred approximately four times per hour and during 44 percent of the intervals observed, respectively. After one month of consistent application, the grabbing was eliminated and the shouting occured during only 8 percent of the intervals observed.

A stimulus control procedure was utilized to reduce inappropriate entries during ambulation. The client was presented with symbols of two different colors, one paired with a primary reinforcer, the other with no discernible reinforcer. The s-delta was then affixed on doors leading to areas considered to be of potential danger. The client was then permitted to ambulate freely, with monitoring. Through a total of 10 hours of observation, the client entered an inappropriate door only once.

Standard toilet training procedures (Hussian, 1981) had been implemented in an attempt to encourage appropriate urination for several months with little change over baseline rates. When a symbol was paired with a positive reinforcer and then mounted over the client's toilet and on his bathroom door, the client's inappropriate urinations were reduced by approximately 75 percent. The total treatment package included positive practice, the stimulus control procedure, and differential reinforcement. When the client urinated in the wrong area a correction procedure was also successfully implemented.

It can be seen from the case illustration that a behavioral approach to management problems can be used in conjunction with medical/pharmacological intervention to form a comprehensive intervention package. Reductions in potentially dangerous wandering (without a reduction in ambulation per se), shouting, grabbing, agitation/combativeness, stereotypy, crying, and motor retardation were observed. Though in no way could the client be considered freed from the disease nor could the prognosis be improved, the client's behavior became much more manageable without restricting the client's movement or reducing adjunctive responses. Staff and family interactions also improved, thereby, it was hoped, improving the quality of his life as well.

References

Baltes, M.M., & Barton, E.M. (1977). New approaches toward aging: A case for the operant model. *Educational Gerontology: An International Quarterly, 2*, 383–405.

Baltes, M.M., Honn, S., Barton, E.M., Orzech, M., & Lago, D. (1983). On the social ecology of dependence and independence in elderly nursing home residents: A replication and extension. *Journal of Gerontology, 38*, 556–564.

Hussian, R.A. (1981). *Geriatric psychology: A behavioral perspective.* New York: Van Nostrand Reinhold.

Hussian, R.A. (1982). Stimulus control in the modification of problematic behavior in elderly institutionalized patients. *International Journal of Behavioral Geriatrics, 1:1*, 33–42.

Hussian, R.A. (1984). Behavioral geriatrics. In M. Hersen, R.M. Eisler, & P. M. Miller (Eds.). *Progress in Behavior Modification* (Vol. XVI). New York: Academic Press, 159–183.

Hussian, R.A., & Davis, R.L. (1983). *Analysis of wandering behavior in institutionalized geriatric patients.* Paper presented at the meeting of the Association for Behavior Analysis, Milwaukee, WI.

Hussian, R.A., & Hill, S.D. (1980). Stereotyped behavior in elderly patients with chronic organic mental disorder. *Journal of Gerontology, 35*, 689–691.

Rosberger, Z., & MacLean, J. (1983). Behavioral assessment and treatment of "organic" behaviors in an institutionalized geriatric patient. *International Journal of Behavioral Geriatrics, 1:4*, 33–46.

5

Sexual Problems

Leslie R. Schover

Despite the sexual revolution, eroticism in America is still regarded as the province of the young and healthy. In media images, the ideal lover is unwrinkled, athletic, and under 30. A sexy man gets instantaneous erections and can sustain them for hours of intercourse. Beautiful teenagers writhe in multiple orgasms. We foster negative stereotypes, however, of men and women who remain sexual in their older years: The senile man molesting young girls, the coercive boss chasing his secretary, the raddled grandmother dressing like an adolescent, or the wealthy old lady duped by a gigolo.

Adults often feel angry and ashamed when their widowed parents find a new love (McKain, 1972). Children of nursing-home residents pressure staff to forbid sexual contact (Wasow & Loeb, 1977). Although some are motivated by fear of losing an inheritance to a new stepparent, much of their dismay arises from the belief that older people should become asexual. A psychoanalyst might see control of an aging parent's sexuality as the ultimate oedipal revenge.

A recent cross-cultural survey of attitudes about sexuality and aging (Winn & Newton, 1982) ranks the United States among the most repressive societies in the world. Continued sexual activity and interest were expected of older men in 70 percent and of older women in 84 percent of 106 cultures. Only 3 cultures actively censured sexual expression in the elderly.

Despite the fact that sex for the elderly remains the last bastion of American puritanism, however, older adults do manage to stay sexually interested and active. In the following sections I will review research on sexual behavior in aging samples, summarize the physiologic changes in the male and female sexual response that occur with aging, and examine the association between sexual dysfunction and aging. Strategies are offered for assessing and treating sexual problems in older individuals and couples and for helping nonclinical aging populations preserve the integrity of their sexuality.

Description of the Problem

In order to treat sexual problems in elderly patients, the clinician needs to be familiar with normative data on sexual interest and activity in older adults, changes in the sexual response cycle with aging, and the incidence and types of sexual dysfunctions in this population. The following sections review some of these basic facts.

Sexual Interest and Activity in Older Adults

Research has repeatedly suggested that the frequency of sexual activity and desire in a person's later years corresponds directly to the importance of sexuality earlier in life (George & Weiler, 1981; Giambra & Martin, 1977; Martin, 1981; Masters & Johnson, 1966; White, 1982b). In an interview study of men aged 60 to 79, Martin (1981) found that frequency of intercourse, responses to erotic stimuli, and the length of time a man would tolerate celibacy were significantly interrelated. Men who had been at the low end of the spectrum of sexual interest and activity in their youth were the most likely to discontinue sex and to report loss of erectile function in old age. These men were not distressed, however, by their sexual incapacity. Martin concludes that lack of motivation is an important factor in sexual dysfunction and inactivity in the elderly.

Methodological flaws in studies of sex in older adults led early researchers to conclude that sexual activity automatically decreased with age. George and Weiler (1981), reviewing evidence from Kinsey's surveys as well as from the cross-sectional interview studies conducted at Duke University in the 1960s, suggested that the age-related sexual decline is really a cohort effect, that is, a result of the era in which a person grew up. Cohort effects are to be expected in sex research, given the rapid changes in sexual behavior and attitudes in the twentieth century. A prime example is the finding that the best predictor of a woman's ability to reach orgasm is the decade of her birth (Morokoff,

1978). The more recently she was born, the more likely she is to be orgasmic. Her era of birth is a more powerful factor than her current age, religion, social class, or education.

George and Weiler (1981) also emphasized other weaknesses in the design of research on aging and sexuality. Studies suffer from lack of longitudinal data, narrow definitions of sexual activity as heterosexual intercourse, biased sampling, and lack of controls for social desirability in subjects' self-reports of sexual behavior.

George and Weiler's own research surmounted some of these problems. Married men and women between 46 and 71 years of age were interviewed at two-year intervals across six years. Participants, recruited from a health insurance program, were more representative of the community than many sex research samples. Subjects who lost a spouse through death or divorce during the six years were excluded from the analyses, to limit the research to patterns of sexual activity in an ongoing relationship.

The most common pattern for an individual man or woman over the six years was stability of sexual interest and activity (58 percent of the sample). Only 20 percent decreased sexual activity with their partner, and a mere 7 percent were celibate across all test dates. Although the oldest subjects were more likely to report a sexual decline, George and Weiler believe that cohort effects are at least partially responsible, concluding that the elderly of the future may well be more sexually active than the current generation of senior citizens.

Even though current research points to sexual stability as the normative pattern for older adults, many men and women do cease sexual activity as they age. In George and Weiler's (1981) research, 18 percent of men and 33 percent of women over age 65 stopped having intercourse during the six years of the study. In Martin's (1981) sample of healthy men aged 60 to 79, 13 percent were sexually inactive. Starr and Weiner's (1981) survey of 800 adults over 60 found that 7 percent of men and 30 percent of women were celibate. At the extreme end, in White's (1982b) group of very elderly nursing-home residents, only 8 percent *had* masturbated or engaged in partner sex within the last month.

Why do older people stop being sexually active? For men, the diseases common in old age, rather than aging per se, seem to interfere with sexual vigor. In a Scandinavian study that followed a cohort of 70-year-olds for five years (Persson, 1981), men who remained sexually active had a lower mortality. Persson regards sexually active aging men as biologically more youthful. This relationship was not observed for women, however. Indeed, studies concur that there is a gender difference in the reasons for becoming celibate (George & Weiler, 1981; White, 1982b). The male partner controls an older couple's sexual frequency. While men stop having sex due to lack of motivation, ill health, or erection problems, women become inactive because of loss of a willing and able partner.

In general, women report lower rates of sexual activity and interest than men at all age levels over 45, although the gender gap narrows after 70. Elderly women who are widowed or divorced face a lonely future, since there are four single women for every single man over age 65 (Corby & Zarit, 1983). Our cultural bias that the male partner should be the elder combined with men's shorter life expectancy contributes to the large number of widows. The problem is compounded when older men turn to younger women as partners for dating and remarriage.

Nevertheless, the majority of men and women remain active sexually well into old age. Thus, changes with aging in the sexual response cycle are a pertinent issue.

The Sexual Response Cycle and Normal Aging

In discussing changes in sexual responsiveness with aging, it is helpful to divide the sexual response cycle into its components of desire, arousal, orgasm, and resolution (Kaplan, 1979; Masters & Johnson, 1966). For each phase we will examine observations of physiologic responsiveness in the elderly and the effects of aging on the biologic systems necessary for adequate function.

Sexual Desire.   The biologic system crucial in maintaining sexual desire is the sex-hormone-feedback cycle. Sex steroids circulate in the blood, acting in the limbic system of the brain to promote sexual desire. Just as earlier studies suggested a decline in sexual activity with age, initial research on sex hormones in men found that the level of testosterone, the steroid produced by the testes, was decreased in older men (Kolodny, Masters, & Johnson, 1979). Since men with abnormally low testosterone levels report loss of sexual desire, erectile dysfunction, and difficulty reaching orgasm, it was believed that a "male menopause" was a normal feature of aging, and that this hormonal decline provoked a decrease in sexual activity.

More recent and methodologically sound hormonal studies, however, have not replicated a decrease in testosterone level with aging (Harman & Tsitouras, 1980; Purifoy, Koopmans, & Mayes, 1981). Older men who remain in good physical health retain testosterone levels as high as those found in younger samples. The early studies included only institutionalized elderly men or patients from Veterans Administration hospitals. Certainly debilitated elderly men, particularly those with a history of alcohol abuse, are likely to produce less testosterone, but this cannot be attributed to the normal aging process. Indeed, testosterone may be a marker of physical fitness. Young men's testosterone levels increase dramatically with regular aerobic exercise (Remes, Kuoppasalmi, & Adlercreutz, 1979).

Mild decreases in testosterone levels such as those typically seen in elderly men in poor health have little impact on sexual behavior. Testosterone seems to work on a threshold model. As long as a man has the minimum hormone value necessary for sexual function, more may be superfluous. When testosterone is within the normal range, few correlations have been found between sexual interest or frequency and hormonal level.

One recent study, however, did find a modest relationship between sexual activity and hormone levels in men over 60 (Tsitouras, Martin, & Harman, 1982). The researchers suggest that elderly men may require a higher serum level of testosterone than younger men, because of reduced ability of target tissues to use the hormone. In younger men, hormone–behavior relationships are perhaps obscured by the easy availability of sex and by almost universal good health. As aging intervenes, those men with high levels of sexual vigor, in both hormonal and motivational realms, remain more active.

In women, even though hormonal menopause does occur, only a minority report a loss of sexual desire (Kolodny, Masters, & Johnson, 1979). Indeed, the end of anxiety about unwanted pregnancy and the additional leisure time afforded by retirement and the "empty nest" spark a renaissance of sexual pleasure for many women (Rubin, 1982).

The major hormonal change accompanying menopause is the decrease in estrogen and progesterone produced by the ovaries. These hormones are actually mild inhibitors of sexual desire and arousability (Schreiner-Engel, Schiavi, Smith, & White, 1981). It is testosterone and its related androgens that seem to spark sexual interest in women, as well as in men (Persky et al., 1982; Schreiner-Engel et al., 1981). The adrenal glands of a menopausal woman continue to produce the usual amount of androgens, but the circulating level drops by 10 to 50 percent because estrogen is no longer available to be metabolized to androgens in target tissues (Persky et al., 1982). Although Persky and colleagues did document a positive correlation between circulating androgens and women's sexual desire and arousal, they found the effect too small to produce significant difference in sexual function between pre- and postmenopausal women.

In summary, then, sexual desire remains relatively stable as a person ages. Although some men and women experience a loss of desire associated with abnormally low androgen levels, a hormonal deficiency is usually associated with a pathologic state rather than being an inevitable concomitant of aging.

Sexual Arousal. Sexual arousal includes both the subjective pleasure in response to an internal or external erotic stimulus and the physiologic changes resulting from activation of the autonomic nervous system (Masters & Johnson, 1966). These include increased heart rate, respiration, and blood pressure as well as the hallmark of arousal—genital vasocongestion. In men, the visible result is penile erection. In women, arousal produces swelling of the external genitals, vaginal expansion both in length and width, vaginal lubrication, and the formation of the "orgasmic platform" to cushion the penis as the walls of the introitus fill with blood.

Masters and Johnson's (1966) original research on arousal and aging remains the standard in the field, even though 20 years have passed since they observed 39 men and 34 women over age 50 respond to sexual stimulation in the laboratory. Their major finding was that, in both men and women, physiologic sexual arousal becomes slower and less intense with aging. A man needs more time, and often more direct penile stimulation, to achieve full erection. If he loses an erection during sexual activity, he may have difficulty regaining it. The maximal firmness of the erection may also decrease slightly, although it is still sufficient for penetration. Women take longer to produce vaginal lubrication and may not lubricate as much as they did when younger. Women also showed less breast engorgement, skin flush, genital swelling, and vaginal expansion. The changes in sexual arousal were mild in both men and women, however, and did not preclude good sexual function.

In aging men, the occurrence of nocturnal penile tumescence (NPT) is further evidence that arousal remains fairly intact even in old age. NPT consists of reflex erections that occur during sleep. From infancy through senescence, men have several episodes of erection during each night. These erections are not evoked by erotic dreams, or by an external stimulus such as a full bladder or friction on the penis. Instead they are part of the generalized autonomic nervous system activation of rapid-eye-movement (REM) sleep (Karacan, Salis, & Williams, 1978). NPT episodes may also coincide with a release of testosterone into the bloodstream (Schiavi et al., 1982).

In healthy men between the ages of 20 and 50, the amount of NPT per night declines gradually; it then remains stable until age 80. The average amount of time spent in erection after age 50 is 90 minutes per night, divided into two or three episodes (Kahn & Fisher, 1969; Karacan, Williams, Thornby, & Salis, 1975). In men over 70, some minor changes occur in the quality of NPT. More of the episodes occur during non-REM sleep, and erections are more likely to be partial rather than fully rigid.

Although women have episodes of increased vaginal blood flow during REM sleep that appear to be the analogue of NPT (Fisher et al., 1983), no research on postmenopausal women is yet available. We can only speculate that older women would show patterns of vaginal blood flow that are similar to, but less intense than, those of younger women.

Orgasm. Orgasm in both men and women is marked by contractions of striated muscles around the genitals, along with a subjective sensation of extreme pleasure. Masters and Johnson (1966) found that older men were better able to delay ejaculation. Although men over 50 occasionally failed to reach orgasm during sexual activity, they did not experience great frustration. As for the quality of the orgasm itself, the sensation of ejaculatory inevitability that accompanies emission of semen into the posterior urethra in younger men is often weakened or lost in an older man. The muscular contractions of ejaculation are also fewer and less intense, so that semen is expelled with less force. The amount of semen may also be reduced. Some men find their orgasmic sensation to be less intense as well.

Orgasmic changes in aging women are less noticeable. The contractions of the outer third of the vagina are fewer (Masters & Johnson, 1966), and the rectal sphincter may not contract at all. There is no documented loss of the ability to have multiple orgasms, however. A few elderly women complain of cramping pain with orgasm that appears to result from contraction of a uterus that has lost elasticity because of estrogen deficiency (Masters & Johnson, 1966).

Resolution.   The resolution phase consists of a return to the un-excited baseline state, in terms of both subjective pleasure and phys-iologic domain. In men, a refractory period follows ejaculation. Dur-ing this time, further sexual stimulation may result in erection but cannot lead to repeated orgasm. The duration of the refractory period increases with age. After age 60 some men need a rest of several days between ejaculations (Masters & Johnson, 1966). Penile detumescence also occurs more rapidly in older men. A man who compensated for premature ejaculation by continuing to thrust until his partner achieved orgasm may be distressed when he can no longer maintain his erection. Other men are upset because they cannot regain an erection and have intercourse twice in one sexual session.

Although women do not have a refractory phase, the vagina returns to its unexcited state much more quickly after orgasm in the postmenopausal woman, which may interfere with pleasure in contin-ued intercourse (Masters & Johnson, 1966).

Use It or Lose It?   Masters and Johnson (1981) have stated that older men and women must "use it or lose it" when it comes to sex. They believe that men or women who go through long periods of celibacy after age 50 actually undergo atrophy of their sexual response, leading to vaginal shrinkage and dryness in women and erectile dys-function in men.

Since this statement can engender much anxiety, it is worth exam-ining. Masters and Johnson base their contention that sexually active postmenopausal women have more vaginal lubrication on three re-search subjects (Masters & Johnson, 1966). A recent study at Rutgers Medical School (Leiblum, Bachmann, Kemmann, Colburn, & Swartz-man, 1983) did confirm that women who continued sexual activity had slightly less vaginal atrophy than celibate women. This relationship, however, could reflect cessation of sex by women who experienced dyspareunia because of vaginal shrinkage.

In men there is even less evidence for a physiologic effect of celibacy. Although testosterone levels may rise slightly after sexual arousal in men, 9 out of 11 monks in one study (Ismail, Davison, & Loraine, 1970) had normal hormone levels.

Until more sophisticated, longitudinal research finds evidence to support the existence of disuse atrophy, older adults should not be pressured to "use or lose it."

Sexual Dysfunction in
Older Adults

Although the age-related changes in the sexual response cycle demand some patience, there is no call for panic. Couples who centered their sexual routine on intercourse may need to include more foreplay. Sexual dysfunctions often begin, however, when lack of knowledge about sexuality and aging leads a man or woman to greet these small adjustments as the harbingers of a sexless old age. In addition to the roles of anxiety and ignorance in promoting sexual problems, some diseases of aging have sexual side effects.

Unfortunately, little is known about the incidence and types of sexual dysfunction in the elderly. The few existent surveys of the aging population have not used modern diagnostic categories to define sexual dysfunctions (Schover, Friedman, Weiler, Heiman, & LoPiccolo, 1982). Each facet of sexuality should be assessed, including problems with desire, arousal, orgasm, pain, or couple disagreements on the frequency and variety of activity. The relative contribution of organic and psychological causes also needs study. Clinical experience suggests that the most common sexual problems in the elderly are loss of sexual desire, erectile dysfunction, and female dyspareunia. Research data, however, are sadly lacking.

Kinsey, Pomeroy, and Martin (1948) interviewed only 126 men older than age 60 out of 5000 subjects. Rates of erectile dysfunction derived from this research are often quoted, however. Kinsey found that only 2 percent of men in their 40s had significant erection problems. The incidence increased to 7 percent of men in their 50s, 18 percent of men in their 70s, and 80 percent of men in their 80s. These results are questionable, however, not only on the grounds of inadequate sample size, but also because of the reluctance of elderly men in the 1940s to admit to continued sexual vigor. A more recent Danish survey of 1163 men aged 51 to 95 (Hegeler & Mortensen, 1977) focused on morning erections as a measure of organic capacity. The data on morning erections closely paralleled men's reports of sexual interest. Only 10 percent of men in their 50s had no morning erections. This figure increased to 39 percent at ages 76 to 80, and 69 percent between ages 91 to 95. These rates of erectile dysfunction are actually surprisingly similar to Kinsey's, albeit a bit more optimistic.

Many older men develop erectile dysfunction because of psychological distress. Fear of a loss of function because of aging or illness can become a self-fulfilling prophecy. Some erection problems in older men begin with a temporary organic cause, such as alcohol intoxication or antihypertensive medication, but persist because of fear of sexual failure even when the cause has been removed.

Another common etiologic factor is the loss of a spouse through divorce or death. The pressure to please a new partner, the anxiety of adapting to a new sexual routine, and bewilderment at societal changes in the rules of dating and sex all contribute to sexual dysfunction. A "widower's syndrome" of erectile dysfunction has been identified in men whose wives die after a lingering illness, necessitating celibacy (Hengeveld & Korzec, 1980; Kolodny et al., 1979). When the widower begins to date, or remarries, an erection problem develops. The cause has been presumed to be a combination of performance anxiety and unresolved mourning.

A recent comprehensive evaluation of 92 widowers (mean age 66), however, revealed that 71 percent who fit the classic pattern had organic causes for their sexual dysfunction (Schover, Karacan, & Hartse, 1982). Men with psychogenic problems were significantly younger and likely to have had wives who died suddenly. They also had higher scores on a state anxiety scale. Although the sample was biased toward the organic by referral patterns, the data emphasize the danger of overlooking medical factors because of a salient psychological picture. In the general population of men over age 50, a conservative estimate would be that one-third of erection problems have an organic component.

Older men with erection problems often develop ejaculatory dysfunction as well. Some ejaculate quickly, losing their previous control. Others ejaculate with a flaccid penis. They complain that their orgasmic pleasure is reduced and that their semen drips out rather than spurting. It is unclear whether these disturbances of ejaculation result from damage to the neurologic control of the urethral sphincters (Newman, Reiss, & Northrup, 1982) or are learned habits (Kaplan, 1983).

No reliable statistics are available on premature ejaculation in aging men. Starr and Weiner (1981) report that 16 percent of men over 60 had at least occasional difficulty reaching orgasm, and 9 percent experienced pain with intercourse.

Clinical experience suggests that low sexual desire is a common problem for both men and women in their later years. Some people have never been particularly interested in sex. Aging becomes an excuse to discontinue their marital obligation. Couple discrepancies in sexual desire may be exacerbated by renewed interest in sex on the part of the postmenopausal wife (Rubin, 1982). If an elderly man or woman enters a new sexual relationship, issues of low desire in one partner may become more problematic. Recently married older couples seem more apt to seek help for a desire problem than are partners in a long-term marriage.

Data on sexual dysfunction in older women are even more scarce than statistics on men. Kinsey, Pomeroy, Martin, and Gebhard (1953) found that only 65 percent of women in their late 50s could reach orgasm. In striking contrast, only 2 percent of a recent sample of unusually healthy and motivated community volunteers over 60 (Starr & Weiner, 1981) were unreliably orgasmic. In the same survey, dyspareunia occurred in 16 percent of women, an incidence lower than one might expect in a postmenopausal sample. A study at Rutgers Medical School reported dyspareunia in one-third of 42 postmenopausal women who remained sexually active but were not taking replacement estrogens (Bachmann, 1983). Again, the incidence of dysfunction of the desire or arousal phase of the sexual response cycle is unknown for older women.

In our own sexual rehabilitation program in a major cancer center, we have been interviewing men with bladder and prostate cancer and, when possible, have included their wives or lovers. The interviews take place before cancer treatment begins. Since this is an elderly group, varying widely in socioeconomic status, the data give an idea of rates of sexual problems, albeit somewhat biased in the dysfunctional direction by the husband's ill health.

A total of 53 men were interviewed, ranging in age from 38 to 78 (mean, 63 years) (Schover & von Eschenbach, 1983). Eighty-nine percent were married. Major sexual dysfunctions occurred with similar frequency in the bladder cancer versus prostate cancer groups. Although only 2 percent admitted to low sexual desire, 40 percent had erectile dysfunction. Erection problems were mild and intermittent in 10 percent and significant in 30 percent. The erection problems were positively correlated with age, as well as with the presence of non-cancer organic factors in a man's medical history that could affect erectile function. Thirteen percent reported premature ejaculation, and 9 percent complained of reduced intensity of orgasmic pleasure.

Among the wives, 28 percent had at least one sexual dysfunction, according to their own or their husband's report. Eleven percent had medical problems curtailing their sexual activity. Twenty-one percent had low sexual desire. Eight percent had difficulty getting aroused and lubricating vaginally, with 6 percent reporting dyspareunia. Eight percent were totally inorgasmic, and another 6 percent rarely could reach orgasm during intercourse.

Although the data reviewed cannot paint a detailed picture of sexual dysfunction in the elderly, they provide a distinct impression that sexual problems are a significant issue in this segment of the population.

Assessment of Sexual Problems in Older Adults

For the most part, assessment of sexual problems in older adults draws on evaluation techniques developed for younger individuals and couples (Kaplan, 1983; LoPiccolo & LoPiccolo, 1978; Meyer, Schmidt, & Wise, 1983). Some special skills and considerations can be helpful, however, in working with the sexual dysfunctions associated with aging. This section will suggest ways to combine interviews, questionnaires, and medical examinations into a comprehensive assessment package.

Interview Techniques

In my view, the sexual assessment interview is the most crucial part of the evaluation of an individual or couple. The interview has several purposes:

1. The patient or couple has a chance to express sexual concerns and to learn that the problem is remediable.
2. Each phase of the man's and woman's sexual response is assessed and a multi-axial diagnosis of sexual dysfunction is made (Schover et al., 1982).
3. The quality of the relationship is observed. Areas for evaluation include couple communication, expression of anger and caring, issues that cause conflict, and relationship strengths.
4. Each spouse's attitudes about sexuality become clear.
5. Each spouse's motivation to change and goals for sex therapy can be addressed.
6. The need for neuropsychological or psychiatric consultation is assessed.
7. The best choice of specialized medical consultation can be made, that is, gynecologic, urologic, endocrinologic, NPT monitoring.

Clinicians who have not been trained in sex therapy are advised to read Kaplan's (1983) text, *The Evaluation of Sexual Disorders* and LoPiccolo and LoPiccolo's (1978) *Handbook of Sex Therapy*. Role-playing with a friend or colleague is also helpful in increasing a clinician's comfort in handling sexual issues. There is no substitute, however, for direct supervision from an experienced colleague.

With older patients, special attention should be given to creating an atmosphere that is as comfortable as possible for discussing sex. It is not my intention to stereotype all older adults as sexually conservative. As with younger patients, their sexual attitudes and readiness to discuss a sexual problem vary widely. Many older adults seeking help for a sexual issue come straight to the point. Others, however, need a period of verbal "foreplay" before they are ready to discuss their sex lives.

Many older adults regard seeking psychotherapy as a stigma (Solomon, Faletti, & Yunik, 1982). Unless the patient or couple is very direct about their agenda, I usually begin by suggesting that they may feel hesitant to talk to a psychologist. I explain that even the most "normal" or "well-adjusted" adult can occasionally use some help in dealing with stressful life events. Although I know they have come to me because of a sexual problem, I would like to take a few minutes first to get to know each spouse as a person, and also to find out a little about their relationship. I ask about occupation, years married, children and grandchildren (an automatic icebreaker with most older adults!), leisure pursuits, social network, and physical health. It is particularly important to ask about symptoms of depression, sleep disorders, any deterioration of social or cognitive skills, and current use of alcohol, psychotropic medication, and pain killers.

I then elicit a brief relationship history, including any previous marriages and their outcomes, how the couple met each other, the qualities that attracted them to each other initially, and the reasons they have stayed together as a couple. If an older couple has married recently, it may help to know whether their children approved, if their income is adequate, and if they are living in one spouse's previous home (often a source of conflict) rather than in a new residence (McKain, 1972; Treas & Van Hilst, 1976).

I ask how each spouse expresses caring, both verbally and nonverbally. I also ask about the cues each gives when annoyed, and the issues that are sources of bickering or disagreement. The discussion of physical ways of showing affection can often lead into an assessment of sexuality.

INTERVIEWER:	As a couple, how much do you express affection by touch? Do you kiss good morning, or cuddle in front of the TV?
MRS. Y.:	Not very much. I would, but he never has.
INTERVIEWER:	(to Mr. Y.) Is that the way you see it?
MR. Y.:	Yes, I guess I've never been a real touchy person. I don't go in for a lot of kissing or hugging.
MRS. Y.:	His whole family is like that. Mine was much warmer. We always hugged and kissed our parents goodnight. His father would rarely even shake hands.
INTERVIEWER:	Mrs Y., have you ever wished Mr. Y was more romantic?
MRS. Y.:	Oh yes! But after 43 years, I've learned not to expect anything. He wants to do everything his way.
INTERVIEWER:	(to Mr. Y.) How do you express your caring for Mrs. Y.?
MR. Y.:	Well, I've worked hard, and I fix things around the house. I never went off drinking or with other women.
INTERVIEWER:	So you feel you've been a good husband, and Mrs. Y. should understand that you love her, without a lot of mushy stuff.
MR. Y.:	That's exactly right.
MRS. Y.:	Well, everyone likes to feel special once in a while.
INTERVIEWER:	Does Mr. Y. make you feel special when the two of you have sex?
MRS. Y.:	No, he's just as selfish then. He wants it when he wants it.
MR. Y.:	(crosses his arms and looks disgusted) Well, if I had to wait for you, we'd never have any.
INTERVIEWER:	It sounds like Mr. Y. is usually the one who starts things when it comes to sex. (Mr. and Mrs. Y. nod agreement.)
INTERVIEWER:	Mrs. Y., how can you tell when Mr. Y. is in the mood for sex?
MR. Y.	(harumphs and his wife laughs:) It's not hard to know.

INTERVIEWER: What does he do?

MRS. Y.: Oh, he just starts grabbing.

INTERVIEWER: Does he wait until you're in bed?

MRS. Y.: Usually. He wakes me up from sleeping, and then he grumbles if I'm not ready.

INTERVIEWER: Couples have all kinds of ways of touching and it helps me to know the kind of patterns you've worked out over the years. When Mr. Y. wakes you up, how and where does he touch you?

MRS. Y.: Oh, I don't know.

MR. Y.: I touch her breasts, usually. She used to like that when we were younger, but now she doesn't like anything I do.

MRS. Y.: Well, you don't do much! I swear it wouldn't matter to you if I slept right through it, as long as you were satisfied!

The interviewer can proceed into more explicit questions about sexual techniques and communication, giving each partner a chance to express his or her perspective on the couple's sex life. It is often easiest to begin with the least emotionally laden material, for example, how often the couple has sex, who initiates, and changes in sexual function over the years. Later the clinician can ask about techniques of caressing, masturbation, sexual jealousy, and knowledge of past affairs. When asking a difficult question, it is often helpful to preface it with a normalizing statement, letting the patient know that he or she will not be judged negatively, no matter what the answer.

INTERVIEWER: So your foreplay often includes Mr. G. caressing your breasts, or stroking your genital area, but you feel a little shy about touching his penis. It is also very common and normal to enjoy oral sex, though not every couple feels comfortable including it in their routine. What has been your experience with oral sex? (Note that an open-ended question was used, so that a simple "yes" or "no" would be insufficient as an answer.)

MR. G.: I might like it, but she won't hear of it.

MRS. G.: I was raised to think that was dirty, and I still feel that way.

INTERVIEWER: Have the two of you talked about your feelings
               about oral sex before?

MRS. G.:   Oh, he's hinted around a few times, but we haven't
               had a long conversation about it.

MR. G.:   We don't really talk a lot about sex.

The clinician should elicit enough information to diagnose dysfunctions in the desire, arousal, or orgasm phase of the sexual cycle for
each partner and also to delineate problems with coital pain and disagreements about sexual frequency or the variety of sexual activities
(Schover et al., 1982). Any traumatic incidents in the couple's relationship should be explored. Specific topics to cover are reviewed in
Schover (1982b).

I generally begin by interviewing the couple conjointly, giving the
clear message that sexual problems are relationship problems and letting each partner know that his or her perspective will be included. A
number of older couples live together, rather than marrying, because
they fear losing retirement benefits. If they are embarrassed about
being unmarried, I try to convey my acceptance of their status. I ask
whether they refer to each other as husband and wife, "boyfriend" and
"girlfriend," or by some other terms. If the patient is seen without a
partner, the same type of interview can be conducted. The main advantage of a couple interview is that it is very revealing about dyadic
communication and conflicts.

If I see partners together, I usually reserve a few minutes for
each individually. I often introduce this segment of the interview as
follows:

> I'd like to spend a few minutes with each of you alone. It's not that I
> think you have a lot of secrets from each other, but when it comes to
> sex, there are some areas that are just easier to discuss without your
> partner. I hold the information from this individual time in confidence. I
> may ask you if it would be OK to discuss something you said privately
> when all three of us are back together, but I won't bring anything up
> without your permission.

During the individual interviews, I may ask about attraction to
the partner, affairs, masturbation, homosexuality, unusual sexual preferences, and the content of sexual fantasies. If the couple is in a new
relationship, the split interview gives me a chance to find out whether
the current partner is being unfavorably compared to the previous

spouse. Widows and widowers often reveal such conflicts. In a more long-term relationship, sexual attraction may have diminished, but the spouse hesitates to admit his or her lack of interest to the partner. Although the split may leave the therapist with the responsibility of concealing a secret (Schover, 1982b), at least the couple's prognosis for treatment is as clearly defined as possible.

Since many professionals trained in sex therapy are young, one issue is whether the patient will feel comfortable with a clinician the age of his or her grandchildren. Changes in sexual mores over the years make therapist–patient age gaps particularly relevant in sex therapy. The impression made by the clinician at the first contact can be crucial in disarming the patient's suspicions about sex therapy and therapists.

I find it helpful to present myself as an expert professional. I use my title of "doctor" and address patients by their last name. When discussing sexuality, I use reasonably clinical terms, such as "intercourse," "penis," and "climax or orgasm," in preference to Latin or technical medical jargon or to sexual slang. When I know the patient better, I may become more informal, but at first I want to convey respect for each person's right to sexual health with dignity. Of course warmth and humor are appropriate at all stages of therapy.

Often patients apologize for being interested in sex "at my age." I use this as an opportunity to discuss myths about sexuality and aging. If a patient says that sex is no longer important in his or her life, I usually respond "Many older people do maintain active sex lives. There is nothing about age, in itself, that means you have to give up sex. Many others, though, find that sex is no longer important to them. They are also normal and healthy." Patients who initially deny any sexual desire often change their story when they know their sexual feelings will be seen as acceptable.

A patient may feel more confident if the clinician displays some familiarity with the special sexual problems of older adults. For example:

PATIENT: After my husband's heart attack, I was afraid that sex would be dangerous for him. He never seemed to be in the mood anymore either.

CLINICIAN: This is a very common problem for couples after a heart attack. Often the doctor doesn't give you any information about resuming sex, or if he does, he talks to your husband alone instead of the two of you together. Then each spouse feels afraid, but they don't discuss it with each other.

PATIENT: Oh yes, I can see that we fit right in.

CLINICIAN: Some simple education and discussion could proba-
             bly help each of you feel more relaxed about your
             sex life.

Clinicians may need to become aware of their own negative attitudes about sexuality in the elderly. Young clinicians may have trouble
regarding a person with wrinkles and gray hair as sexual. Watching and
discussing films about sexuality and aging,* including *Ripple in Time,
Rose by Any Other Name,* and *Love in Later Life,* can help in examining one's own feelings. The clinician may also imagine how he/she will
feel about sex in future years. I see no reason why a sensitive and
competent clinician of any age cannot provide effective sex therapy for
an elderly patient.

It is wise to allow 1½ to 2 hours for the initial assessment interview. This can be accomplished either in one session or spread across
two separate days. I usually prefer one session, if the patient has the
stamina, since we can arrive at some closure by the end. The interview
should conclude with an agreement on some concrete and specific
behavioral changes that the individual or couple wants to make and
with feedback on the types of treatment options available.

Questionnaire Assessment

Although many paper-and-pencil inventories are undoubtedly useful
and valid as research tools, they may not help a clinician working with
older adults to plan treatment for sexual dysfunction. A questionnaire
is useful in the present context if it elicits information difficult to
obtain from an interview or if it obviates the clinician's spending additional, expensive time in face-to-face assessment. Questionnaires also
can provide an objective measure of symptom change from pre- to
post-therapy.

Several well-validated and helpful inventories are available to the
sex therapist, but none is specifically geared for older adults. The most
comprehensive is the Derogatis Sexual Function Inventory (DSFI)
(Meyer et al., 1983). It includes sections on sexual knowledge, sexual

---

*Available from the Multi-Media Resource Center, 1525 Franklin St., San Francisco,
CA 94109.

attitudes, psychological symptoms, positive and negative affect, gender role, sexual fantasy, body image, and sexual satisfaction. One weakness of the DSFI is the lack of a scale measuring behavioral sexual dysfunction. The norms for the DSFI are also based on groups with a mean age in the early 30s (Derogatis & Meyer, 1979). An older adult's scores may appear dysfunctional when compared to this inappropriate reference group. The DSFI is also long. Some elderly patients may get fatigued or have difficulty understanding the instructions.

A briefer inventory that provides information more relevant for behavioral sex therapy is the Sexual Interaction Inventory (SII) (Lo-Piccolo & Steger, 1978). The SII scores depend on both partners' responses to items concerning 17 types of sexual activity. Patients indicate actual and ideal frequencies for engaging in each activity as well as their own and their partner's actual and ideal pleasure from the activity. Subscales derived from these responses assess the accuracy of each partner's perception of the other's preferences, each partner's general level of pleasure, acceptance of one's own sexual enjoyment, acceptance of the mate's pleasure levels, dissatisfaction with the frequency of various activities, and the couple's overall sexual disagreement.

The SII norms, too, are based on a sample of young to middle-aged couples. Older patients who are conservative about the variety of caresses they enjoy may appear to be maladjusted in terms of pleasure levels, even though each partner is satisfied with his or her narrow range of behaviors. The SII also may be offensive to some elderly patients, particularly if administered before their initial therapy session. The questionnaire includes a drawing of each sexual activity. The illustrations ensure that the patient understands the event in question, but may be too explicit for some couples. The emotional impact of the SII can be softened if it is presented by the therapist after rapport has been established, with the caveat that it is "x-rated." Patients can be reminded that couples vary tremendously in the sexual activities they find comfortable, and that in answering the SII they should be honest about their preferences rather than try to conform to some artificial standard of sexual conduct.

I often find it helpful to have each partner fill out a brief multiple-choice questionnaire about sexual function, the Sex History Form (SHF) (Schover et al., 1982), before the initial assessment interview. The SHF provides enough information to make a preliminary sexual-problem diagnosis and is a helpful guide for the interview. As with previously cited questionnaires, the normative sample for the

SHF was composed primarily of young research subjects. For clinical purposes, however, the norms are not crucial. It is helpful to know that a man has difficulty maintaining erections in 75 percent of his sexual encounters, even if erection problems are not prevalent in men his age.

One sexual questionnaire has been specifically designed for elderly men and women (White, 1982a). Its scales measure knowledge about sex and aging and attitudes toward sex and the elderly. Although this instrument is suited to research with large groups, I do not believe it would help a clinician to plan treatment for an individual's or a couple's sexual problem.

In assessing the quality of a marriage relationship, the Dyadic Adjustment Inventory (DAI) (Spanier, 1976) can be helpful. It yields a global marital satisfaction score. Individual items also reveal areas of conflict in the relationship. The normative sample for the DAI had a mean age of about 35. Although one might expect that age would not affect self-reports of relationship happiness, my clinical impression is that older couples exhibit more social-desirability bias in filling out the DAI. I have seen couples who clearly had been miserable for decades in long-term marriages whose DAI scores were in the normal range.

Other inventories can be used in individual cases to assess psychopathology or cognitive deficits that could interfere with the success of sex therapy. A detailed consideration of such instruments is beyond the scope of this chapter. Even when a sexual dysfunction is the presenting problem, however, it is especially important to look for depression and cognitive changes, using brief, problem-focused assessments (Solomon et al., 1982).

Medical Assessment

For most sexual dysfunctions in older patients, a complete medical examination is an indispensable part of the evaluation. Changes in a man's erectile or orgasmic function can be symptoms of diabetes or multiple sclerosis. Loss of sexual desire in a man or woman can signal a hormonal abnormality or debilitation from an undiagnosed systemic illness. Dyspareunia can result from a variety of gynecologic diseases. A responsible sex therapist requires a recent physical examination before treating most sexual symptoms, particularly new dysfunctions in a person who has previously been sexually adequate.

The clinician evaluating a sexual problem can glean important information from the patient's history of major illnesses and surgery, current prescription medications, and alcohol, tobacco, and tranquilizer use. Many of the diseases associated with aging and the medications used to treat them affect sexual function (Kaplan, 1983; Kolodny et al., 1979; Wagner & Green, 1981). The clinician should stay familiar with the burgeoning sexual medicine literature so that medical factors are not overlooked in making treatment decisions.

The clinician can take an active role in referring the patient for specialized medical evaluations. For women the choices are limited. Most problems involving pelvic pain or vaginal dryness are best referred to a gynecologist. Unfortunately, many gynecologists have little interest or expertise in sexual problems. Clinicians should be aware of good referrals in their community. Occasionally an endocrinologist may be helpful in assessing symptoms of menopause or loss of sexual desire.

In the past 5 to 10 years, a wide array of diagnostic examinations has been developed to find the cause of an erection problem (Wagner & Green, 1981). In men older than 50 the contribution of organic causes becomes major, so that some specific screening examinations are crucial in planning appropriate treatment. As we will see, in addition to behavioral sex therapy, our armamentarium now includes hormonal therapy, as well as revascularization and penile prosthesis surgery. Many urologists now perform a comprehensive examination for erectile dysfunction. Sexual dysfunction clinics also offer such services.

In addition to performing a thorough physical examination and routine blood tests,, the physician should check the integrity of the pelvic vascular system. Vascular insufficiency is probably the most common organic cause of erection problems in men over 50. Arteriosclerosis in the pelvic or penile arteries can reduce blood flow to the penis (Wagner & Green, 1981; Virag, 1982a). Risk factors for this condition include diabetes (Jevtich, Edson, Jarman, & Herrera, 1982; Ruzbarsky & Michal, 1977), pelvic radiotherapy for cancer (Goldstein, Feldman, Deckers, Siroky, & Krane, 1982), radical pelvic cancer surgery (Bergman, Silvertsson, & Suurkala, 1982), aorto iliac surgery (Flanigan, Schuler, Keifer, Schwartz, & Lim, 1982), and smoking (Jarman, Edson, & Elist 1982; Wagner & Green, 1981). Penile blood pressure or pulse measurements may reveal these deficits (Wagner & Green, 1981). The blood pressure or pulse in the penis is measured with a special strain gauge sensor or Doppler stethoscope and is then compared to similar measurements taken from the arm. If the results indicate vascular insufficiency, the pelvic blood vessels can be visualized by arteriography, usually performed under a general anesthetic (Juhan, Padula, & Huguet, 1982; Wagner & Green, 1981). The cavernous bodies and venous drainage system of the penis can also be seen on an x-ray when dye is pumped directly into the erectile tissue, creating an artificial erection. These invasive tests carry a risk of serious side effects and are mainly used in planning vascular surgery. If sex therapy or a penile prosthesis are the only treatment options being considered, detailed studies of the pelvic blood vessels are probably unjustified.

The neurologic component of the erection response should also be assessed (Wagner & Green, 1981). The autonomic nervous system controls blood flow to the penis. Erection problems may occur after damage to important pathways at any point from cortex to penis. The most common culprits are sacral spinal cord injuries (Amelar & Dubin, 1982), or such pelvic cancer surgery as radical prostatectomy (Walsh & Donker, 1982), radical cystectomy (Bergman, Nilsson, & Peterson, 1979), or abdominoperineal resection (Yaeger & Van Heerden, 1980). Some chronic illnesses, including diabetes (Jevtich et al., 1982), obstructive lung disease (Fletcher & Martin, 1982), and alcoholism (Wagner & Green, 1981), can also damage the parasympathetic and sympathetic fibers. Most antihypertensive medications (Moss & Procci, 1982) have sexual side effects because they interfere with neurotransmission in the parasympathetic or sympathetic pathways. Tricyclic antidepressants and monoamine oxidase inhibitors can have similar effects on erection. Given the tremendous numbers of medications often prescribed for the elderly, drug effects should always be assessed when a man complains of erectile dysfunction.

A few older men have erection problems that can be traced to a loss of sensation on the penile skin. Minor decreases in genital sensation seem to be common with aging (Wagner & Green, 1981). A significant loss of tactile pleasure is rare, however, except after spinal cord injury or with severe diabetic neuropathy, neurologic diseases such as multiple sclerosis (Goldstein, Siroky, Sax, & Krane, 1982), or local trauma.

The physician can elicit several genital reflexes and measure sensory thresholds on the skin of the penis. The speed of the bulbocavernosus reflex can be measured with an electromyograph. If the reflex is abnormally slow or absent, the nerves involved in erection may be damaged (Wagner & Green, 1981).

In making decisions about the organic versus psychogenic nature of an erection problem, monitoring of nocturnal erections has been the most accepted diagnostic test (Marshall, Morales, & Surridge, 1982; Wagner & Green, 1981). A full sleep-laboratory evaluation includes not only continuously measuring the changes in the circumference of the penis during the night but also monitoring to make sure that REM sleep and respiration are normal. The normality of the sleep erections, indicating a psychological cause for an erection problem, is determined by the size of the penis, its shape and rigidity, and the duration of the erection episodes.

Since sleep-laboratory evaluations are expensive and often not covered by insurance, several abbreviated screening methods for NPT have been tried. One group of researchers (Ek, Bradley, & Krane, 1982) have created a "snap-gauge" that fits snugly around the penis. If a man has a rigid sleep erection, three plastic snaps on the gauge break; partial erection breaks only one or two snaps. Of course this test provides no information about the shape or duration of the erection, which can lead to a false assumption of normality. A diagnosis implicating an organic cause could also be erroneous if, for example, the lack of erection resulted from disturbed sleep. An even more primitive form of erection monitoring is the stamp test (Barry, Blank, & Boileau, 1980), which substitutes a ring of special stamps for the snap gauge. If the stamps tear, the NPT is considered adequate. Although the stamp test has some utility as a first step in screening, surprisingly some insurance companies accept it as proof that an erection problem is organic and should be treated with a penile prosthesis.

Hormonal abnormalities are fairly common in men with erectile dysfunction. A low testosterone level was seen in 15 percent of such patients in two sex therapy clinics (Schwartz, Bauman, & Masters, 1982; Segraves, Schoenberg, & Ivanoff, 1983), in 19 percent of sexually dysfunctional men in a VA outpatient clinic (Slag, Morley, & Elson, 1983), and in a full 28 percent of men with erection problems seen at an endocrine clinic (Spark, White, & Connolly, 1980). Rates of hyperprolactinemia (overproduction of prolactin by the pituitary), another hormonal cause of sexual dysfunction, ranged from 0 to 8 percent in the same four series.

Both low testosterone and high prolactin are associated with health problems that become more common with aging, including alcohol abuse, thyroid abnormalities, hormone treatment for metastatic prostate cancer, renal dialysis, and medications such as cimetidine, antihypertensives, digoxin, tricyclic antidepressants, and major tranquilizers.

The diagnosis of hormonal deficits in both men and women has been revolutionized by radioimmune assays, which can accurately measure tiny amounts of circulating hormones (Spark, 1983). Men with erection problems, particularly when accompanied by low sexual desire, should have screening blood tests for serum testosterone and prolactin. Given the wide variation of a man's hormone levels on an hourly, daily, weekly, and even seasonal basis, one test value is not definitive but can indicate the need for a further hormonal workup.

The clinician who coordinates the sexual assessment may be a physician, psychologist, or other health professional. No matter what his/her specialty is, however, the clinician should understand the meaning of the medical test results. The clinician's job is to integrate the medical, interview, and questionnaire data into patient feedback, couched in language that the patient can understand. Only then can the patient make an informed decision about pursuing recommended treatments.

Intervention in Sexual Problems of Older Adults

This section reviews issues in intervention in older adults' sexual problems. We will examine problems in care delivery, look at strategies for reaching out to the elderly in the community, and summarize the state of the art in both sex therapy and medical treatments.

Community Outreach: Sexuality and the Elderly

Despite all the media attention given to sexuality and sexual problems over the past decade, older men and women rarely seek sex therapy. When the entire sample of couples seen over a 10-year period at the Johns Hopkins sexual dysfunction clinic was examined, only 3 percent were found to be 60 or older, and none was over 70 (Wise, 1983), although treatment success appeared to be similar for older and younger patients. In Masters and Johnson's (1970) first 6 years of practice, 26 percent of couples contained one partner older than 50, but only 10 percent included a spouse over 60. Masters and Johnson documented a higher failure rate for sex therapy with older couples: if the husband was over 50, he had a 25 percent chance of failing to reverse his symptoms, and 41 percent of women over 50 failed to improve. Some of these failures may be attributed to undiagnosed organic factors, however, since sophisticated medical assessments of sexual function were not available in the 1960s.

Older men, in particular, often search for a medical solution to a sexual problem in preference to trying counseling. In a sexual dysfunction clinic within the urology department at University of California, San Francisco, 38 percent of patients were 50 years or older, including 27 percent aged 60 or above (Finkle & Jackson, 1982). The medical orientation of this clinic may have contributed to this higher proportion of elderly patients. The clinic at the University of Chicago (Segraves, Schoenberg, Zarins, Knopf, & Camic, 1982) offered a multidisciplinary sexual evaluation, but men with erection problems could enter the system by calling either the Psychiatry Department or the Urology Department. Sixty-two percent consulted the urologist, and of this group 38 percent refused to visit the psychiatrist as part of their workup. The authors mentioned that the mean age of the urology-referred men was 50 years.

Thus clinicians wishing to provide sexual counseling to elderly patients may need to reach out to the community with educational programs or sexual enrichment groups geared specifically for senior citizens.

Several goals should be kept in mind:

1. Educate potential therapy consumers about the normal sexual response cycle and the variety and efficacy of treatments available for sexual dysfunctions in older adults.
2. Counter the stereotypes that only severely disturbed people can benefit from counseling and that older adults should not be distressed by a sexual problem.
3. Emphasize that some older adults prefer not to be sexually active. Both celibacy and continued sexual activity can be adaptive. Each person's choice should be respected.
4. Offer services that are affordable by older adults on fixed incomes.

Public lectures are a good way to promote sexual health for senior citizens. Groups who are glad to have expert speakers include senior citizens' centers, organizations of retired persons, and local chapters of national groups for persons with cardiac disease, diabetes, Parkinson's disease, and cancer, and for their families. In my experience, the audiences are lively and interested in dispelling myths about sexuality and the elderly. Of course, the lecture should provide helpful and accurate information, rather than be a mere advertisement for clinical services.

Physicians and allied health care professionals such as nurses and social workers may also be receptive to a presentation at weekly rounds, or at monthly meetings of a professional society. Such an educational lecture can not only improve the quality of patient care, but also increase a clinician's therapy referrals. A physician's reluctance to ask patients about sexual function often reflects a lack of knowledge about how to treat a problem once it is diagnosed. With the knowledge that a competent specialist is available, primary-care physicians may be more interested in assessing sexual problems.

Hospitals and clinics may provide sexual enrichment programs or therapy especially geared for older adults. Sviland (1978) describes a "flood of couples" over 60 who wanted to be part of a hospital-based sexual enrichment program. A weekend enrichment group might be a useful place to start.

Some older adults can benefit from educational reading materials about sex. Several self-help books of general interest are available. For women, *Becoming Orgasmic* (Heiman, LoPiccolo, & LoPiccolo, 1976), *For Yourself* (Barbach, 1975), and *For Each Other* (Barbach, 1982) provide solid and helpful information. Unfortunately, however, they are written for younger women and include little discussion of menopause or of the special difficulty an elderly woman may have in becoming comfortable with self-stimulation or noncoital partner caressing. For men, *Male Sexuality* (Zilbergeld, 1978) provides excellent self-help programs for dealing with mild sexual dysfunctions. My own book, *Prime Time: Sexual Health for Men over Fifty* (Schover, 1984) presents information about normal sexual function and aging in men and women and about the medical and psychological causes of and treatment for sexual problems in older men.

Sex Therapy for Older Adults

The behavioral sex therapy treatment programs for specific dysfunctions can, of course, be applied to the problems of older patients. Clinicians unfamiliar with basic sex therapy are referred to texts by Kaplan (1974, 1979), Leiblum and Pervin (1980), and LoPiccolo and LoPiccolo (1978). Some modifications in format may be needed, however, in working with older couples.

Many sex therapists begin treatment by taking a chronological sex history individually with each partner. With older patients, the discussion of childhood and adolescence should be shortened and more attention paid to the evaluation of the patient's sex life over the adult years. Otherwise the sex history may take hours and become frustrating for a patient who prefers to focus on the current problem.

One intervention that should always be included in sexual counseling with older adults is a sex education session. Using pictures or three-dimensional models of the genitals,* the clinician explains the function of each part of the genitals, summarizes the sexual response cycle, and describes how it changes with aging. Many older men and women have little understanding of their own bodies and no information about the minor sexual slowing that occurs with normal senescence. If a medical factor is contributing to a sexual dysfunction, for instance, organic causes for erectile dysfunction or postmenopausal dyspareunia, the clinician can explain exactly what has gone wrong and detail the risks and benefits of medical treatment.

The education session helps the patient to formulate realistic treatment goals. It may not be sensible to expect instant, 100 percent erections at age 75, or to hope that sex therapy will restore vaginal lubrication in an older woman. Sometimes the couple wishes to become comfortable with a wider range of noncoital caressing, so that their sexual routine is less centered on intercourse. The sensate focus exercises (Kaplan, 1975; Masters & Johnson, 1970) are invaluable in promoting this kind of attitude and behavioral change. Books and movies may also be helpful adjuncts to in-session discussion.

Specific behavioral homework exercises have been developed for the sexual dysfunctions (Kaplan, 1974; Leiblum & Pervin, 1980; LoPiccolo, 1978). These can be adapted for use with older patients.

An example is sex therapy for erectile dysfunction. In young men, or older men without organic impairment, the goal is to restore reliable, firm erections. Even if an erection problem has some organic basis, however, sex therapy can help the couple enjoy mutual noncoital stimulation to orgasm. With less pressure to attain full erections and more time spent on caressing, a man may still be able to achieve enough tumescence for penetration.

The treatment program (Kaplan & Moodie, 1982; Schover, 1984)

---

*Good models are produced by Jim Jackson & Co., 33 Richdale Ave., Cambridge, MA 02140.

usually includes sensate focus exercises gradually progressing toward intercourse; cognitive behavioral interventions such as the use of fantasy and coping self-statements; and practice in achieving, losing, and regaining erections. If a man is comfortable with masturbation, many of the homework exercises are completed on an individual basis first, before the partners try them together. Many elderly men and women reject masturbation as an option. If gentle attitude change is ineffective, the therapist should tailor the homework to couple activities, rather than forcing the issue.

Although premature ejaculation grows less common with age, a number of men have a lifelong problem with it. If they have compensated by achieving a second erection and thus prolonging intercourse, the lengthening refractory period can cause renewed distress in the later years. The stop–start or squeeze techniques are highly successful in helping men learn to delay ejaculation. Both treatment methods involve teaching the man to monitor his arousal. Before he reaches the point of ejaculatory inevitability, he or his partner either simply stops the stimulation, or actually squeezes the penis to reduce arousal and delay ejaculation. Variations of these exercises are discussed in Perelman (1980) and should be part of the repertoire of every sex therapist.

For men who have developed the syndrome of ejaculation with a flaccid penis, Kaplan (1983) reports enhancing orgasm by teaching men to delay ejaculation until they have a full erection. In a technique similar to the stop–start method, the patient stimulates himself or is stimulated by a partner, but does not continue the caressing to orgasm unless his erection is firm

Treatment techniques for low sexual desire have been discussed by Kaplan (1979) and Schover (1982a). Goals of therapy, irrespective of the patient's age, include removing pressure to perform, increasing the patient's attention to erotic stimuli, and resolving the marital conflict which often contributes to this sexual dysfunction.

Treatment programs to increase sexual arousal and orgasmic capacity in women have depended heavily on masturbation exercises (LoPiccolo & Lobitz, 1978; McGovern, McMullen, & LoPiccolo, 1978). As with therapy for erectile dysfunction, the focus on self-stimulation may need to be altered for older couples. In contrast to young women who complain of difficulty reaching orgasm during intercourse, older women often need help in learning to have orgasms through noncoital stimulation, especially if aging interferes with vigorous, intercourse-centered sex. Older men often are skeptical that a woman can feel satisfied with noncoital orgasms. They fear their wives will seek extramarital affairs if the husband cannot "perform." The wives are affronted by this lack of trust, but are also embarrassed and ashamed to be touched or kissed on the genitals, or to provide penile caressing. The therapist needs considerable patience and diplomacy in teaching such couples, through sensate focus exercises and educational materials, that old dogs *can* learn new tricks.

Dyspareunia in postmenopausal women should be managed as conservatively as possible. Hormonal therapy may not be necessary if the couple can learn to increase the woman's arousal through extensive foreplay and to use a water-based gel for extra vaginal lubrication. Applying the gel can become a part of the mutual pleasuring. Women may benefit from learning to relax their pubococcygeal muscles with Kegel exercises (Heiman et al., 1976). Kegels involve gaining voluntary control over the muscles that surround the vaginal entrance. Once the woman has learned to contract the muscles, she also can recognize the difference between tension and relaxation. A few women may need to work with a series of graduated vaginal dilators (Leiblum, Pervin, & Campbell, 1980), or go through a course of systematic desensitization (Lazarus, 1980) in order to feel relaxed again during intercourse.

One final target for behavioral intervention is the problem of the demented elderly person who is inappropriately sexual. A literature search revealed few data on the incidence of such symptoms in the demented, though Wise (1983) ascribes them to frontal lobe damage as opposed to sexual apathy seen in persons with more global cortical atrophy. A combination of neuroleptic medication and restructuring of the environment to extinguish inappropriate sexual advances and to increase alternate sources of reinforcement may help.

Many older couples prefer medical treatment to counseling, particularly in dealing with an erection problem. The sex therapist can still help by guiding the couple's choice of medical therapy, by promoting clear couple communication while they are making that choice, and by helping the partners adjust sexually after medical treatment. As the case history in the final section of this chapter illustrates, sexual counseling in conjunction with medical treatments is often short term. Follow-up sessions at standard intervals after medical treatment can help patients maintain an improvement in the quality of their sex lives. First, however, each clinician needs a working knowledge of medical treatments available for sexual dysfunctions in older adults.

Medical Treatments for
Sexual Problems

An in-depth description of medical therapy for sexual problems is beyond the scope of this chapter. I will present a brief summary of each type of treatment, however, and provide references for the clinician who would like a more thorough grounding.

Hormone Replacement Therapy for Women. Women whose vaginas appear atrophied on pelvic examination and who complain of lack of vaginal lubrication and painful intercourse may be helped by hormone replacement therapy, particularly if conservative behavioral treatment is unsuccessful.

Currently, the high doses of estrogen used during the 1960s and 1970s are not considered necessary. Either a local estrogen cream or low-dose estrogen combined with progesterone are usually sufficient to alleviate such symptoms of menopause as hot flashes and vaginal atrophy and to prevent osteoporosis. One recent study (Leiblum et al., 1983) suggests that vaginal atrophy is not correlated with the estrogen levels of untreated postmenopausal women, but rather with the level of circulating androgens. If replicated, this research may have implications for hormone therapy. Replacement estrogens, if used for over two years, do increase a woman's risk of uterine cancer. Correlations with breast cancer are still controversial. Gall bladder disease is also increased, but no changes have been demonstrated in the incidence of cardiovascular disease with replacement estrogens (American Council on Science and Health, 1983).

Can replacement estrogens increase a woman's desire for sex? Dennerstein and Burrows (1982) observed increased sexual desire and arousability when women whose ovaries had been surgically removed were given estrogen rather than placebo. Natural menopause does not cause as abrupt and severe an estrogen deficiency as oophorectomy, however, so results may not generalize to postmenopausal women. As was mentioned previously, research by Persky et al. (1982) failed to identify a major loss of sexual pleasure in postmenopausal women, despite their lower serum androgen levels. Given our current state of knowledge, replacement estrogens should probably be reserved for vaginal atrophy rather than prescribed for low sexual desire.

Hormone Therapy for Older Men. One very common physician error is to prescribe replacement testosterone without even ordering a screening blood test when an older man complains of erection problems. If a man already has normal hormone levels, as is usually the case, replacement testosterone does not cure his erection problem and actually produces worse results than a placebo (Benkert, Witt, Adam, & Leitz, 1979; Salmimies, Kockott, Pirke, Vogt, & Schill, 1982). The extra testosterone may give a slight boost to a man's sexual desire, leaving him even more frustrated than ever with his lack of erections. In addition, unnecessary testosterone therapy may have serious side effects such as activating an occult prostate cancer, interfering with the man's natural testosterone production, inducing hypercalcemia, and causing liver damage.

When an older man actually does have an abnormally low level of testosterone, replacement therapy may help resolve low sexual desire, erectile dysfunction, or difficulty reaching orgasm (Spark et al., 1980). These symptoms are occasionally also the result of an abnormally high level of prolactin. Hyperprolactinemia can be successfully treated by surgery to remove a pituitary tumor, or by bromocriptine, a drug that blocks the production of prolactin. The sexual dysfunction often resolves with appropriate hormone treatment (Schwartz et al., 1982). For some couples, however, particularly after years of sexual problems, sex therapy must be combined with hormonal therapy to completely restore sexual function. Problems of erection and orgasm in older men also often have multiple organic causes. If a vascular or neurologic deficit exists, the patient may be a candidate for a penile prosthesis.

Surgery to Implant a Penile Prosthesis. Penile prostheses are rapidly gaining popularity. Two basic types are available. The semirigid prosthesis consists of two silicone rods implanted in the twin cavernous bodies that form the erectile tissue in the penile shaft. The result is a permanent erection, rigid enough for intercourse but flexible enough to hide cosmetically. Several versions of the semirigid prosthesis are now available. The Finney flexirod is hinged for easier concealment (Finney, 1982). The Jonas prosthesis has a core of silver wire in each rod so that the penis can assume a straight position for intercourse but be bent into a less obtrusive curve during nonsexual activities (Bennett, 1982). The semirigid prostheses have a 90 to 95 percent rate of technical success (Wagner & Green, 1981).

The second type of prosthesis is inflatable (Bennett, 1982). The inflatable prosthesis currently in use consists of two silicone cylinders implanted in the cavernous bodies and connected inside the pelvis with tubing to a small pump in the scrotum and to a reservoir positioned under the abdominal muscles. The reservoir is filled with saline solution. When it is full, and the cylinders in the penis are empty, the penis is flaccid. When the man desires an erection, he or his partner locates the pump inside the scrotum and squeezes it 10 to 15 times, inflating the cylinders with saline solution. The shaft of the penis becomes fully rigid, staying erect until a release valve on the bottom of the pump is pressed. The fluid then returns to the reservoir. The inflatable prosthesis has a higher rate of complications than the semirigid one because it has more parts to break. Reoperation rates have been reported to be between 6 percent (Furlow, 1981) and 44 percent (Kaufman, Lindner, & Raz, 1982). A new and simpler inflatable prosthesis is currently being readied for general use (Finney, 1983).

Although the surgery necessary to insert a penile prosthesis is considered minor, can be performed under local anesthetic (Kaufman, Lindner, & Raz, 1982), and entails few complications, it can be followed by infection (sometimes requiring removal of the prosthesis), erosion of penile tissue by the semirigid rods, and long-term pain. Once either type of prosthesis has been inserted, a man will not be able to recover natural, full erections if it is removed. Patients need to understand these drawbacks clearly, as well as to realize that the prosthesis will not improve penile sensation, orgasm, or the desire for sex.

Men often see the prosthesis as an easy answer to an erection problem. Sadly enough, wives or sexual partners are often not included either in the decision to have the operation or in the physician's explanations of the process. Advice on incorporating the prosthesis into a couple's sexual routine is rarely given. The case example in this chapter illustrates the way sexual counseling can enhance a couple's satisfaction with the prosthesis. A guide for patients interested in this procedure, which includes suggestions on making an informed decision and getting used to the new prosthesis, may be found in *Prime Time: Sexual Health for Men over Fifty* (Schover, 1984).

Revascularization Surgery for Erection Problems. If an erection problem is caused solely by vascular disease, a physician may suggest a new surgical procedure to increase baseline blood flow to the penis (Virag, 1982b). If circulation is adequate in the nonaroused state, erection becomes possible when autonomic nerves signal for rapid arterial inflow. When the large central aorta or iliac arteries are blocked, vascular surgery can restore erectile function, along with improvement in circulation to the legs, about one-third of the time (Flanigan et al., 1982). In the more common case, however, where the arteriosclerosis is in the smaller arteries closer to the penis, new experimental bypass surgery has had disappointing results (Wagner & Green, 1981; Zorgniotti, 1982). Often it results in too much blood flow, which produces priapism (a permanent erection that damages the penile tissue), or the new bypass scars or clots shut. Until such time as these techniques are perfected, the man who chooses revascularization surgery is gambling against very unfavorable odds. The follow-up data are also still sparse on surgery to correct abnormal venous drainage from the penis (Virag, 1982b). Nevertheless, these operations continue to have an appeal because they promise a "natural" correction of the erection problem, in contrast to the artificial penile prosthesis.

Case Illustration

Mr. J., a 74-year-old retired insurance salesman, was referred to me along with Mrs. J., age 70, who had worked for many years as a secretary. They had been married for 40 years. Mr. J. wanted to have a penile prosthesis inserted, but his wife was opposed to the idea.

Mr. J. had been having mild erectile dysfunction for 15 years. He had had coronary bypass surgery 10 years before and had been taking propranolol since that time. The couple continued to have sexual activity about once every two weeks, although Mrs. J. had never been as interested in sex as her husband. She labeled herself as "neurotic and inhibited." Mr. J. was always the sexual initiator, and his wife often refused to have sex. When she was in a sexual mood, however, she had no difficulty with arousal or vaginal lubrication, even after menopause, and was usually orgasmic during intercourse.

One year prior to my assessment, Mr. J. had been treated for bladder cancer with radical cystectomy, that is, surgical removal of the bladder, prostate, seminal vesicles, and posterior urethra. As is typical, his erectile dysfunction worsened after the operation, which damages the parasympathetic nerves surrounding the prostate. He no longer could obtain more than the most partial erection. The couple continued noncoital caressing, although even less frequently than their sexual activity before cystectomy. They learned to cope with Mr. J.'s urinary ostomy appliance during sex. Mrs. J. was orgasmic on these occasions. Mr. J. could still experience the sensation of orgasm, but it was weak and centered in his lower back rather than in his penis. No semen was ejaculated, of course, since the prostate and seminal vesicles that manufacture the fluid had been removed.

Mr. J. still felt as much desire for sex as always, but hesitated to initiate it. Mrs. J. expressed relief at the cooling of their sex life, which annoyed her husband. Mrs. J. did feel upset, however, by her husband's social withdrawal since the surgery. Instead of going square dancing, which she enjoyed despite her arthritis, he would "sit in his rocking chair like an old granny." He also was uncharacteristically irritable. He complained of insomnia and mild difficulty with memory. He had trouble following square dance calls or filling out his income tax forms. Although I believed that Mr. J. was depressed, he did not see himself in that light and refused to consider antidepressant medication.

It was clear that Mr. J. was dissatisfied with the sexual function possible to him. The couple had tried extensive noncoital stimulation, with no improvement in Mr. J.'s erections. Since a penile prosthesis appeared to be the only chance of restoring erections, I gave a detailed explanation of the surgical procedure to the couple. Mrs. J.'s major fear had been that the surgery might reactivate Mr. J.'s cancer or be a significant cardiac risk. She felt reassured when she understood the procedure more fully. She also thought Mr. J. was a bit foolish to be so concerned about sex at age 74. She knew, however, that the cystectomy had left her husband feeling that he was no longer a whole person. If a penile prosthesis would give him some "get up and go," she was willing to resume a more active sex life.

Mr. J.'s urologist felt he would be a good surgical candidate. A semirigid prosthesis of the simplest Small-Carrion type was implanted. During the surgical recovery period, Mr. J. took great delight in making seductive jokes to the nurses. Since he was a warm and humorous person, his role of "dirty old man" was generally greeted with amusement rather than anger. When I went to visit him in his room, he insisted on showing me the excellent cosmetic result of his surgery. I decided to react with calm acceptance, rather than to refuse to look or to interpret the meaning of his behavior. Mrs. J. stayed with her husband during the hospitalization. She rarely seemed embarrassed by his behavior, but was in general more reserved than her husband. Mr. J. seemed to be testing all of us to see whether his sexuality would be accepted.

I next saw Mr. J. when he returned alone for a follow-up examination, 10 weeks after surgery. He was proud of his erect penis, and in fact had decided that the elasticized briefs we recommended for concealment were too confining. He wore boxer shorts so that his erection made a slight bulge in his inner pants leg when he sat down. Mr. J. was disappointed, however, by his sexual function. The couple had tried having intercourse three times. Although Mrs. J. was cooperative, she was unenthusiastic, and had not been orgasmic. Mr. J. feared that his penis was too small to give his wife pleasure. He himself was able to have a weak orgasm, still unsatisfactory to him, after 15 to 20 minutes of intercourse.

Although we discussed the lack of importance of penis size in a woman's reaching orgasm, this session focused on the emotional quality of the couple's sexual interaction. Mr. J. was making sex into work. He watched his wife's reactions minutely and secretly resented her "clumsiness" in stimulating his penis during foreplay. I suggested that the couple inject some playfulness and romance into their sexual routine. I asked Mr. J. when he had last brought his wife flowers or written her a love note. He looked at me in astonishment. "At our age? She'd think I was nuts!" I advised the couple to try a sensate focus exercise, spending a long time exchanging caresses, without going on to intercourse or orgasm. Since the couple lived several hundred miles from the hospital, I could not see them weekly, as I would have preferred. I sent written instructions for the exercise home with Mr. J. and asked him to call if the sexual problems persisted.

I next saw Mr. and Mrs. J. three months later. Mr. J. brought some camellias from his greenhouse for our clinic staff, offering me first choice. Although the couple had discussed the sensate focus exercise, they had not tried it. Instead they had, in Mrs. J.'s words, "gotten down to business." Mrs. J. was now orgasmic with intercourse, which was taking place weekly. It took her a little longer to reach orgasm than in previous years, but she found herself more able to match her husband's sexual desire. Mr. J. was having orgasms that felt more normal in intensity and were centered in his penis. The couple attributed these improvements to practice and to healing of the postsurgical soreness. In the previous weeks, however, Mr. J. had developed some chest pain and fatigue. He was diagnosed as anemic. He appeared a bit more depressed. We discussed ways to deal with his depression behaviorally, with a program of light exercise and more social activity, along with better sleep hygiene.

Mr. J.'s enjoyment of sex continued for two more months. The next time I saw him, we discussed his fear of dying from a coital heart attack. He sometimes became breathless during intercourse and then had trouble reaching orgasm. I tried to reassure him about the safety of intercourse and suggested that he focus on his pleasurable sensations or on a sexual fantasy rather than on his breathing. I reminded him that older men may feel less urgency about having to reach orgasm on every sexual occasion.

Mr. J. continued to have some worrisome physical symptoms that seemed to indicate an intermittent obstruction of his urinary ostomy. When he was feeling well, he enjoyed sexual activity, but if he felt ill and fatigued, his sexual desire decreased.

My most recent session with Mr. J., now a year post–penile prosthesis surgery, concerned a recurring dream that was troubling him. In the dream he begins a project at work, but cannot accomplish the task. He feels a sense of personal failure and frustration. Mr. J. could not connect the dream to any particular area of his current life. At first I suggested that the dream might reflect his disappointment with his continued lack of sexual desire. This did not seem to be the whole story, however; Mr. J. was clearly worried about his health in general and the possibility of a cancer recurrence. "Could your dream be about preparing for death?" I asked.

"Oh, I never think about death," Mr. J. protested. "Although now that you mention it, I have been a little worried that I never made a will." He went on to discuss his physical symptoms further.

This interview suggested to me that Mr. J.'s desire for a penile prosthesis, and his assumed role of "dirty old man," were not just an indication of disinhibition with mild dementia. Sex meant more to Mr. J. than merely the physical pleasure of orgasm, or even the traditional concept of being a real man. For Mr. J., focusing on sexuality was a protest against debility and impending death. I believe that Mrs. J. recognized her husband's fears, and thus was able to be a loving sexual partner, even though she would have preferred the tranquility of celibacy. No matter how long or short a time Mr. J. has left, I believe the penile prosthesis has had a positive influence, because it has encouraged him to live his life rather than waiting passively to die.

Conclusion

Sexuality is a significant concern to many older adults. Recent developments in behavioral sex therapy and in medical treatments for organic sexual dysfunction offer effective treatment for the problems of aging men and women. The clinician who works with older patients should coordinate the interview, questionnaire, and medical assessments to arrive at a comprehensive treatment plan. The clinician needs sensitivity to the special sexual concerns of the elderly, along with a commitment to the right of persons of all ages to sexual health.

References

Amelar, R.D., & Dubin, L. (1982). Sexual function and fertility in paraplegic males. *Urology, 20,* 62–65.

American Council on Science and Health (1983). *Postmenopausal estrogen therapy* (Research Rep.). Summit, NJ: Author.

Bachmann, G. (April 25, 1983). Painful coitus in the postmenopausal woman. *Sexuality Today,* p. 3.

Barbach, L. (1975). *For yourself.* New York: Doubleday.

Barbach, L. (1982). *For each other.* New York: Doubleday.

Barry, J.M., Blank, B., & Boileau, M. (1980). Nocturnal penile tumescence monitoring with stamps. *Urology, 15,* 171–172.

Benkert, O., Witt, W., Adam, W., & Leitz, A. (1979). Effects of testosterone undecanoate on sexual potency and the hypothalamic-pituitary-gonadal axis of the impotent males. *Archives of Sexual Behavior, 8,* 471–479.

Bennett, A.H. (1982). The inflatable and malleable penile prosthesis. In A. H. Bennett (Ed.), *Management of male impotence* (pp. 210–218). Baltimore: Williams & Wilkins.

Bergman, B., Nilsson, S., & Peterson, I. (1979). The effect on erection and orgasm of cystectomy, prostatectomy and vesiculectomy for cancer of the bladder: A clinical and electromyographic study. *British Journal of Urology, 51,* 114–120.

Bergman, B., Silvertsson, R., & Suurkala, M. (1982). Penile blood pressure in erectile impotence following cystectomy. *Scandinavian Journal of Urology and Nephrology, 16,* 81–84.

Corby, N., & Zarit, J.M. (1983). Old and alone: The unmarried in later life. In R. B. Weg (Ed.), *Sexuality in the later years: Roles and behavior* (pp. 131–147). New York: Academic Press.

Dennerstein, L., & Burrows, G.D. (1982). Hormone replacement therapy and sexuality in women. *Clinics in Endocrinology and Metabolism, 11,* 661–679.

Derogatis, L.R., & Meyer, J.K. (1979). A psychological profile of the sexual dysfunctions. *Archives of Sexual Behavior, 8,* 201–223.

Ek, A., Bradley, W., & Krane, R.J. (April, 1982). *A new concept in the measurement of penile rigidity.* Paper presented at the meeting of the American Urologic Association, Kansas City, MO.

Finkle, A.L., & Jackson, S. (1982). Urology/sexuality clinic: Results of counseling of 67 men. *Western Journal of Medicine, 137,* 95–98.

Finney, R.P. (1982). Rigid and semirigid penile prostheses. In A.H. Bennett (Ed.), *Management of male impotence* (pp. 198–209), Baltimore: Williams & Wilkins.

Finney, R.P. (April, 1983). *New totally intra-penile inflatable prosthesis for impotence.* Paper presented at the annual meeting of the American Urologic Association, Las Vegas, NV.

Fisher, C., Cohen, H.D., Schiavi, R.C., Davis, D., Furman, B., Ward, K.,

Edwards, A., & Cunningham, J. (1983). Patterns of female sexual arousal during sleep and waking: Vaginal thermoconductance studies. *Archives of Sexual Behavior, 12,* 97–122.

Flanigan, D.P., Schuler, J.J., Keifer, T., Schwartz, J.A., & Lim, L.T. (1982). Elimination of iatrogenic impotence and improvement of sexual function after aortoiliac revascularization. *Archives of Surgery, 117,* 554–549.

Fletcher, E.C., & Martin, R.J. (1982). Sexual dysfunction and erectile impotence in chronic obstructive pulmonary disease. *Chest, 81,* 413–421.

Furlow, W.L. (1981). Use of the inflatable prosthesis in erectile dysfunction. *Urologic Clinics of North America, 8,* 181-193.

George, L.K., & Weiler, S.J. (1981). Sexuality in middle and late life: The effects of age, cohort, and gender. *Archives of General Psychiatry, 38,* 919–923.

Giambra, L.M., & Martin, C.E. (1977). Sexual daydreams and quantitative aspects of sexual activity: Some relations for males across adulthood. *Archives of Sexual Behavior, 6,* 497–505.

Goldstein, I., Feldman, M.I., Deckers, P.J., Siroky, M.B., & Krane, R.J. (May, 1982). *Radiation-induced impotence: A clinical study.* Paper presented at the meeting of the American Urologic Association, Kansas City, MO.

Goldstein, I., Siroky, M.B., Sax, D.S., & Krane, R.J. (1982). Neurourologic abnormalities in multiple sclerosis. *Journal of Urology, 128,* 541–545.

Harman, S.M., & Tsitouras, P.D. (1980). Reproductive hormones in aging men. I. Measurement of sex steroids, basal luteinizing hormone, and Leydig cell responnse to human chorionic gonadotropin. *Journal of Clinical Endocrinology and Metabolism, 51,* 35–40.

Hegeler, S., & Mortensen, M. (1977). Sexual behavior in elderly Danish males. In R. Gemme & C.C. Wheeler (Eds.), *Progress in sexology* (pp. 285–292). New York: Plenum.

Heiman, J., LoPiccolo, L., & LoPiccolo, J. (1976). *Becoming orgasmic: A sexual growth program for women.* Englewood Cliffs, NJ: Prentice-Hall.

Hengeveld, M.W., & Korzec, A. (1980). Mourner's impotence. In R. Forleo & W. Pasini (Eds.), *Medical sexology* (pp. 243–248). Littleton, MA: P.S.G. Publishing.

Ismail, A.A.A., Davison, D.W., & Loraine, J.A. (1970). Assessment of gonadal function in impotent men. In W. J. Irvine (Ed.), *Reproductive endocrinology.* Edinborough, Scotland: Livingstone.

Jarman, W.D., Edson, M., & Elist, J. (1982). *A clinical study of the medical management of impotence.* Paper presented at the meeting of the American Urologic Association, Kansas City, MO.

Jevtich, M.J., Edson, M., Jarman, W.D., & Herrera, H.H. (1982). Vascular factors in erectile failure among diabetics. *Urology, 19,* 163–168.

Juhan, C.M., Padula, G., & Huguet, J.H. (1982). Angiography in male impotence. In A. H. Bennett (Ed.), *Management of male impotence* (pp. 73–107). Baltimore: Williams & Wilkens.

Kahn, E., & Fisher, C. (1969). REM sleep and sexuality in the aged. *Journal of Geriatric Psychiatry, 2,* 181–199.

Kaplan, H.S. (1974). *The new sex therapy.* New York: Brunner/Mazel.

Kaplan, H.S. (1975). *The illustrated manual of sex therapy.* (pp. 29–59). New York: Quadrangle.

Kaplan, H.S. (1979). *Disorders of sexual desire.* New York: Brunner/Mazel.

Kaplan, H.S. (1983). *The evaluation of sexual disorders.* New York: Brunner/Mazel.

Kaplan, H.S., & Moodie, J.L. (1982). Sex therapy. In A. H. Bennett (Ed.), *Management of male impotence* (pp. 237–243). Baltimore: Williams & Wilkins.

Karacan, I., Salis, P.J., & Williams, R.L. (1978). The role of the sleep laboratory in diagnosis and treatment of impotence. In R.L. Williams & I. Karacan (Eds.), *Sleep disorders: Diagnosis and treatment* (pp. 353–382). New York: Wiley.

Karacan, I., Williams, R.L., Thornby, J.I., & Salis, P.J. (1975). Sleep-related penile tumescence as a function of age. *American Journal of Psychiatry, 132,* 932–937.

Kaufman, J.J., Lindner, A., & Raz, S. (1982). Complications of penile prosthesis surgery for impotence. *Journal of Urology, 128,* 1192–1194.

Kinsey, A.C., Pomeroy, W., & Martin, C.E. (1948). *Sexual behavior in the human male.* Philadelphia: W. B. Saunders.

Kinsey, A.C., Pomeroy, W., Martin, C.E. & Gebhard, P. (1953). *Sexual behavior in the human female.* New York: Simon & Schuster.

Kolodny, R.C., Masters, W.H., & Johnson, V.E. (1979). *Textbook of sexual medicine.* Boston: Little, Brown.

Lazarus, A.A. (1980). Psychological treatment of dyspareunia. In S.R. Leiblum & L.A. Pervin (Eds.), *Principles and practice of sex therapy* (pp. 147–166). New York: Guilford.

Leiblum, S., Bachmann, G., Kemmann, E., Colburn, D., & Swartzman, L. (1983). Vaginal atrophy in the postmenopausal woman: The importance of sexual activity and hormones. *JAMA, 249,* 2195–2198.

Leiblum, S.R., & Pervin, L.A. (1980). *Principles and practices of sex therapy.* New York: Guilford.

Leiblum, S.R., Pervin, L.A., & Campbell, E.H. (1980). The treatment of vaginismus: Success and failure. In S.R. Leiblum & L.A. Pervin (Eds.), *Principles and practice of sex therapy* (pp. 167–194). New York: Guilford.

LoPiccolo, J. (1978). Direct treatment of sexual dysfunction. In J. LoPiccolo and L. LoPiccolo (Eds.), *Handbook of sex therapy* (pp. 1–18). New York: Plenum.

LoPiccolo, J. & Lobitz, W.C. (1978). The role of masturbation in the treatment of organic dysfunction. In J. LoPiccolo & L. LoPiccolo (Eds.), *Handbook of sex therapy* (pp. 187–194). New York: Plenum.

LoPiccolo, J., & LoPiccolo, L. (Eds.). (1978). *Handbook of sex therapy.* New York: Plenum.

LoPiccolo, J., & Steger, J.C. (1978). The sexual interaction inventory: A new instrument for assessment of sexual dysfunction. In J. LoPiccolo & L. LoPiccolo (Eds.), *Handbook of sex therapy* (pp. 113–122). New York: Plenum.

Marshall, P., Morales, A., & Surridge, D. (1982). Diagnostic significance of penile erections during sleep. *Urology, 20,* 1–6.

Martin, C.E. (1981). Factors affecting sexual functioning in 60–79-year-old married males. *Archives of Sexual Behavior, 10,* 399–420.

Masters, W.H. & Johnson, V.E. (1966). *Human sexual response.* Boston: Little, Brown, & Co.

Masters, W.H., & Johnson, V.E. (1970). *Human sexual inadequacy.* Boston: Little, Brown, & Co.

Masters, W.H., & Johnson, V.E. (1981). Sex and the aging process. *Journal of the American Geriatrics Society, 9,* 385–390.

McGovern, K.B., McMullen, R.S., & LoPiccolo, J. (1978). Secondary orgasmic dysfunction. I. Analysis and strategies for treatment. In J. LoPiccolo & L. LoPiccolo (Eds.), *Handbook of sex therapy* (pp. 209–218). New York: Plenum.

McKain, W.C. (1972). A new look at older marriages. *Family Coordinator, 21,* 61–69.

Meyer, J.K., Schmidt, C.W., & Wise, T.N. (Eds.) (1983). *Clinical management of sexual disorders.* Baltimore: Williams & Wilkins.

Morokoff, P. (1978). Determinants of female orgasm. In J. LoPiccolo & L. LoPiccolo (Eds.), *Handbook of sex therapy* (pp. 147–166). New York: Plenum.

Moss, H.B., & Procci, W.R. (1982). Sexual dysfunction associated with oral antihypertensive medication: A critical survey of the literature. *General Hospital Psychiatry, 4,* 121–129.

Newman, H.F., Reiss, H., & Northrup, J.D. (1982). Physical basis of emission, ejaculation, and orgasm in the male. *Urology, 19,* 341–350.

Perelman, M.A. (1980). Treatment of premature ejaculation. In S.R. Leiblum & L.A. Pervin (Eds.), *Principles and practice of sex therapy* (pp. 199–234). New York: Guilford.

Persky, H., Dreisbach, L., Miller, W.R., O'Brien, C.P., Khan, M.A., Lief, H.I., Charney, N., & Strauss, D. (1982). The relation of plasma androgen levels to sexual behaviors and attitudes of women. *Psychosomatic Medicine, 44,* 305–319.

Persson, G. (1981). Five-year mortality in a 70-year-old urban population in relation to psychiatric diagnosis, personality, sexuality, and early parental death. *Acta Psychiatrica Scandinavica, 64,* 244–253.

Purifoy, F.E., Koopmans, L.H., & Mayes, D.M. (1981). Age differences in serum androgen levels in normal adult males. *Human Biology, 53,* 499–511.

Remes, K., Kuoppasalmi, K., & Adlercreutz, H. (1979). Effect of long-term physical training on plasma testosterone, androstenedione, luteinizing hormone and sex-hormone-binding globulin capacity. *Scandinavian Journal of Clinical Laboratory Investigation, 39,* 743–749.

Rubin, L.B. (1982). Sex and sexuality: Women at midlife. In M. Kirkpatrick (Ed.), *Women's sexual experience: Explorations of the dark continent* (pp. 61–82). New York: Plenum.

Ruzbarsky, V., & Michal, V. (1977). Morphologic changes in the arterial bed of the penis with aging. Relationship to the pathogenesis of impotence. *Investigative Urology, 15,* 194–199.

Salmimies, P., Kockott, G., Pirke, K.M., Vogt, H.J., & Schill, W.B. (1982). Effects of testosterone replacement on sexual behavior in hypogonadal men. *Archives of Sexual Behavior, 11,* 345–354.

Schiavi, R.C., Fisher, C., White, D., Beers, P., Fogel, M., & Szechter, R. (1982). Hormonal variations during sleep in men with erectile dysfunction and normal controls. *Archives of Sexual Behavior, 11,* 189–200.

Schover, L.R. (1982a). Assessment and treatment of low sex desire. In A.S. Gurman (Ed.), *Questions and answers in the practice of family therapy* (Vol. 2, pp. 128–131). New York: Brunner/Mazel.

Schover, L.R. (1982b). Enhancing sexual intimacy. In P.A. Keller & L.G. Ritt (Eds.), *Innovations in clinical practice* (Vol. 1, pp. 53–66). Sarasota, FL: Professional Resource Exchange.

Schover, L.R. (1984). *Prime time: Sexual health for men over fifty.* New York: Holt, Rinehart, & Winston.

Schover, L.R., & von Eschenbach, A.C. (April, 1983). *Erectile function in bladder and prostate cancer patients before treatment.* Paper presented at the meeting of the American Urologic Association, Las Vegas, NV.

Schover, L.R., Friedman, J.M., Weiler, S.J., Heiman, J.R., & LoPiccolo, J. (1982). Multiaxial problem-oriented system for sexual dysfunctions: An alternative to *DSM-III. Archives of General Psychiatry, 39,* 614–619.

Schover, L.R., Karacan, I., & Hartse, K.M. (June, 1982). *The widower's syndrome: Psychogenic or organic erectile dysfunction?* Paper presented at the meeting of the Association for the Psychophysiological Study of Sleep, San Antonio, TX.

Schreiner-Engel, P., Schiavi, R.C., Smith, H., & White, D. (1981). Sexual arousability and the menstrual cycle. *Psychosomatic Medicine, 43,* 199–214.

Schwartz, M.F., Bauman, J.E., & Masters, W.H. (1982). Hyperprolactinemia and sexual disorders in men. *Biological Psychiatry, 8,* 861–876.

Segraves, R.T., Schoenberg, H.W., & Ivanoff, J. (1983). Serum testosterone and prolactin levels in erectile dysfunction. *Journal of Sex and Marital Therapy, 9,* 19–26.

Segraves, R.T., Schoenberg, H.W., Zarins, C.K., Knopf, J., & Camic, P. (1982). Referral of impotent patients to a sexual dysfunction clinic. *Archives of Sexual Behavior, 11,* 521–528.

Slag, M.F., Morley, J.E., & Elson, M.K. (1983). Impotence in medical clinic outpatients. *JAMA, 249,* 1736–1740.

Solomon, J., Faletti, M., & Yunik, S. (1982). The psychologist as a geriatric clinician. In T. Millon, C. Green, & R. Meagher (Eds.), *Handbook of clinical health psychology* (pp. 227–250).

Spanier, G.B. (1976). Measuring dyadic adjustment: New scales for assessing the quality of marriage and similar dyads. *Journal of Marriage and the Family, 38*, 15–28.

Spark, R.F. (1983). Neuroendocrinology and impotence. *Annals of Internal Medicine, 98, 103–105.*

Spark, R.F., White, R.A., & Connolly, P.B. (1980). Impotence is not always psychogenic: Newer insights into hypothalamic-pituitary-gonadal dysfunction. *JAMA, 243*, 750–755.

Starr, B.D., & Weiner, M.B. (1981). *The Starr-Weiner report on sex and sexuality in the mature years.* New York: Stein & Day.

Sviland, M.A.P. (1978). Helping elderly patients become sexually liberated: Psychosocial issues. In J. LoPiccolo & L. LoPiccolo (Eds.), *Handbook of sex therapy* (pp. 351–360). New York: Plenum.

Treas, J., & Van Hilst, A. (1976). Marriage and remarriage rates among older Americans. *The Gerontologist, 16*, 132–136.

Tsitouras, P.D., Martin, C.E., & Harman, S.M. (1982). Relationship of serum testosterone to sexual activity in healthy elderly men. *Journal of Gerontology, 37*, 288–293.

Virag, R. (1982a). Arterial and venous hemodynamics in male impotence. In A. H. Bennett (Ed.), *Management of male impotence* (pp. 108–126). Baltimore: Williams & Wilkins.

Virag, R. (1982b). Revascularization of the penis. In A.H. Bennett (Ed.), *Management of male impotence* (pp. 219–233). Baltimore: Williams & Wilkins.

Wagner, G., & Green, R. (1981). *Impotence: Physiological, psychological, surgical diagnoses and treatment.* New York: Plenum.

Walsh, P.C., & Donker, P.J. (1982). Impotence following radical prostatectomy: Insight into etiology and prevention. *Journal of Urology, 128*, 492–497.

Wasow, M., & Loeb, M.B. (1977). Sexuality in nursing homes. In R.L. Solnick (Ed.), *Sexuality and aging.* Los Angeles: University of Southern California Press.

White, C.B. (1982a). A scale for the measurement of attitudes and knowledge regarding sexuality in the aged. *Archives of Sexual Behavior, 11*, 491–502.

White, C.B. (1982b). Sexual interest, attitudes, knowledge, and sexual history in relation to sexual behavior in the institutionalized aged. *Archives of Sexual Behavior, 11*, 11–23.

Winn, R.L., & Newton, N. (1982). Sexuality in aging: A study of 106 cultures. *Archives of Sexual Behavior, 11*, 283–298.

Wise, T.N. (1983). Sexual disorders in medical and surgical conditions. In J.K. Meyer, C.W. Schmidt, Jr., & T.N. Wise (Eds.), *Clinical management of sexual disorders* (pp. 317–332). Baltimore: Williams & Wilkins.

Yeager, E.S., & Van Heerden, J.A. (1980). Sexual dysfunction following proctocolectomy and A-P resection. *Annals of Surgery, February,* 169–170.

Zilbergeld, B. (1978). *Male sexuality.* Boston: Little, Brown, & Co.

Zorgniotti, A.W. (1982). An appraisal of penile revascularization. In A. H. Bennett (Ed.), *Management of male impotence* (pp. 234–236). Baltimore: Williams & Wilkins.

Afterword

Peter M. Lewinsohn and Linda Teri

In selecting topics for inclusion in this book we were concerned that the area of clinical application be timely and clinically important and that there be some empirical basis for the assessment intervention procedures. We were also concerned that the individuals we chose to write the chapters be experts in their fields and doing work considered to be on the leading edge. We hope the reader agrees that we made outstanding selections.

In this section we will briefly comment on issues relevant to each of the chapters, pointing to common threads and directing the reader to other sources of information.

Common Threads

While focused on specific problems, there are nevertheless certain common threads that run through all of the chapters, which deserve to be emphasized. For one, the problems of the elderly are rarely simple. Ideally clinicians would like to be able to work with patients who have specific problems for which an efficacious treatment exists. The chapters are organized in this way and reflect the considerable body of knowledge that can be brought to bear on each of the specific problems. As indicated in our introduction and by the chapter authors themselves, in the real world, problems of the elderly are usually multiple, requiring additional assessment and treatment skills beyond those described in each of the chapters. Thus, the mental health worker dealing with older adults needs to be trained and familiar with the total range of potential problems afflicting the elderly and to be focused on treating the total patient.

Second, it is always important to develop an integrated approach. This is explicitly or implicitly recognized by all of the authors in their emphasis, for example, on the importance of a recent and thorough medical examination. The reader needs to be aware that regardless of whether the patient's problems are approached within Lawton's global functional assessment framework, or Hussian's pinpointing of specific problems and use of behavioral interventions, the clinician must be concerned with achieving a degree of integration and overall planning which is sensitive to the short- and long-term needs of the patient.

Third, there are general attitudinal and ethical issues that are especially important with older adults. These issues have been addressed by numerous authors (e.g., Santos & VandenBos, 1982; Birren & Sloane, 1980; Busse & Blazer, 1980) as well as succinctly summarized by Lewinsohn, Teri, & Hautzinger (1984). These authors suggest general principles that should guide one's work with older adults; while these principles were aimed specifically at psychologists, they are applicable to all who seek to provide clinical services to older adults. To wit:

1. Psychological services aimed at the elderly population must recognize and incorporate ways of addressing the multiplicity of problems shown by older people.
2. Psychologists working with older people must be familiar with the phenomenology of aging.
3. Psychologists working with elderly clients should make a conscious effort to maintain realistic expectations.
4. Psychologists should strive to maintain and to preserve the elderly person's independence.
5. Psychologists should provide intervention that does not foster dependency.
6. Psychologists working with elderly clients should make a conscious effort to distinguish the various needs represented in any one case.
7. Psychologists should provide services which are readily accessible to elderly clients.
8. Psychologists working with elderly clients should facilitate comprehensive care.

9. Psychologists should provide services which include assessment, intervention, and prevention.

With these general considerations in mind, we will now address the chapters individually.

Neuropsychological Assessment

Muriel D. Lezak

In a relatively small number of pages, Lezak provides a succinct summary of a body of knowledge and application for which the clinical importance will become increasingly recognized as clinicians attempt to disentangle cognitive dysfunction from functional disabilities in older patients. Dr. Lezak is the author of what is probably the most useful textbook in the field of clinical neuropsychology (Lezak, 1983). Lezak's chapter presents a concise summary and conveys a great deal of useful information of special relevance to the elderly. Lezak carefully describes different kinds of approaches to neurological assessment, and while Lezak's preference for individualized rather than standardized approaches is clear, her discussion serves to confront the reader with the importance of having to make his/her own judgments.

The focus on "executive function" is especially valuable because assessment of this more subtle but specifically important aspect of functioning is usually neglected. One would expect that in the future there will be further refinements of this component of the neuropsychologist's armamentarium as the importance of people's ability to provide direction to their lives, to be able to strive toward short- and long-term goals, and to maintain organization, integration, and planning in their daily life is recognized. Reading Lezak's chapter (as well as Lezak's book) should help to dispel the notion that cognitive impairments due to organicity are not susceptible to psychological intervention. Even in the absence of efficacious cognitive remediation procedures (which we hope will be developed soon), there is quite a bit that one can do to assist patient and caregiver with cognitive difficulties. (For further discussion of this approach, readers are referred to Zarit and Zarit, 1983). Lezak's chapter also serves to emphasize the importance of the differential diagnosis between dementia and depression. The reader who is interested in this issue from another vantage point is referred to Gallagher and Thompson (1983).

While focused on assessment, Lezak is sensitive to the uses to which neuropsychological information is put and the importance of meeting the needs of the referral source. The utility of neuropsychological procedures for repeated assessment to evaluate change, to reevaluate hypotheses, and to confirm diagnoses is also evident. One would hope that many of the relatively sensitive and easy-to-use neuropsychological procedures described by Lezak will find increasing use in the longitudinal study of patients.

Functional Assessment

M. Powell Lawton

Ideally the patient has a relatively specific and clearly identified problem: the person has become very inactive, is dissatisfied with specific aspects of his/her sexual behavior, shows evidence of cognitive impairments, or engages in behaviors that are distressing to the caregivers or to others in the person's environment. Unfortunately, typically things are not this simple. People usually come to treatment with multiple, ambiguous, and often diffuse problems, and it sometimes takes considerable clinical effort and skill to identify the most salient and important problems. Lawton's approach addresses this rather common situation in which the clinician needs to become informed about everything that might have influence on the problem situation. Lawton's description of functional assessment and the relevant techniques is thus quite valuable. Lawton provides a framework that enables the reader to approach the problem of assessment and to collect and organize the data. Functional assessment should be viewed as an attempt to generate hypotheses about possible causes and possible interventions. While future research may lead to methodological and conceptual refinements, the continued need for functional assessment will undoubtedly loom large.

Excess Disability in the Elderly: Exercise Management

Alan Roberts

The major assumption underlying Roberts' approach is that being active is critical for people's mental health. We heartily agree. While specifically focused on patients with excess disability that is often, but not necessarily, related to physical illness, Roberts' chapter also has implications that are more general and point to the role psychologists can play to help people optimize their activities. There are a number of other aspects which are noteworthy about Roberts' chapter. His use of the term "excess disability" instead of "chronic pain" allows for the extension of knowledge about the treatment of "chronic pain" to a much wider range of clinical problems, for example, patients who have become excessively passive and withdrawn for any number of reasons. Roberts demonstrates how the principles and techniques developed by Fordyce (1976) can be used with outpatients, providing sufficient detail to guide the clinician in working with such patients.

Severe Behavioral Problems

Richard A. Hussian

The types of behavioral problems addressed in Hussian's chapter are encountered most often in working with institutionalized elderly, but their importance is not restricted to those who are institutionalized since such difficulties are equally problematic when they occur in the home. In fact, family members are more likely to need help coping with these problems than are trained staff. As Hussian indicates, these are the types of problems that often precipitate the elderly person losing his/her independence and being viewed by others and by him-/herself as out of control and dangerous. Thus, the availability of efficacious methods for dealing with such problems is critical.

In his book, Hussian (1981) provides a more detailed discussion of many of these problems and of the importance of providing systematic training for the nursing home staff and of the potential contributions of the psychologist as a consultant.

Sexual Problems

Leslie R. Schover

Dr. Schover provides an excellent overview of sexual problems. Not only does this chapter familiarize the reader with the major issues, approaches, and problems, but it also provides many valuable suggestions based on Schover's clinical experience. As Schover points out, sexual difficulties of various kinds are probably experienced by a substantial proportion of elderly, many of whom would benefit from the approaches described here. This is an area in which there is considerable reluctance on the part of the elderly as well as professionals to discuss sexual problems and to become involved in their solution. Clearly it is an area in which there is a need for considerable consciousness raising among the potential clientele as well as among the professional audience, and Schover describes many ways of accomplishing these goals.

We hope the reader agrees that the topics we included in this volume are timely and important and represent a significant and growing body of knowledge. While the chapters have been focused on specific problems, we wish to end by pointing to the fact that the elderly underutilize mental health services. Thus, clinicians must not only be knowledgeable and experienced, they must also strive to make their services timely, relevant, and available to older adults. The best treatments are useless if they are not used by the people who can benefit from them. Educational programs aimed at community audiences to familiarize people with services before they actually need them and to change attitudes about service utilization are seriously needed.

References

Birren, J., & Sloane, R.B. (1980). *Handbook of mental health and aging.* Englewood Cliffs, NJ: Prentice Hall.

Busse, E.W., & Blazer, D. (1980). *Handbook of geriatric psychiatry.* New York: Van Nostrand Reinhold.

Fordyce, W.E. (1976). *Behavioral methods for chronic pain and illness.* St. Louis: C.V. Mosby.

Gallagher, D., & Thompson, L.W. (1983). Depression. In P. Lewinsohn & L. Teri (Eds.), *Clinical geropsychology.* New York: Pergamon Press.

Hussian, R.A. (1981). *Geriatric psychology: A behavioral perspective.* New York: Van Nostrand Reinhold.

Lewinsohn, P., Teri, L., & Hautzinger, M. (1984). Training clinical psychologists for work with older adults: A working model. *Professional Psychology, 15,* 187–202.

Lezak, M.D. (1983). *Neuropsychological assessment.* New York: Oxford Press.

Santos, J.F., & VandenBos, R. (1982). *Psychology and the older adult.* Washington, DC: American Psychological Association.

Zarit, S., & Zarit, J. (1983). Cognitive impairment. In P. Lewinsohn & L. Teri (Eds.), *Clinical geropsychology.* New York: Pergamon Press.

Index

Index